The ANNOTATED Godfather ™

JENNY M. JONES

The ANNOTATED Godfather™

THE COMPLETE SCREENPLAY

BLACK DOG
& LEVENTHAL
PUBLISHERS
NEW YORK

PUBLISHED BY

Black Dog & Leventhal Publishers, Inc.
151 West 19th Street / New York, NY 10011

DISTRIBUTED BY

Workman Publishing Company
225 Varick Street / New York, NY 10014

Manufactured in China
Cover and interior design by Ohioboy Art & Design

ISBN-13: 978-1-57912-739-8

h g f e d c b a

Library of Congress Cataloging-in-Publication Data available on file.

CONTENTS

"What are they getting so excited about? It's only another gangster picture."

—Marlon Brando, 1971

Looking back thirty-five years after the release of *The Godfather*, one can't help but marvel how the film ever got made, when every conceivable obstacle stood in its way.

A writer who didn't want to write it.

Mario Puzo was broke and needed to pen something commercial in order to write the kind of books he really cared about.

A studio that didn't want to produce it.

The box-office failure of previous gangster movies made Paramount Pictures reluctant to pick up their option, but with the novel a runaway success, and other studios showing interest, they couldn't let it slip away.

A film no director would touch.

Twelve directors turned it down, including, at first, Francis Ford Coppola. But, Coppola, too, was broke, and needed a job directing a Hollywood production in order to make the kind of personal films he really cared about.

A cast of unknowns.

Except for one renowned actor, Marlon Brando, who was considered box office poison by studio executives.

A community against it.

Before filming even began, Italian-American groups protested what they perceived was to be the movie's characterization of their culture, and amassed a war chest to stop the production.

And, yet, *The Godfather* succeeded beyond anyone's wildest imagination, to become one of the greatest cinematic masterpieces in history—a film that continues to captivate us, decades after its release.

The Godfather is a unique film in that it bridges many audiences, appealing to both erudite film buffs and TV couch potatoes alike. As film critic Kenneth Turan says, it is irresistible: "Like one of those potato chips, you can't have only one of it. It is a film that, once started or stumbled upon on TV, demands to be seen all the way to the end. It is that well-constructed, that hypnotic, simply that good." Even Al Pacino admits that, when he's flipping the channels and comes across *The Godfather*, he can't help but keep watching.

But why is the film still so compelling today? Certainly the thrill of looking inside the particular subculture that *The Godfather* explores, in conjunction with the movie's intense action and drama, is endlessly entertaining. There are two other central reasons to love the film. The first is in the details. With each new viewing, a different, distinct detail reveals itself: the jarring crunch of gravel under Michael's feet after Carlo is murdered; the blustery performance of Sterling Hayden; the exquisite marriage of Nino Rota's haunting score with the dazzling Sicilian landscape. The details are no accident. In addition to Coppola's dogged efforts to infuse the film with the flavor and intricacies of his own Italian-American experiences, he assembled an incredible collection of talent to create the film. From the cinematographer to the production designer, from the makeup artist to the special-effects wizard, from the costume designer to the casting director, from Brando to Pacino—only today can the wonder of such a gifted group, working together on one movie set, be fully appreciated.

Another reason *The Godfather* is such a powerful film is that it works both on the grand level of an epic—with its stunning cinematography, magnificent performances, and comment on the rise of postwar America and capitalism—and on the very intimate level of the story of one family. The father-son relationship, sibling dynamics, and the quest to find oneself within the context of the family, are themes that are not only relatable, they are infinitely mineable. Michael's soulful struggle of how to react to, reject, resolve, and ultimately become part of his family is a struggle for the ages—and one that deepens with each viewing.

The Annotated Godfather: The Complete Screenplay endeavors to tell the story of *The Godfather* by offering behind-the-scenes stories and insight in tandem with the screenplay of *The Godfather*. The screenplay of the 1972 film featured herein incorporates much of Francis Ford Coppola and Mario Puzo's own wording from their final, pre-production draft or *shooting script* (officially titled "Third Draft," complete on March 29, 1971). This look back at the monumental film also traces the development of the screenplay and explores the evolution of several subsequent versions and re-edits of the film that appeared after 1972. Among those different versions are *The Godfather Saga*, a four-part miniseries broadcast on NBC in 1977, which combined *The Godfather* and its sequel, *The Godfather: Part II*, in mostly chronological order, with some restored scenes that did not appear in the original theatrical release; *The Godfather 1902-1959: The Complete Epic* (a.k.a. *Mario Puzo's The Godfather: The Complete Novel for Television*), a video boxed set released in 1981 in the same format as *Saga* but with fewer restored scenes; and *The Godfather Trilogy: 1901-1980*, a re-editing of all three *Godfathers* in mostly chronological order, with even more additional footage, released in 1992.

This book offers a cohesive story of the making of the film by analyzing a wide range of source material. In addition to the various versions of the script, alternate and deleted scenes, and modified releases of the film, *The Annotated Godfather: The Complete Screenplay* also draws upon Puzo's original novel, production documents housed at the American Zoetrope Research Library in Rutherford, California, and interviews with some of the cast and crew. Onetime Paramount executive Peter Bart has likened the story of *The Godfather's* production to the Akira Kurosawa film *Rashômon*, in which each time a single event is described by a different witness, it comes out as an entirely different story. Looking at it through the refracted lens of time and perspective, the volatile mix of personalities involved and the struggles to complete the film according to Coppola's vision proved, in the end, to be instrumental in making *The Godfather* what it is today—a landmark of American cinema.

GENESIS OF
THE GODFATHER

MARItags...

"None of the grown-ups I knew were charming or loving or understanding. Rather they seemed coarse, vulgar, and insulting. And so later in my life when I was exposed to all the clichés of lovable Italians, singing Italians, happy-go-lucky Italians, I wondered where the hell the moviemakers and storywriters got all their ideas from."

— Mario Puzo, *The Godfather Papers: and Other Confessions*

Mario Puzo was born in 1920 in impoverished Hell's Kitchen, the son of Italian-born parents. His first two novels, *The Dark Arena* (1955) and *The Fortunate Pilgrim* (1965), earned good reviews but weak sales and a mere $6,500 for Puzo's bank account. Puzo had written about a character influenced by the world of organized crime in *Pilgrim,* and an editor suggested it could have done better with more of that "Mafia stuff." At age forty-five, Puzo owed $20,000 in gambling debts, so he wrote a ten-page book outline entitled *Mafia*—an attempt at a more commercial novel. Eight publishers turned it down.

At a meeting at G. P. Putnam's Sons, Puzo regaled the editors with Mafia stories, impressing them enough to give him a $5,000 book advance. Puzo had never known a mobster or gangster, so he had to do exhaustive research for the book.

Two years before the book was completed, Puzo remained strapped for cash. Paramount Vice President of Creative Affairs Peter Bart received a tip from George Weiser, a story editor who freelanced as a literary scout for Paramount, and based on sixty pages, he set Puzo up at the studio. In an interview with the author, Bart reported: "It was not a real manuscript, just a few chapters, into which he had crammed a lot of the plot. It was a long way from a finished manuscript. At that point I said to Bob [Evans], 'Look, even though you're not enthusiastic, it is much beyond a Mafia story,' so I optioned it at Paramount." Puzo was so broke, he agreed—against his agent's advice—to accept a deal of a paltry $12,500 option, $80,000 if it was made into a film, with escalators. Paramount kept giving him little advances—said Robert Evans, senior vice president of Paramount, in *Variety:* "We had to give him the bread to keep him alive while he was writing the book. We never expected it to be the huge success it has turned out to be."

In March 1967 Paramount announced their deal to back Puzo's material in the hopes of eventually making it into a movie. Two years later, *The Godfather* was published. It was a smash, spending sixty-seven weeks on *The New York Times* bestseller list. Three

MARIO PUZO, IN HOLLYWOOD IN JUNE 1970, WHILE WORKING ON *THE GODFATHER* SCRIPT.

CRAFTING *THE GODFATHER* SCRIPT

Puzo was thrilled with his office at Paramount, which had a refrigerator with an unlimited supply of soda. He cut the 446-page novel down to a 150-page first draft of a screenplay (dated August 10, 1970), and mailed a copy to the one man he envisioned as Vito Corleone, Marlon Brando. The screenplay opened with Michael and Kay driving to the wedding, followed by a courthouse scene of Bonasera's daughter's attackers being acquitted. A reedited version begins with a love scene between Michael and Kay (suggested by the studio). When Francis Ford Coppola first saw the screenplay, he was aghast. It was set in the 1970s, complete with hippies. He described it in *Time* magazine: "Puzo's screenplay had turned into a slick, contemporary gangster picture of no importance. It wasn't Puzo's fault. He just did what they told him to do."

After thoroughly analyzing and dissecting the novel, Coppola crafted his own treatment of a screenplay. He gave it to Puzo, and they proceeded to swap halves of the script to edit from their respective home bases. A second draft of a screenplay emerged, at 173 pages and dated March 1, 1971. The third and final preshooting draft (referred to in this book as the shooting script), was dated March 29 and ran 158 pages—suggesting a longer picture than Paramount had imagined.

MARIO PUZO ON SET

Puzo felt excluded from the filming, and Paramount didn't allow him to see the final cut when he wished to. He grudgingly realized he had no final say over the film, and said in *The Hollywood Reporter:* "You can't say I'm delirious with joy over what they've done to my book for the movie, even though I've done the screenplay." He even swore a Sicilian vendetta against Paramount vice president Robert Evans (most likely in jest). Speculation was that *The Godfather Papers: and Other Confessions,* Puzo's memoir published just before the film's release, was going to be an angry exposé. It turned out to be fairly tame in its criticism. While he vowed never to do another film unless he had final approval, Puzo did go on to write the screenplay for *The Godfather: Part II,* and *Part III,* and the first draft of *Superman,* among others.

months after publication, when other studios started showing interest, Paramount confirmed their rights to produce the film. According to *Variety:* "Paramount Pictures probably made the prime deal for a bestseller in modern film history with its $80,000 ceiling for Mario Puzo's *The Godfather*." They called it, quite rightly, a "bargain-basement literary buy."

Against convention, producer Al Ruddy wanted to keep the author involved in the movie project. They lunched at the Plaza, where Ruddy cautioned him about the pitfalls of feeling too much ownership over the book. Puzo, who has always said he penned *The Godfather* to finance the writing he really wanted to do, threw the book on the floor, professing he never cared to read it again. So in April, Puzo was contracted to turn out *The Godfather* screenplay for an additional $100,000, expenses, and a few percentage points of the profits. It took Paramount a long five months to actually sign a director to the project.

"Making *The Godfather* was such an extraordinarily unpleasant experience in every aspect that I've avoided thinking about it or talking about it for thirty years."

—Peter Bart, at the 2006 South by Southwest Film Festival

Through the 1960s, Hollywood was in an economic downturn, with dwindling movie attendance and declining production. Major takeovers ruled the day: MCA and Universal Pictures merged; Warner Bros. was bought by Kinney National Company (which had previously primarily owned funeral parlors and parking lots); and the conglomerate Gulf+Western bought Paramount Pictures. As the 1970s began, Paramount was ranked a dismal ninth among film studios.

Paramount's 1968 big-budget Kirk Douglas vehicle *The Brotherhood,* a Mafia picture, opened to anemic ticket sales. Although *The Godfather* novel was selling well, *The Brotherhood*'s weak box office made Paramount gun-shy about mob movies, and they shelved the project.

Paramount had its fair share of recent big-budget disasters, exemplified by the aptly titled *Waterloo.* Then, over Christmas of 1970, *Love Story* burst onto the movie scene. With a $106 million return on a $2.2 million investment, *Love Story* changed the fortunes of Paramount Pictures. Paramount had nurtured the bestselling novel through the writing process, and the small-budget film excelled without major star power. As gangbuster sales of Puzo's book forced Paramount to take another look at their film option, they would try to re-create *Love Story*'s success using the same formula on *The Godfather.* In late 1969, Paramount announced they would make the film. And, as producer Al Ruddy says today, "they saw it as a low-budget gangster movie."

THE PLAYERS

The new young executives at Paramount strove to adapt the company to the current climate in Hollywood with fewer movies, smaller budgets, and less extravagant stars.

CHARLES G. BLUHDORN, CHAIRMAN OF GULF+WESTERN INDUSTRIES, IN 1971.

CHARLES G. BLUHDORN,
COMPANY FOUNDER AND CHAIRMAN OF THE BOARD, GULF+WESTERN

The brash and vulgar Bluhdorn took a failing auto parts distributor and built it into Gulf+Western Industries, Inc., subsuming some sixty-five companies, Paramount Pictures included. Mel Brooks's *Silent Movie* features a parody of the company, called Engulf and Devour. Dubbed "The Mad Austrian," Bluhdorn was a hot-tempered, heavily accented executive who liked to bark orders. Although Paramount was only a small part of Gulf+Western, he took great interest in it. He compared Coppola's work on *The Godfather* to having the secret to Coca-Cola.

STANLEY JAFFE,
CEO, PARAMOUNT PICTURES

At the young age of twenty-eight, Stanley Jaffe produced *Goodbye, Columbus* and was appointed executive vice president and chief corporate officer of Paramount Pictures shortly thereafter. Jaffe left Paramount in early April, just as production on *The Godfather* was about to begin. Rumors that his resignation (or firing) was connected to *The Godfather*'s production abound, but both Robert Evans and Peter Bart have suggested he left because of a fight with Bluhdorn over the casting of a woman in another picture. Oddly enough, Jaffe returned as CEO of Paramount again, in 1991.

FRANK YABLANS,
HEAD OF MARKETING/VICE PRESIDENT FOR DOMESTIC SALES, BECAME PRESIDENT OF PARAMOUNT

The young, hard-nosed Yablans oversaw Paramount for four years, often called "The Golden Age of Paramount," during which time the studio released such critical and financial successes as *The Godfather* and *The Godfather: Part II, Serpico, Paper Moon, Chinatown, Murder on the Orient Express,* and *The Longest Yard.* He masterminded a groundbreaking distribution plan for *The Godfather* that helped make it one of the most successful films in history.

ROBERT EVANS,
SENIOR VICE PRESIDENT IN CHARGE OF WORLDWIDE PRODUCTION, PARAMOUNT

Bob Evans lived large. As a youth, he worked for Evan-Picone sportswear ("I'm in ladies' pants," he liked to say) and was "discovered" by Norma Shearer at The Beverly Hills Hotel pool. After a few acting gigs he decided to become a producer. When Bluhdorn offered him the highly visible job at Paramount, he had yet to make a single film. *The New York Times* called it "Bluhdorn's Folly," one of the nicer assessments at the time. Very hands-on with his pet projects, Evans clashed with the also opinionated Coppola throughout the making of *The Godfather.* Evans also presided over some of the best films in Paramount's history.

PETER BART,
VICE PRESIDENT OF PRODUCTION, PARAMOUNT

Bart, a West Coast correspondent for *The New York Times,* wrote a piece on Robert Evans for the Sunday edition. Evans contends this is how he first caught Bluhdorn's eye, which Bart finds amusing, as the piece was rather snarky. Once he became a vice president, Evans picked Bart to be his right-hand man. Bart was the creative side of the team, shepherding projects like *The Godfather* through a long development process. Over eight years, he developed such films as *Paper Moon, Harold and Maude, True Grit,* and *Rosemary's Baby.* His book-smart personality was a great fit with Evans's business acumen and gut-level instinct. It was Bart's idea to hire Francis Ford Coppola. "I began advocating Coppola because I felt that Francis was a brilliant young filmmaker, even though he hadn't shown his prowess yet. He was extraordinarily intelligent and well spoken—so I was indeed the most aggressive advocate of Francis as the person to direct the picture."—Peter Bart, 2007.

ALBERT S. RUDDY,
PRODUCER, ALFRAN PRODUCTIONS

Affable Al Ruddy rose through the ranks in the entertainment business with few qualifications but his moxie. After a chance meeting with a Warner Bros. executive, he co-created the successful television show *Hogan's Heroes,* and three movies: *Little Fauss and Big Halsy, Wild Seed,* and *Making It.* Although all were unsuccessful at the box office, they were made on the cheap and came in under budget, just what Paramount wanted for *The Godfather.* Rather than go through a lengthy pitch of how he was going to adapt the book into a movie, he convinced Bluhdorn to hire him by announcing, "Charlie, I want to make an ice-blue terrifying movie about people you love." Bluhdorn said, "That's brilliant!" banged on the desk, and ran out of the room. Ruddy succeeded, but as he said shortly after the film was released: "It was the most miserable film I can think of to make. Nobody enjoyed one day of it." Today, while he admits the shoot was rough, he calls it "a great experience that started everyone's career. It was magic."

ABOVE: PRODUCER AL RUDDY, IN 1971.
BELOW: MARIO PUZO, FRANCIS FORD COPPOLA, ROBERT EVANS AND AL RUDDY AT THE PARAMOUNT PICTURES PRESS CONFERENCE ANNOUNCING *THE GODFATHER* (PHOTO COURTESY OF RUDDY MORGAN ORGANIZATION).

THE ARCHITECT: FRANCIS FORD COPPOLA

"It was my intention to make this an authentic piece of film about gangsters who were Italian, how they lived, how they behaved, the way they treated their families, celebrated their rituals."

—Francis Ford Coppola, in *Time* magazine

When Paramount gave *The Godfather* the green light, finding a director turned out to be a difficult task. Twelve directors turned down the job—many, including Peter Yates (*Bullitt*) and Richard Brooks (*In Cold Blood*), because they didn't want to romanticize the Mafia. Arthur Penn (*Bonnie and Clyde, Little Big Man*) was too busy. Costa-Gavras (*Z*) thought it was too American.

Robert Evans, Paramount's head of production, sat down with Peter Bart, his creative second in command, to determine why previous organized crime films hadn't worked, and decided it was because Jews made them, not Italians. So, they sought an Italian-American director, a commodity in short supply. Bart thought of a twenty-nine-year-old he had met when he had written a little piece for *The New York Times* on a young wannabe director who paid his way through college by making "nudies," otherwise known as skin flicks.

Francis Ford Coppola was born in Detroit in 1939. His father, Carmine, was the conductor and arranger for the *Ford Sunday Evening Hour* radio program (hence Francis's middle name). Because the ambitious musician worked traveling shows, the Coppola family was often uprooted. Francis was grounded by an upbringing steeped in his Italian heritage.

At age nine Francis contracted polio and spent a year in virtual isolation. During this time, he developed an interest in mechanical things. He got an 8mm camera and started making movies, and by a young age knew that he wanted to be a director. He was a theater arts major at Hofstra University, and then enrolled at UCLA for a master's in fine arts. While he was attending UCLA, prolific B-movie filmmaker Roger Corman recruited him, as he did so many young filmmakers of great potential, to work on several schlock films. Coppola married fellow UCLA graduate Eleanor Neil in 1963 while working on his directorial debut, the Corman-financed *Dementia 13*.

ABOVE: COPPOLA AND CREW WATCHING FOOTAGE ON LOCATION AT THE SCENE OF PAULIE GATTO'S MURDER.
BELOW: COPPOLA AND PACINO DISCUSS THE SOLLOZZO/MCCLUSKEY MURDER SCENE.

After winning a screenwriting competition, Coppola got a job as a screenwriter and wrote the script for *Patton,* among other projects. He directed *You're a Big Boy Now,* a precursor of sorts to *The Graduate,* which garnered him a Golden Palm nomination at the Cannes Film Festival. Warner Bros. offered Coppola the musical *Finian's Rainbow.* Young George Lucas was a production assistant there and became a protégé who was also interested in working outside the studio system.

Coppola went on to write and direct his own film, *The Rain People,* about a young pregnant wife (Shirley Knight) and her search for personal fulfillment. In 1969, Coppola set his dreams in motion: he sold his house, moved to San Francisco, obtained a loan from Warner Bros., and started an independent film studio with Lucas and other young idealistic filmmakers. American Zoetrope was founded with the utopian vision of creating personal, artistic films.

The first project the company produced was Lucas's futuristic sci-fi drama *THX 1138.* The unsuccessful film was ruinous for American Zoetrope. Warner Bros. recut the film, eventually releasing it with little marketing backing. The studio went through a major restructuring, and the new brass weren't impressed by American Zoetrope's proposed projects. They asked for their $600,000 back. Coppola tried to raise money doing commercials and educational films, but soon he was desperate enough to listen to the pitch to direct *The Godfather.*

Peter Bart first approached Coppola to direct *The Godfather* in the spring of 1970. Coppola tried to read the book but found it sleazy. His father advised him that commercial work could fund the artistic pictures he wanted to make. His business partner, George Lucas, begged him to find something in the book he liked. He went to the library to research the Mafia, and became fascinated by the families that had divided New York and run it like a business. Coppola reread the novel and came to see a central theme of a family—a father and his three sons—that was in its own way a Greek or Shakespearean tragedy. He viewed the growth of the 1940s Corleone Family as a metaphor for capitalism in America. He took the job.

Coppola was announced as director on September 28, "by default," according to Bob Evans. With the inexperienced Coppola, Paramount thought they were hiring an Italian-American director who would also come in on budget and be pliable. Although indeed Italian American, Francis Ford Coppola would not be the director the studio had envisioned.

The first battle was over the picture being a period piece. Coppola was adamant that the film be set in the 1940s. In a recent interview he explained, "One of the reasons it was so important to me to get Paramount to agree to set the movie in the forties instead of the seventies is that so much of the story connects with what was going on in America during that period: the birth of America after World War II; Michael's service in the Marines; the imagery of America; what was going on in America; the rise of corporate America. All of that was very much part of the story, and I couldn't imagine how you would tell the story in the way they were planning to do it." Paramount had asked Puzo to set the screenplay in the seventies because contemporary films were cheaper to make: no 1940s cars to find, sets to create, costumes to make. Eventually, Coppola's desire to preserve the book's period quality won out.

The second battle was over location. Coppola wanted to shoot in New York, an expensive proposition because of the unions. Producer Al Ruddy had suggested Cleveland,

Kansas City, and Cincinnati as possible sites—or perhaps a studio backlot. (In an interview with the author, he indicates it was also because "some of 'the boys' [read: Mafia] told us we couldn't come to New York.") In an October 1970 *Variety* piece, Coppola stated: "I very much want to do it in New York. The atmosphere is strictly New York, and since I want to do the film as a period piece, if possible—say the 1940s—any other locale is going to make it more difficult to capture the special flavor of New York." Ruddy countered: "We're watching the pennies and we think we can make the picture for much less on other locations and not sacrifice any quality." In the end, the studio gave in, and the film was shot on location in New York.

In September 1970, Robert Evans announced on behalf of Paramount: "*The Godfather* will be our big picture of 1971." At this point, the book had sold more than one million copies in hardcover and six million in paperback, forcing Paramount to reconsider a modest film. The $2 million budget was increased to $3 million, and then to $4 million, and eventually to $6 million. Coupled with the book's runaway success, Coppola's sheer force of will overcame the objections of the studio brass.

The third battle, and it was a long and bloody one, was over casting. Coppola recalls Charles Bluhdorn wondering, after the multitude of screen tests (and all the money that was spent on them), how fifty-odd actors could all be terrible. He suggested that with just one director, it must actually be the *director* who was terrible. When it was all over, Coppola had the principals he wanted all along. However, the arguments had left the combative Coppola exhausted and the studio wary. Paramount kept a close eye on Coppola throughout the filming, making for a very pressurized situation.

The *Godfather* production was rough going. Coppola was disorganized, indecisive, and scattered. (His struggles with the studio would have understandably left little time for planning.) He didn't film in the conventional way of adhering to the shooting script—much of the movie was in his head. Production fell behind schedule, and each day cost $40,000. Many members of the crew were not supportive; they thought Coppola was in over his head. While in a bathroom stall, he overheard some of the crew griping, "Where did they find this kid? Did you ever see such a bad director in your life?" To make matters worse, from the start he battled with the stubborn cinematographer, Gordon Willis, who during production once exclaimed that Coppola "couldn't do anything right."

When the first rushes (the first positive prints made on the night of shooting and used to gauge progress) came in, Paramount was underwhelmed. Although Coppola and Willis had deliberately planned the interplay between dark and light scenes, as Peter Bart reports, some of the early dailies were so dark that Paramount had trouble seeing what was going on. This, in Bart's words, exacerbated Coppola's "difficult relationship with the studio." Brando mumbled in the Sollozzo meeting scene. (According to Coppola, the actor said that just because he was Marlon Brando, that didn't mean he didn't get nervous on his first day.) Evans had trouble understanding him in the scene and haughtily suggested subtitles.

The Paramount executives were concerned. They sent the script to Elia Kazan—another director—but Bart coaxed an art director friend of Kazan's into reporting the director's senility to Evans. This put the kibosh on plans for Kazan to take over, but Coppola had nightmares of the great Kazan awkwardly informing him of his firing.

COPPOLA'S FAMILY

On March 17, 1971 Coppola arranged for the full cast of Corleones to have an informal, improvisational "rehearsal" meal at Patsy's Restaurant in New York. He arranged for a home-style table with home-style dishes. The cast stood around, anxious and uncertain. Coppola recalls, "It was the first big time that the actors were to meet Brando, and although Brando was sort of washed up in the eyes of the Paramount executives, to people like Al Pacino and the rest of the cast, he was more than a god—he was God."

"We were all new to each other," said John Cazale in an interview. "We stood there not knowing what to do. Brando broke the ice. He just went over, opened a bottle of wine, and started the festivities. I think we all realized then that he was acting with us the way the Don would have acted with his own family." Coppola had hoped that a sensual activity such as eating would give the cast a chance to relate to one another as a family—and it did. Brando, wordlessly going into character, sat at the head of the table; Talia Shire (the female family member) served the food; and the "sons," Robert Duvall, James Caan, and Al Pacino, each in his own way tried to impress the "father," Brando. "Jimmy Caan was cracking jokes and trying to impress him, Al was trying to outbrood him, and whenever Brando would turn away, Duvall would imitate him, although he was clearly not really part of the group," Coppola reminisces. Throughout the process of that first improvisation, the actors all found their characters.

(i) so you know everyone's thinking "we have plenty of our own, why did Michael have to bring 'her'". Maybe families with eligible daughters should be introduced to Michael and Kay. "The American girl", an oddity. Michael and Kay think its funny; but they are really, underneath a bit uneasy about it. You'd have to be, especially Kay.

I think there should be a point where Michael introduces Kay to his Mother and Father. That could be economic and tell us a lot about Michael's relationship to his Father. Also, important that Michael is serious about Kay, and has brought her to the Wedding to ease her into the knowledge of who his father is.

[margin note: maybe use. Michael introducing KAY?]

(j) The Sex scene with Sonny and Lucy should go very far. I like Puzo's screenplay image of the Maid-Of-Honor's gown up, practically over her head. *[margin note: 1946 morals? mine.]*

(k) The scene with Bonasera is good and very important. It further defines the Don's power, and puts forth the essence of what it is the Don refers to as 'friendship' i.e. a pledge of loyalty. It is the gathering and manipulations of these pledges which give the Don his extraordinary power in the first place.
It is very important that after Bonasera gives his pledge, that we understand he feels he is now under a grave and frightening obligation to the Godfather. Bonasera must be a super, super actor.

Textures:

(l) Fat, older man dancing with a ten year old girl in a confirmation dress. Her little shoes on his big ones.

Older couple, having just danced a Tarentella; he is around the back of her with a white handkerchief, mopping her back, even down her dress, for her. *[margin note: yes — more impressions and less exposition.]*

Guest in an inappropriate tux, uncomfortable, adjusting it so he'll just look right. (Luca Brasi?)

Kids in little suits 'sliding around the sandwich man'.

Someone being asked to sing (Nino)? refusing and refusing as he is walking up to the bandstand.

Throwing the sandwiches.

(m) where we are. Also, it would be clear that we are viewing the overlap or repeated action through the eyes of a new character: one who had exited during the first time we had seen it; sort of like Rosenkrantz and Guildenstern Are Dead; repeating and reviewing the action from the perspective of other than the character's principally involved. We already know and experienced the whispering from the point of view of Sonny, Lucy, perhaps Sonny's wife; of what significance it is to Hagen, and therefore to the Don. This is an important stylistic decision.

4. THE CORE:

The core of the scene: Introduce the Don, and gradually reveal the breadth of his power, make clear his relationship to Michael.
Establish the fusion of family and business.
Introduce all the main characters and sub-plots of the film.

5. PITFALLS: *[margin note: corns.]*

Cliches, Italians who-a, talka lika-dis; failure to make a convincing setting. People must feel that they are seeing a real thing, with hundreds and hundreds of interesting specifics, like the children sliding around the 'sandwich man', throwing the sandwiches: "Hey Bino, two copagole and one prociutto!" etc. Failing to intoxicate with the formidability of the Don and his power.
Losing a basic 'humanity' to all these people.
Failing to set up a tension between the godfather and Michael re: the nature of their relationship.
[margin note: Too much exposition.]

THE BIBLE: COPPOLA'S NOTEBOOK

When Coppola embarked on adapting *The Godfather* novel into a feature film, he created a document analogous to a theater prompt book (Coppola had a background in theater). He took the novel and sliced out all the pages, pasting each one into the middle of a blank notebook page, and leaving a wide margin for his own notes. He used this massive document, which he called *The Godfather* Notebook, to analyze the novel and determine what would be included in the film.

In the notebook, he dissected the entire novel by diagramming the story—breaking down each of fifty scenes according to the following categories: Synopsis, The Times (how to preserve the 1940s period quality), Imagery and Tone, The Core (the essence of the scene), and Pitfalls (issues to watch out for, such as pacing or clichés). This approach to breaking down dramatic work was inspired by an Elia Kazan piece in *Directors on Directing: A Source Book of the Modern Theatre,* a collection of essays edited by Toby Cole and Helen Krich Chinoy.

Coppola peppered the notebook with his own ideas and concerns about how the scenes should play out, and how to make the film authentic to Italian and Mafia culture while remaining true to Puzo's novel. He also jotted down little pep talks to himself, such as this note on the characters' reactions to death: "This is tough. Think about it AND BE PREPARED, FRANCIS." Coppola now recalls, "I actually schlepped this with me every day of *The Godfather.*"

When it came time to direct *The Godfather*, Coppola relied on the notebook rather than the shooting script for inspiration. It's an amazing testament to his rigorous adaptation of the novel.

Paramount assigned Vice President Jack Ballard to keep an eye on costs. Coppola calls him "a grotesque guy with a bald head who was sent to make me miserable." Another issue: editor Aram Avakian and assistant director Steve Kesten, both of whom Coppola had hired, had designs on the director and producer jobs. Rumors of footage sabotage were even floated. Regardless, at this point, very little was necessary to fuel both Coppola and the studio's paranoia and antipathy toward each other. As Bart suggests, "Francis did feed into that skepticism."

Evans's and Coppola's stories diverge here. Evans said he found Coppola's footage brilliant, so he fired the interlopers. According to Coppola, associate producer Gray Frederickson told him that Avakian was bad-mouthing the footage to the higher-ups at Paramount. In addition, the studio refused to allow him to reshoot the Sollozzo scene—indicating to Coppola that they intended to sack him. Coppola didn't believe a studio would fire a director in the middle of the week, because they would need the weekend to get a new one on board, so he took matters into his own hands. He fired Kesten, Avakian, and a host of others midweek and quickly reshot the Sollozzo scene, in order to make the cost of hiring another director to reshoot it more prohibitive.

Undoubtedly, Paramount was taken aback by Coppola's counter-coup. They watched the new scene and concluded it was much better (although Coppola believes the original scene might actually be the one that ended up in the film). Paramount's concern about the PR implications of firing the *Godfather* director also worked in Coppola's favor. In addition, according to Marlon Brando's autobiography, he returned Coppola's favor of casting him by threatening to walk off the picture if Coppola was fired. While Brando had said that Coppola didn't give the actors much direction, in general Brando supported Coppola's artistic vision. Coppola stayed. Peter Bart has said that, after years of purposely avoiding thinking about it, he's come to the realization that, as he said at the South by Southwest Film Festival, "there really was a plot afoot during the third week of shooting *The Godfather* to fire Francis Coppola." In a recent interview, he states: "I honestly did feel from the second week that this was a remarkable movie being made, but the number of people seeing the dailies began to shrink." He explains, "You can always tell when a studio is giving up on a picture—you look around the room and there's nobody there." The tally of Coppola's near-firings: five—over casting Brando; when Paramount saw the first rushes; when Coppola insisted on shooting scenes on location in Sicily; when he went over budget; and during the editing process.

In August 1971, Coppola went home to San Francisco to edit a first cut of the film. It came in at two hours and forty-five minutes, but he knew that Paramount was unwilling to market a long epic to the moviegoing public, and had been told directly by Evans that if it were longer than two hours and fifteen minutes, Paramount would take the film and edit it themselves in Los Angeles. Coppola didn't want to go to L.A., because he would have less control and preferred to work from his home base. So he edited his first cut down to a two-hour, twenty-minute version of the film.

When Evans saw the shorter version, he went ballistic, as all of the texture had been left on the cutting-room floor. According to Al Ruddy, Evans got on the phone with the president of the studio, Frank Yablans, and told him the film seemed longer at two hours twenty minutes than at three hours. In his self-aggrandizing but very entertaining memoir, *The Kid Stays in the Picture,* he reported his admonishment to Coppola: "You shot a saga, and you turned in a trailer. Now give me a movie." So Paramount took the film to L.A. after all (as Coppola surmises they intended to do all along). During the editing process Evans had sciatica and was wheeled around on a hospital bed.

Debates rage as to who was ultimately responsible for the completed film. Shortly after the release, Coppola acknowledged in a *Time* interview: "Bob forces you to come up with alternatives. He pushes you until you please him. Ultimately, a mysterious kind of taste comes out; he backs away from bad ideas and accepts good ones." Evans even blamed the long hours he put in editing *The Godfather* for the disintegration of his marriage to Ali MacGraw.

But Coppola took umbrage at Evans's claims, even sending Evans a now-famous telegram (which Evans reportedly framed and displayed in his bathroom), that was reprinted in part by *The New York Times:* "Your stupid blabbing about cutting *The Godfather* comes back to me and angers me for its ridiculous pomposity. I've been a real gentleman regarding your claims of involvement. . . . You did nothing on *The Godfather* other than annoy me and slow it down." As he recently said, "After fighting me on Brando, fighting me on Pacino, fighting me on the music, and on whether or not it would be period, and on whether it would be in New York—now you say *you* made the movie because you put back in the half hour!"

As Stanley Jaffe, then president of the studio, now sums up, "The best move made by us at the studio was to hire Francis. . . . With Evans really overseeing the filming and Francis's strong vision and personality, there were moments of tension but always evolving into what made the movie better."

This much is true: Evans, to his credit, fought the higher-ups at Paramount for the longer version, and for the extra time needed to edit it properly (it was originally slated for a Christmas release). What is also apparent is that the magnificence of *The Godfather: Part II,* over which Coppola had complete control, is evidence that Coppola's rich artistic vision made its mark on *The Godfather.* As Al Ruddy says, "Francis was born to do this movie."

THE GODFATHER
THE COMPLETE ANNOTATED SCREENPLAY

THE NUTS AND BOLTS: PRODUCTION DETAIL

The slow camera movement that begins the film, which starts with a close-up of Bonasera's face and ends up behind Don Vito Corleone's head, takes more than two minutes to complete. This visual effect was created with a recently invented computer-timed lens, until then used only in commercials, which could be programmed to zoom for specific time increments. There are actually very few zoom shots in the picture—both Coppola and cinematographer Gordon Willis eschewed them for a more realistic perspective.

ADAPTATION AND THE CUTTING ROOM FLOOR

Coppola's original conception was to begin the film with the wedding, immediately introducing all of the characters. Then a friend pointed out how interestingly he had written the opening scene for *Patton,* in which the general gives a rousing speech to the viewer in front of a flag. Coppola rewrote the opening with the key Bonasera scene. From his notes: "It further defines the Don's power and puts forth the essence of what it is the Don refers to as 'friendship,' i.e., a pledge of loyalty." In starting with this scene, the film is actually more congruous with the novel, which opens with Bonasera in an American court of law, being denied justice. The book also includes extensive scenes in which the button man Paulie Gatto exacts Bonasera's justice on the men who hurt his daughter.

THE NUTS AND BOLTS: PRODUCTION DETAIL

Production notes indicate that ten percent of *The Godfather* was shot on sound stages at Filmways Studio lot located on 127th Street in East Harlem. The Corleone home was constructed for the film to include two stories, complete with a living room, dining room, full kitchen, paneled study, and a foyer with stairs leading to the bedroom.

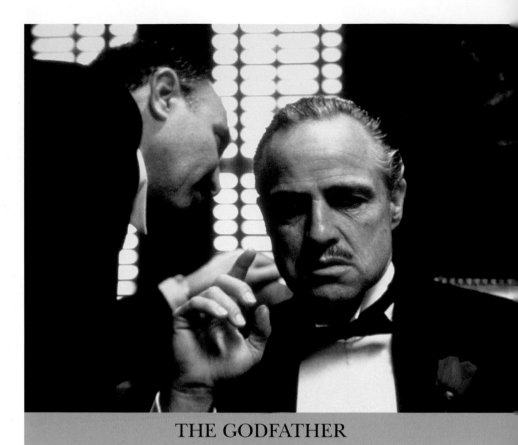

THE GODFATHER

INT DAY: DON'S OFFICE (SUMMER 1945)

The PARAMOUNT logo is presented austerely over a black background. There is a moment's hesitation, and then the simple words in white lettering:

Mario Puzo's
THE GODFATHER

While the black remains, we hear: "I believe in America." Suddenly we are watching in CLOSE VIEW, AMERIGO BONASERA, a man of sixty, dressed in a black suit, on the verge of great emotion.

BONASERA
I believe in America. America has made my fortune.

As he speaks, THE VIEW imperceptibly begins to loosen.

BONASERA
And I raised my daughter in the American fashion. I gave her freedom, but I taught her never to dishonor her family. She found a boyfriend— not an Italian. She went to the movies with him; she stayed out late. I didn't protest. Two months ago, he took her for a drive, with another

boyfriend. They made her drink whiskey, and then . . . they tried . . . to take advantage of her. She resisted; she kept her honor. So they beat her—like an animal. When I went to the hospital, her nose was a-broken, her jaw was a-shattered—held together by wire. She couldn't even weep because of the pain.

He can barely speak; he is weeping now.

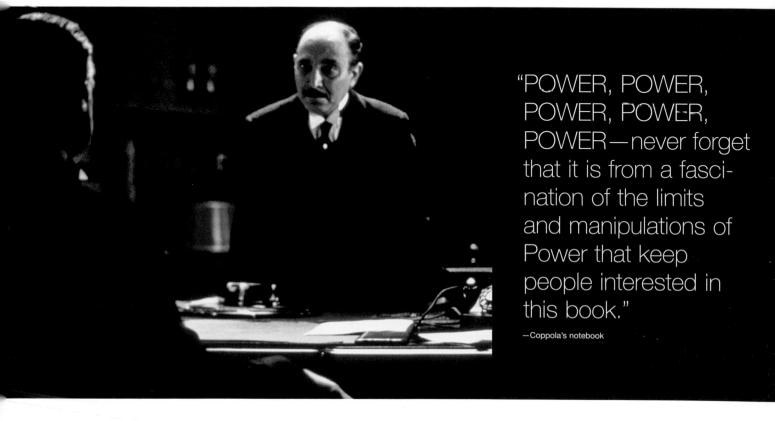

"POWER, POWER, POWER, POWER, POWER—never forget that it is from a fascination of the limits and manipulations of Power that keep people interested in this book."
—Coppola's notebook

BONASERA

But I wept. Why did I weep? She was the light of my life. Beautiful girl. Now she will never be beautiful again. Sorry. I—I went to the police, like a good American. These two boys were brought to trial. The judge sentenced them to three years in prison, and suspended the sentence. Suspended the sentence! They went free that very day! I stood in the courtroom like a fool, and those two bastards, they smiled at me. Then I said to my wife, 'For Justice, we must go to Don Corleone.'

By now, THE VIEW is full, and we see DON CORLEONE's office in his home. The blinds are closed, and so the room is dark and with patterned shadows. We are watching BONASERA over the shoulder of DON CORLEONE.

DON CORLEONE

Why did you go to the police? Why didn't you come to me first?

BONASERA

What do you want of me? Tell me anything, but do what I beg you to do.

DON CORLEONE

What is that?

BONASERA rises and whispers into THE DON's ear.

BONASERA

I want them dead.

DON CORLEONE

(shakes his head)

That I cannot do.

TOM HAGEN sits nearby at a small table, examining some paperwork. SONNY CORLEONE stands impatiently by the window nearest his father, sipping from a glass of wine.

BONASERA

I will give you anything you ask.

DON CORLEONE

(strokes a cat in his lap)

We've known each other many years, but this is the first time you ever came to me for counsel or for help. I can't remember the last time that you invited me to your house for a cuppa coffee, even though my wife is godmother to your only child. But let's be frank here. You never wanted my friendship, and you were afraid to be in my debt.

BONASERA

I didn't want to get into trouble.

DON CORLEONE

I understand. You found Paradise in America. You had a good trade, you made a good living, the police protected you, and there were courts of law; and you didn't need a friend like me. But now you come to me and you say, 'Don Corleone, give me Justice.' But you don't ask with respect; you don't offer friendship; you don't even think to call me Godfather. Instead, you come into my house on the day my daughter's to be married and you ask me to do murder—for money.

BONASERA

I ask you for Justice.

DON CORLEONE

That is not Justice; your daughter's still alive.

BONASERA

Let them suffer, then—as she suffers. How much shall I pay you?

Both HAGEN and SONNY react.

DON CORLEONE

(standing)

Bonasera, Bonasera, what have I ever done to make you treat me so disrespectfully? If you'd come to me in friendship, then the scum that

 BEHIND THE SCENES

The cat appearing in this scene was one of the many who lived at the old Filmways Studio. During the shooting, Coppola picked it up and placed it in Marlon Brando's lap. It is an example of how Coppola worked with Brando—rather than discoursing with him on acting, he would often provide Brando with stimulation by simply making props available to him. This improvised detail added texture to the scene by suggesting the character of Vito Corleone to be a gentle man with hidden claws. Of course, the downside of improvisation is the inevitable technical problems; the cat's loud purring drowned out Brando's dialogue, which later had to be dubbed into the film.

BEHIND THE SCENES

Salvatore Corsitto, the novice who portrays undertaker Amerigo Bonasera, was hired from an open casting call. According to Coppola, Brando considered Corsitto's performance to be among the best in the film, because it was so genuine. During this scene's shaky rehearsal, Brando recommended dialogue changes. Coppola reworked the scene, which was scheduled to be shot the very next day. Absurdly last-minute rewrites were a common occurrence during the film's production—dialogue changed so frequently that Coppola would often come to the set in the morning with freshly prepared cue cards for Marlon Brando, who refused to learn his lines.

ITALIAN CLICHÉS

Bonasera's thick Italian accent is rare in the American sequences of the film, and it was the actor's actual way of speaking. Coppola strove for authenticity throughout the making of *The Godfather*, emphasizing in the prompt book he called *The Godfather* Notebook to avoid the pitfall of clichéd Italians, "who-a talk-a like-a dis."

ruined your daughter would be suffering this very day. And if by chance an honest man like yourself should make enemies, then he would become *my* enemies.

> *(shakes his finger)*

And then they will fear you.

Slowly, BONASERA bows his head and murmurs.

BONASERA

Be my friend? . . . Godfather?

BONASERA kisses DON CORLEONE's hand.

DON CORLEONE

Good.

> *(walks BONASERA to the door)*

Some day, and that day may never come, I'll call upon you to do a service for me. But until that day, accept this Justice as a gift on my daughter's wedding day.

BONASERA

Grazie, Godfather.

DON CORLEONE

Prego.

BONASERA exits, HAGEN closes the door.

DON CORLEONE

Ahh give this to . . . Clemenza. I want reliable people—people that aren't gonna be carried away. I mean, we're not murderers, in spite of what this . . . undertaker says.

THE DON smells his rose boutonniere.

EXT DAY: MALL (SUMMER 1945)

A HIGH ANGLE of the CORLEONE MALL in bright daylight. There are at least five hundred guests filling the main courtyard and gardens. There is music and laughter and dancing, and countless tables covered with food and wine.

The entire family, all dressed in the formal attire of the wedding party, poses for a family portrait: DON CORLEONE, MAMA, son SONNY, his wife, SANDRA, and their CHILDREN, TOM HAGEN, his wife, THERESA, and their BABY, son FREDO, CONSTANZIA, the bride, and her bridegroom, CARLO RIZZI. As they move into the pose, THE DON seems preoccupied.

DON CORLEONE

Where is Michael?

SONNY

Huh? Don't worry, it's early yet.

DON CORLEONE

We're not taking the picture without Michael.

(SPEAKS ITALIAN to the PHOTOGRAPHER)

HAGEN

What's the matter?

SONNY

It's Michael . . .

DON CORLEONE warmly shakes and squeezes the hands of the friends and guests, and makes them all welcome. MAMA dances with the guests. CONNIE and CARLO laugh and talk at the wedding table. OVERHEAD shot of GUESTS dancing.

EXT DAY: MALL ENTRANCE (SUMMER 1945)

Outside the main gate of the MALL, SEVERAL MEN in suits, working together with a MAN in a dark sedan, walk in and out of the rows of parked cars, writing license plate numbers down in their notebooks. We HEAR the music and laughter coming from the party in the distance.

◉ THE NUTS AND BOLTS: PRODUCTION DETAIL

In Mario Puzo's novel, Constanzia Corleone's wedding invitations listed the event as the last Saturday in August 1945 in Long Beach, Long Island.

◉ THE NUTS AND BOLTS: PRODUCTION DETAIL

The Corleone Compound (aka the Mall) shooting location was on Longfellow Road, a quiet side street in residential Staten Island. Although it was already secluded, the crew constructed an eight-foot-high faux stone wall made from Styrofoam to further isolate the area. The wedding was staged on the sprawling lawn behind the wall. Studio reports varied on the number of extras bused in (up to 750), and included local residents and their children, a passel of Coppolas, and even other cast members' families. The feast included thousands of cookies, yard-wide trays of lasagne, huge baskets of fruit, barrels of beer, gallons of wine, and a six-foot-high, four-tiered wedding cake. The food had to be replenished for each of the four days of filming. Richmond Floral Company provided over two hundred pure white orchids for the bridal bouquets and one hundred Canhamiana orchids (a popular flower in the 1940s) for corsages.

EXT DAY: MALL

PETER CLEMENZA dances the tarantella joyously.

EXT DAY: MALL ENTRANCE

A MAN stops at a limousine and copies down the number.

EXT DAY: MALL

SAL TESSIO playfully tosses an orange into the air.

                                                    CUT TO:

BARZINI, dignified with a black homburg, is always under the watchful eyes of TWO BODYGUARDS as he makes his way to embrace DON CORLEONE in the courtyard.

DON CORLEONE
Don Barzini. You know Santino.

                                                    CUT TO:

CLEMENZA, sweating, stumbles away from the dancing.

CLEMENZA
Hey, Paulie!

Lemme have some wine! Paulie! More wine.

PAULIE hustles, gets a pitcher of icy black wine, and brings it to him.

PAULIE

Excuse me, please. Aw, you look terrif on the floor!

CLEMENZA

(out of breath)

What are ya, a dance judge or somethin'?

(SPEAKS ITALIAN)

Go take a walk around the neighborhood; do your job.

PAULIE walks through the crowd.

CUT TO:

SONNY pinches the cheek of the maid of honor, LUCY MANCINI, who returns his delicious smile. Then he moves to his wife.

SONNY

Hey, Sandra, come on, do me a favor—watch the kids. Don't let 'em run wild, all right?

SANDRA

(annoyed)

Well, you watch yourself, all right?

CUT TO:

TESSIO, a tall, gentle-looking man, dances with a NINE-YEAR-OLD GIRL, her little white party shoes planted on his enormous brown shoes.

CUT TO:

THE DON dances with MAMA.

CUT TO:

CONNIE CORLEONE, the bride, thanks the various GUESTS for the white envelopes they are putting into the large white purse she holds. CARLO has his blue eyes trained on the bulging envelopes and is trying to guess how much cash they hold.

PAULIE

(looking on)

Twenty, thirty grand, in small bills, *cash*—in that little silk purse. Aw, and if this were somebody else's wedding, sweet tomato!

MAN

(throws cappocolo sandwiches in his direction)

Hey, Paulie!

(SPEAKS ITALIAN)

 ITALIANISMS

In the novel, Puzo wrote that Connie agreed to a "guinea" wedding to appease her father, who was unhappy with her choice of husband. There are many authentic Italian touches in the wedding sequences: Clemenza dancing the tarantella; Connie's money-filled silk purse; the colored lightbulbs mounted on a lacy network of wires—reminiscent of Italian street fairs like the Feast of San Gennaro; the throwing of wrapped meat sandwiches (a memory of weddings from Coppola's childhood). Coppola sketched out the feel for the scene in his notebook: "There are many, many guests . . . the bigger the better for this scene. They come from all walks of life, as the Don is a just man. Most of them have come from the city, on the train, or have driven. They have brought their children with them, and so, of all the guests, one-fourth of the number should be children of all ages, even infants. Italian people do not leave their children at home. The ones who are old enough to walk wear little suits, and pretty dresses, some if not many of the boys wear short pants and shiny shoes. Perhaps even a confirmation outfit here or there. Even the children drink wine."

 THE NUTS AND BOLTS: PRODUCTION DETAIL

Six cameras were used to shoot the wedding sequences, including four around the garden to capture cinema verité shots, as well as a soundman wandering around to record improvised dialogue. There was also a camera in a helicopter, but many of those shots were too jumpy and weren't used.

ADAPTATION AND THE CUTTING ROOM FLOOR

In both the novel and the shooting script written prior to filming, it is Michael who tells Kay about the Sicilian tradition of never refusing a request on a daughter's wedding day. The original version actually makes more sense, as Theresa Hagen is herself Italian and wouldn't need this explained to her.

CAST AND CREW: TERE LIVRANO

Tere Livrano, an assistant music editor in Paramount's television music department, was chosen for the part of Theresa Hagen after a friend submitted her photograph to Coppola.

PAULIE

(catching the sandwiches)

Stupid jerk!

CUT TO:

A PHOTOGRAPHER snaps a picture of BARZINI seated at one of the tables. BARZINI sends his two BODYGUARDS to rip the film out of the camera, and BARZINI destroys it.

PHOTOGRAPHER

Hey, what's a matter?

CUT TO:

HAGEN kisses his WIFE.

HAGEN

Have to go back to work.

THERESA

Oh, Tom!

HAGEN

It's part of the wedding. No Sicilian can refuse any request on his daughter's wedding day.

HAGEN walks back to the house, where a group of MEN nervously wait. HAGEN crooks a finger at NAZORINE, who quickly runs after him into the house.

LUCA

(practicing)

Don Corleone, I am honored and grateful that you have invited me to your home . . .

EXT DAY: MALL ENTRANCE

The MEN move on to other parked cars. SONNY storms out of the gate, his face flushed with anger, followed by PAULIE and CLEMENZA.

SONNY

Hey, what's this? Get outta here! It's a private party. Go on! What is it?
Hey, it's my sister's wedding.

The MAN doesn't answer, but points to the DRIVER of the sedan. SONNY menacingly thrusts his reddened face at him. The DRIVER merely flips open his wallet and shows a card, without saying a word. SONNY steps back, spits on the ground, turns, and walks away, followed by CLEMENZA and PAULIE.

SONNY

Goddamn FBI don't respect nothin'.

SONNY spots a PHOTOGRAPHER on the walk back to the courtyard.

"The wedding reception that opens the film functions beautifully on multiple levels. It is first of all a warm and completely convincing Italian family wedding, shot with loving attention to detail. But it also serves as a vehicle to introduce us to the film's major characters, all of whom appear at both the public part of the wedding and the behind-the-scenes palavering in Vito Corleone's private study. And this split between the public and the private, between what is seen and what is known, turns out to be one of the film's great themes."

— Kenneth Turan, film critic

 ADAPTATION AND THE CUTTING ROOM FLOOR

The film version of the wedding includes more shots of the festivities than the preproduction shooting script initially indicated: Connie and Carlo dancing, Mama Corleone singing, Mama and Vito dancing, Tessio tossing an orange into the air—light and lively touches. The additions make the contrast between the gaiety and the underlying tension more pronounced, for example, the crosscutting between FBI agents noting license numbers and the dancing. Some dark interludes not in the shooting script were added to the movie as well, such as rival family head Barzini destroying film from a photographer's camera, and Michael's shocking explanation of how his father helped Johnny's career.

CAST AND CREW: GORDON WILLIS AND THE LOOK OF *THE GODFATHER*

Cinematographer Gordon Willis was fairly new to the feature-film scene when he was hired for *The Godfather*. He had been the cinematographer on six films, all in the span of two years. Willis and Coppola had a combustible relationship during the production of *The Godfather*. They've both been characterized as stubborn and single-minded, and they would often have screaming fights, with a few broken props as a result. After one incident, such a loud noise exploded from Coppola's office that the crew thought Coppola had shot himself (he had only broken a door). The two also conflicted because Willis was very hard on the actors about hitting their marks—with his low lighting scheme, if they missed, they would be filmed in darkness. Coppola, on the other hand, considered himself a protector of the actors. He felt he could get the most out of them by nurturing them.

Despite the fireworks, Willis and Coppola turned out to be the perfect foil for each other: Willis a slow and meticulous perspective purist and rationalist, looking for the beauty in simplicity, and Coppola with the theatrical, grand ideas. The result of the collaboration was stunning cinematography that broke the rules of traditional Hollywood filmmaking. Willis's low light levels and selective masking of Brando's eyes gave an ominous undercurrent to Don Corleone's scenes—very controversial for the time. His intent was to hide from the audience what Vito Corleone was thinking, and use the darkness to personify his evil. Filming in dark conditions helped earn Willis the nickname "The Prince of Darkness." Willis also infused the picture with a golden amber aura, a kind of visual metaphor for the past. Countless period films have copied this technique.

In an amazing seven-year span from 1971 to 1977, seven of the films that he worked on amassed thirty-nine Oscar® nominations and nineteen wins. Coppola recounts that he learned many things from Willis that continue to influence his own filmmaking.

SONNY

Hey, c'mere, c'mere—c'mere, c'mere—c'mere. C'mere! Gimme!

SONNY pushes the PHOTOGRAPHER against a car and smashes his camera on the ground. PAULIE kicks the camera while CLEMENZA restrains SONNY. SONNY throws a few bills at the PHOTOGRAPHER's feet and walks quickly away, followed by PAULIE and CLEMENZA.

INT DAY: DON'S OFFICE

DON CORLEONE sits quietly behind his massive desk in the dark study. Across from him: NAZORINE, TOM HAGEN, and ENZO (NAZORINE's prospective son-in-law).

NAZORINE

. . . but towards the end, he was paroled to help with the American war effort—so, for the last six months, he's been workin' in my pastry shop.

DON CORLEONE

Nazorine, my friend, what can I do for you?

NAZORINE

Well, now that the war is over, this boy, Enzo, they want to repatriate him back to Italy. Godfather, I have a daughter. See, she and Enzo . . .

DON CORLEONE

You want Enzo to stay in this country, and you want your daughter to be married.

Relieved, NAZORINE rises and clasps THE DON's hands in gratitude.

NAZORINE

You understand everything.

DON CORLEONE

Prego.

NAZORINE

(rising)

Thank you.

(to HAGEN)

Mr. Hagen, thank you, huh?

(backing out, enthusiastically)

And wait till you see the beautiful wedding cake I made for your daughter. Oof! Like this.

(LAUGHS)

The bride and the groom and the angel . . .

NAZORINE backs out, all smiles, and nods to the GODFATHER. DON CORLEONE rises and moves to the Venetian blinds.

ADAPTATION AND THE CUTTING ROOM FLOOR

In the novel, another person given an audience by Don Corleone is a young man coincidentally named Anthony Coppola, who asks for help to open a pizzeria.

HAGEN

Who should I give this job to?

DON CORLEONE

Not to our paisan. Give it to a Jew congressman in another district. Who else is on the list?

THE DON is peeking out through the window blinds.

EXT DAY: MALL

WHAT THE DON SEES:

MICHAEL CORLEONE, dressed in the uniform of a marine captain, leading KAY ADAMS through the wedding crowd, is occasionally stopped and greeted by FRIENDS of the family.

GIRL'S VOICE

Hello!

GIRL'S VOICE

Michael.

THE DON, inside the office, peering through the blinds, watching MICHAEL and KAY.

MICHAEL dances with KAY.

INT DAY: DON'S OFFICE

> **HAGEN**
>
> He's not on the list, but Luca Brasi wants to see you.

THE DON turns to HAGEN.

> **DON CORLEONE**
>
> Is this—is this necessary?

> **HAGEN**
>
> He didn't expect to be invited to the wedding, so he wanted to thank you.

> **DON CORLEONE**
>
> All right.

EXT DAY: MALL

LUCA BRASI sitting alone, grotesque, and quietly rehearsing what he will say to DON CORLEONE. Nearby, KAY and MICHAEL are eating at a table at the edge of the wedding. She is smoking a cigarette.

> **LUCA**
>
> Don Corleone, I am honored and grateful . . . that you have invited me to your home . . . on the wedding day of your daughter. May their first child be a masculine child.

> **LUCA**
>
> Don—

> **KAY**
>
> Michael . . .

> **LUCA**
>
> Don—Corleone . . .

> **KAY**
>
> . . . that man over there's talking to himself.

She has picked out LUCA BRASI.

> **LUCA**
>
> I am honored and grateful that you invited me . . .

> **KAY**
>
> See that scary guy over there?

> **LUCA**
>
> . . . on the wedding day of your daughter . . .

> **MICHAEL**
>
> He's a very scary guy.

CAST AND CREW: LENNY MONTANA

Lenny Montana—at six feet six inches tall and three hundred twenty pounds—was a former World Champion wrestler, nicknamed The Zebra Kid. Producer Al Ruddy "discovered" him among a group of onlookers at an early shooting. Not a professional actor, Montana repeatedly botched his lines. Coppola had the inspired idea of adding these short scenes of Brasi practicing what he will say to Don Corleone— these illustrations of Brasi's nervousness thereby explain his subsequent fumbling in his scene with the Don. Apparently Montana's nerves didn't prevent him from playing prankster: at one point he opened his mouth to speak to the Don and stuck out his tongue, which had on it a "fuck you" note. Brando, always one for a good joke, laughed uproariously.

GOOFS, GAFFES, AND BLOOPERS

Look for the cigarette in Kay's hand, which disappears and reappears again.

BELOW: DICK SMITH (LEFT) WITH PHILIP RHODES, BRANDO'S PERSONAL MAKEUP ARTIST, TRANSFORMING HIM INTO THE DON.

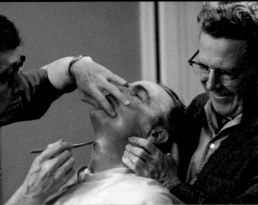

CAST AND CREW: DICK SMITH AND MARLON BRANDO'S MAKEUP

Dick Smith was the head of the New York NBC-TV makeup department from 1945 to 1959, and was television's first significant makeup artist, with nearly one hundred productions under his belt. Prior to *The Godfather,* he made a name for himself in film by doing Dustin Hoffman's 121-year-old makeup in *Little Big Man.* His fifty-film career includes *The Exorcist* and *Amadeus,* for which he won an Oscar®. For *The Godfather,* Smith pioneered the use of Karo syrup as blood (which he first tested in *Midnight Cowboy*). Over the course of a rich career, he has developed countless new materials and techniques, written books that have inspired many of today's talented makeup artists, and is considered to be the "godfather" of modern-day special effects. In an interview with the author, he describes the process of transforming Marlon Brando into the Don:

"I was sent over to England to talk to Marlon Brando about what kind of makeup to use for the film. We have a nice luncheon and he lets me do all the talking. He doesn't explicitly agree to anything—very cagey, this guy. I assume he's agreeing with me, but he hasn't said anything. Time passes and he's back in the States, and now we come to doing a real makeup test. I try putting on some appliances, and he's not too anxious to do it. From a makeup standpoint, he wants to do more or less nothing. 'Plumpers' are definitely in; he's going to have some real dentures made

KAY

Well, who is he? What's his name?

MICHAEL

His name is Luca Brasi—he helps my father out sometimes.

KAY

(smiling nervously)

Oh, Michael, wait a minute; he's coming over here.

LUCA comes toward them to meet TOM HAGEN halfway, just near their table.

HAGEN

(approaching MICHAEL and KAY)

Mikey!

MICHAEL

Oh! Tom!

HAGEN

Hey!

They embrace.

HAGEN

You look terrific.

MICHAEL

My brother Tom Hagen, Miss Kay Adams.

KAY and HAGEN shake hands.

HAGEN

How do you do.

KAY

How do you do.

HAGEN

(privately to MICHAEL)

Your father's been asking for you.

HAGEN

(to KAY)

Very nice to meet you.

KAY

Nice to meet you.

HAGEN smiles and moves back toward the house, LUCA ominously following.

GIRL'S VOICE

(SPEAKS ITALIAN)

KAY

If he's your brother, why does he have a different name?

MICHAEL

Oh, when my brother Sonny was a kid, he found Tom Hagen in the street—and he had no home—and so my father took him in. And he's been with us ever since. He's a good lawyer. Not a Sicilian, but . . . I think he's gonna be consigliere.

KAY

What's that?

MICHAEL

That's like a counselor, an advisor. Very important to the Family. You like your lasagna?

INT DAY: DON'S OFFICE

LUCA

Don Corleone . . .

THE DON lets the stiffly formal LUCA move forward to kiss his cheek. He takes an envelope from his jacket and holds it out, but does not release it until he makes a formal speech.

LUCA

(with difficulty)

I am honored and grateful . . . that you have invited me to your daughter's wedding. On the day of your daughter's wedding. And I hope that their first child . . . will be a masculine child. I pledge . . . my ever—

A group of CHILDREN run into the office. HAGEN quietly corrals them out the door.

LUCA

—ending loyalty.

(he offers the envelope)

For your daughter's bridal purse.

DON CORLEONE

Thank you, Luca, my most valued friend.

THE DON takes the envelope, and then LUCA's hand. They shake hands, each nodding.

LUCA

Don Corleone, I'm gonna leave you now, because I know you are busy. Thank you.

LUCA backs away and HAGEN shows him out.

for the effect. Kind of like a removable bridge that clamps onto his lower teeth, and attached to the outer sides of it are two pink, plastic lumps that are shaped so as to make bulges where his cheeks or jowls would be. I take casts of his upper and lower teeth and get a dentist to do what I think is proper. The only trouble is Marlon is going out to Hollywood for something else, and it quickly gets out of my hands. There is no time to fit him. I gave the dentures to Marlon to take with him. The next time we're gonna see Marlon is the first day of shooting in Staten Island for quite a few scenes. Marlon comes in at nine in the morning, takes the dentures out of his pocket, and I see that the dentist has flattened the blobs so they're ruined. It's gonna take a few hours to fix them. This holds up shooting for three hours while I take a dental acrylic and mold it on to fatten it up, and then polish them. They're fixed around noon and shooting proceeds. I'm watching Marlon like a hawk, and of course I see the dailies. They're okay, but the bulges are just a little overboard. It's not serious—he can get away with it—but every day I grind a little more off so as not to have a precipitous change. All that section of the film on Staten Island is done with the overdone dentures. If you look sharply you can see that it is a little bit much; it becomes subtler later on. . . . Incidentally, many people, both in the business and out of it, attributed Marlon's way of talking for the character to his wearing the plumpers, but it was not that at all. The voice was his creation."

"The kids at an Italian wedding have the run of the place."

—Coppola, in a preproduction meeting

A MOMENT OF LEVITY DURING THE PRODUCTION OF THE WEDDING SCENES.

▶ BEHIND THE SCENES

This Italian wedding was truly a family affair. Not only did his father lead the band, but Coppola's cousin sang the aria, and other relatives were extras. Richard Castellano's (Clemenza's) brother appears in the background of several scenes. Even the man in charge of supplying police officers for the production, Sonny Grosso, reports that his whole family served as extras.

CAST AND CREW: CARMINE COPPOLA

Francis's father, Carmine Coppola, organized an actual six-piece Italian band for the wedding, which made for a lively (if more expensive) set. He composed the tarantella at the start of the sequence, as well as a foxtrot and mazurka. The musically talented Carmine had once played in the NBC Symphony Orchestra under the direction of Arturo Toscanini. Francis has rightly pointed out that *The Godfather* helped Carmine's career immensely, as he went on to do other movie work. When accepting his Academy Award® for *The Godfather: Part II,* Carmine pointed out—just as correctly—that without *him,* Francis wouldn't even be here (to which Carmine's wife Italia sharply responded, as reported in *California* magazine, "Gee, Carmine . . . I hope the labor pains weren't too bad").

EXT DAY: MALL

CONNIE dances with CARLO.

SONNY is sitting at the wedding dais. Every once in a while he glances across the courtyard, where his WIFE is talking with some WOMEN. He bends over and whispers something into the ear of the maid of honor, LUCY MANCINI.

SANDRA and the WOMEN are in the middle of a big, ribald laugh. SANDRA's hands separate with expanding width, farther and farther apart, until she bursts into a peal of laughter. Through her separated hands she sees the wedding dais. SONNY and LUCY are gone.

CROWD

(SINGING)

LA LA LA LA LA LA

MAN

(SPEAKS ITALIAN)

Some of the MALE GUESTS surround MAMA, begging her for a song. They bring her to the dais to sing as she playfully protests.

MAMA

No! . . . No!

MAMA

(SINGS) SERA LUNA . . .

The crowd joins in the singing, clapping hands.

MAMA

Nazorine!

INT DAY: DON'S HALL AND STAIRS

SONNY walks through THE DON's hallway and up the stairs.

EXT DAY: MALL

OLD MAN

(SINGS IN ITALIAN)

The crowd claps, shouts, yells, and laughs to the old man's song.

INT DAY: DON'S HALL AND STAIRS

LUCY MANCINI looks around nervously, lifts her petticoat off the ground, and hurries upstairs, where SONNY is standing on the second landing, motioning for her to come up.

EXT DAY: MALL

The OLD MAN dances.

CAST AND CREW:
MORGANA KING

A variety of actresses, from Anne Bancroft to Alida
Valli, were considered for the part of Carmella
"Mama" Corleone. Morgana King, born Maria Grazia
Morgana Messina de Berardinis, was a jazz singer of
Sicilian descent. *The Godfather* was her first film.

INT DAY: DON'S OFFICE

> HAGEN
>
> Senator Cauley apologized for not coming personally, but said you'd
> understand. Also some of the judges; they've all sent gifts.
>
> *(lifts a glass of wine)*
>
> *Salud.*

We can HEAR SCREAMING.

> DON CORLEONE
>
> What is that outside?

 **ADAPTATION AND THE CUTTING
ROOM FLOOR**

In the pre-film shooting script, Tom Hagen tells the
Don of Sollozzo's background in the drug trade
during this scene when they discuss the senator and
judges. In the movie, this exposition happens just
before their meeting with Sollozzo.

EXT DAY: MALL

JOHNNY FONTANE has arrived at the MALL. He is mobbed by screaming young girls
wanting his autograph as he makes his way into the crowd.

> CONNIE
> *(runs and embraces JOHNNY)*
>
> Johnny! Johnny! I love you!

CONNIE leads JOHNNY to the dais.

INT DAY: DON'S OFFICE

DON CORLEONE at the window, looks through the blinds to see who has arrived.

MANY WEDDING SCENES WERE SHOT AND LEFT ON THE CUTTING ROOM FLOOR.

ADAPTATION AND THE CUTTING ROOM FLOOR

The novel devotes many pages to the Johnny Fontane story line: his relationship with women; Woltz's vendetta against him; getting into the producing game; and inviting an Italian singing buddy from the neighborhood to work with him in Hollywood.

THE NUTS AND BOLTS: PRODUCTION DETAIL

Despite the fading light, Coppola was under orders from the studio to keep shooting. The shots in which Michael appears to the right of Kay were all shot at night, with lamps blazing down to keep continuity with the bright sunlight in the other shots. To cinematographer Gordon Willis's credit, the transitions are fairly seamless.

> DON CORLEONE
> *(pleased)*
>
> He came all the way from California to come to the wedding. I told ya he was goin' to come.
>
> HAGEN
>
> It's been two years; he's probably in trouble again.
>
> DON CORLEONE
>
> He's a good godson.

EXT DAY: MALL

> MAMA
>
> Johnny! Johnny!
>
> (SPEAKS ITALIAN)
>
> . . . then sing a song!

The crowd shouts and applauds JOHNNY.

> KAY
> *(at her table with MICHAEL)*
>
> Michael, you never told me you knew Johnny Fontane.
>
> MICHAEL
>
> Sure. You want to meet him?
>
> KAY
>
> Huh? Oh, ah . . . sure.
>
> MICHAEL
> *(takes her hand)*
>
> My father helped him with his career.
>
> JOHNNY
>
> *O Marenariello.*
>
> KAY
>
> He did? How?

JOHNNY FONTANE is on the bandstand, singing to the delight and excitement of the wedding guests.

> JOHNNY
> *(amid intermittent girlish screams)*
>
> *(SINGS)* I HAVE BUT ONE HEART . . .
>
> MICHAEL
>
> Let's listen to the song.

KAY

No, Michael.

JOHNNY

(SINGS) THIS HEART I BRING YOU

I HAVE BUT ONE HEART

TO SHARE WITH YOU

I HAVE BUT ONE DREAM

THAT I CAN CLING TO

YOU ARE THE ONE DREAM

I PRAY COMES TRUE

KAY

Please, Michael, tell me.

JOHNNY

(SINGS) MY DARLING, UNTIL I SAW YOU . . .

MICHAEL

(over Johnny's song)

Well, when Johnny was first starting out, he was signed to this . . . personal service contract, with a big bandleader. And as his career got better and better, he wanted to get out of it. Now Johnny is my father's godson. And my father went to see this bandleader. And he offered him ten thousand dollars to let Johnny go. The bandleader said no. So the *next* day, my father went to see him, only this time with Luca Brasi. Within an hour he signed a release for a certified check of one thousand dollars.

JOHNNY

(singing through MICHAEL's speech)

. . . *VICINO MARE* . . .

MARIO PUZO'S ENCOUNTER WITH FRANK SINATRA

The Johnny Fontane character is seemingly inspired by Frank Sinatra, an Italian singer whose career was also revived by a movie role (*From Here to Eternity*). After *The Godfather* was published, Puzo went to a birthday party at Chasen's. When the millionaire host insisted on introducing him to Sinatra, all hell broke loose. Puzo chronicled the famous encounter in his book *The Godfather Papers: and Other Confessions*: " . . . Sinatra started to shout abuse. . . . But what hurt was that there he was, a Northern Italian, threatening me, a Southern Italian, with physical violence. This was roughly equivalent to Einstein pulling a knife on Al Capone. It just wasn't done. Northern Italians never mess with Southern Italians except to get them put in jail or deported to some desert island. Sinatra kept up his abuse and I kept staring at him. He kept staring down at his plate. Yelling. He never looked up." Some reports suggest that John Wayne, seated nearby, offered to punch Puzo if necessary.

> KAY

How did he do that?

> MICHAEL

My father made him an offer he couldn't refuse.

> KAY

What was that?

> MICHAEL

Luca Brasi held a gun to his head, and my father assured him that either his brains or his signature would be on the contract.

> (*pauses*)

That's a true story.

> JOHNNY

(SINGS) MA P'ALLEREZZA

STONG'A MURI . . .

KAY is silent.

> MICHAEL

That's my family, Kay; it's not me.

JOHNNY finishes the song and the CROWD screams with delight.

> MAMA

Beautiful.

> VOICE

Bravo!

THE DON and HAGEN walk outside amid the applause, and THE DON embraces JOHNNY. The crowd raise their glasses in a toast.

THE DON indicates for JOHNNY to come with him to the office so that no one will notice. He turns to HAGEN, as the music starts again.

Michael's disturbing description of how his father launched Johnny's career was not in the shooting script written prior to filming. Neither was the comical scene of Fredo's introduction.

CAST AND CREW: JEANNIE LINERO

Jeannie Linero was a dancer before appearing as Lucy Mancini in *The Godfather,* her first film.

DON CORLEONE

Tom . . . I want you to find Santino. Tell him to come to the office.

They go, leaving HAGEN scanning the party looking for SONNY.

A drunken FREDO approaches MICHAEL and KAY's table, surprising MICHAEL. He drops onto his knees, down to their level.

MICHAEL

How are you, Fredo?

(to KAY)

Fredo? My brother Fredo, this is Kay Adams.

KAY

Oh. Hi.

FREDO

(leaning in to kiss KAY)

How do you do?

KAY

(laughs)

Hello.

FREDO

This is my brother Mike.

MICHAEL

Are ya having a good time?

FREDO

Huh? Yeah. This is your friend, huh?

INT DAY: DON'S OFFICE

THE DON is at his desk, listening to JOHNNY.

JOHNNY

I don't know what to do. My voice is . . . is weak. It's weak. Anyway, if I had this part in the picture, you know? It puts me right back up on top again. But this—this man out there, he—he won't give it to me, the head of the studio.

DON CORLEONE

What's his name?

JOHNNY

Woltz. Woltz, he—he won't give it to me, and he says there's no chance. No chance.

INT DAY: DON'S HALLWAY

HAGEN glances up the staircase.

> ### HAGEN
>
> Sonny? Sonny!

Then he goes up.

INT DAY: DON'S UPSTAIRS ROOM

SONNY and LUCY are in a room upstairs; he has lifted her gown's skirts up and has her standing up against the door. Her face peeks out from the layers of petticoats around it, like a flower in ecstasy.

> ### LUCY
> *(gasping)*
>
> Uh uh uh . . .

Her head is bouncing against the door with the rhythm of her body. But there is a knocking as well. They stop; freeze in that position.

> ### HAGEN
> *(from hallway)*
>
> Sonny. Sonny, you in there?

> ### SONNY
>
> What?

INT DAY: DON'S UPSTAIRS HALLWAY

Outside, HAGEN by the door.

> ### HAGEN
>
> The old man wants to see you.

INT DAY: DON'S UPSTAIRS ROOM

> ### SONNY
>
> Yeah. One minute.

INT DAY: DON'S UPSTAIRS HALLWAY

HAGEN hesitates. We hear LUCY's HEAD bouncing against the door again. TOM smiles and leaves.

> ### LUCY
> *(grunts)*
>
> Oh oh oh . . . Oh, Sonneeee! Oh oh oh . . .

 BEHIND THE SCENES

While Sonny was having his way with Lucy, Coppola's wife, Eleanor, went into labor with their third child. After the scene was completed, Coppola went to the hospital, and future filmmaker Sofia was born. The movie spawn of the Sonny/Lucy union was Vincent, portrayed by Andy Garcia in *The Godfather: Part III,* who becomes involved with Michael's daughter, Mary—played by none other than the grown-up Sofia Coppola.

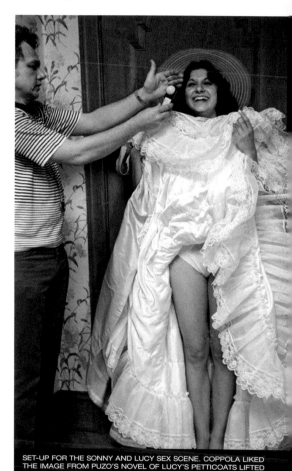

SET-UP FOR THE SONNY AND LUCY SEX SCENE. COPPOLA LIKED THE IMAGE FROM PUZO'S NOVEL OF LUCY'S PETTICOATS LIFTED IN THE AIR.

ADAPTATION AND THE CUTTING ROOM FLOOR

The novel's extensive Lucy Mancini plotline is all but eliminated from the film. In the book, her affair with Sonny is described in great detail. With the Corleone family's help, she eventually moves to Las Vegas. She embarks on a relationship with Jules Segal, a doctor who eagerly helps her correct a weakening of her pelvic floor—although Puzo most often describes her condition, aka her "large box," in sexual rather than medical terms. Coppola viewed the story line as extraneous, and such salacious descriptions initially dissuaded him from accepting the project.

ITALIANISMS

Finocchio is a derogatory term for a homosexual.

BEHIND THE SCENES

Alex Rocco, who played the part of Moe Greene, was on the set the day of this scene between Johnny and the Don. He reports that Al Martino (Johnny Fontane) approached Marlon Brando before the scene, obsequiously calling him a great actor and asking for pointers on how to bring out his emotion for the scene. Brando told him not to worry, "I'll help you." When they proceeded to shoot the scene, Brando gave Martino a real whack across the face—which indeed helped bring tears to Martino's eyes.

EXT DAY: MALL

> WOMAN
>
> (SINGS ITALIAN ARIA)

INT DAY: DON'S OFFICE

HAGEN enters THE DON's office silently, while JOHNNY speaks.

> JOHNNY
>
> A month ago he bought the movie rights to this book, the bestseller. And the main character is a guy just like me. Why, y'know, I wouldn't even have to act—just be myself.

JOHNNY buries his head in his hands.

> JOHNNY
>
> But, oh, Godfather, I don't know what to do. I don't know what to do.

THE DON erupts out of his chair, grabs JOHNNY's hands, and slaps his face.

> DON CORLEONE
>
> *You can act like a man!* What's the matter with you?! Is this how you turned out? A Hollywood *finocchio* that cries like a woman? *(IMITATES CRYING)* What can I do, what can I do? What is that nonsense? Ridiculous.

Both HAGEN and JOHNNY cannot refrain from laughing. THE DON smiles. SONNY enters as noiselessly as possible, still adjusting his clothes. THE DON glances at SONNY, who makes himself as inconspicuous as possible. THE DON is stern.

> DON CORLEONE
>
> You spend time with your family?

> JOHNNY
>
> Sure I do.

> DON CORLEONE
>
> Good. Because a man who doesn't spend time with his family can never be a real man. C'mere. You look terrible. I want you to eat, I want you to rest well and a month from now this Hollywood big shot's gonna give you what you want.

> JOHNNY
>
> That's too late; they start shooting in a week.

> DON CORLEONE
>
> I'm gonna make him an offer he can't refuse.

He takes JOHNNY to the door.

> DON CORLEONE
>
> Now you go outside, enjoy yourself and . . . I want you to leave it all to me.

 GOOFS, GAFFES, AND BLOOPERS

As Johnny leaves the Don's office, watch for a female extra who appears in the doorway, smiles nervously, and steps back out of sight.

JOHNNY

All right.

They embrace, and THE DON closes the door.

DON CORLEONE

Well . . .

EXT DAY: MALL

Now all the wedding GUESTS excitedly clap their hands over the entrance of the cake: NAZORINE is beaming as he wheels in a serving table containing the biggest, gaudiest, most extravagant wedding cake ever baked—an incredible monument of his gratitude. The CROWD is favorably impressed: they begin to clink their knives or forks against their glasses, in the traditional request for the bride to cut the cake and kiss the groom.

"Every character, every major character in the book should get some [introduction], except Sollozzo, who is impossible. But even he is introduced in the wedding in a line. To get some little memorable introduction so that later on when you see them, Martini or Clemenza or Tessio, you can always have that wedding where you first saw him to refer back to."

—Coppola, in a preproduction meeting

COPPOLA DISCUSSES THE SCENE WITH DUVALL AND BRANDO.

INT DAY: DON'S OFFICE

DON CORLEONE
What time does my daughter leave with the bridegroom?

HAGEN
(checks his watch)

In a few minutes; right after they cut the cake. Now, your new son-in-law . . . do we give him something important?

DON CORLEONE
Never. Give him a living but never discuss the Family business with him. What else?

HAGEN
Virgil Sollozzo called. Now we're gonna have to give him a day sometime next week.

DON CORLEONE
We'll discuss him when you come back from California.

HAGEN
(chuckles)

When am I goin' to California?

DON CORLEONE
I want you to go tonight. I want you to talk to this movie big shot and settle this business for Johnny. Now if there's nothing else, I'd like to go to my daughter's wedding.

EXT DAY: MALL

The FAMILY has assembled again to take the picture, this time with MICHAEL on the end.

MAMA
Carlo, we're gonna take the picture.

MICHAEL
Wait a minute.

MICHAEL walks swiftly to KAY, grabbing her hand and bringing her into the group.

KAY
(protesting)

No, Michael, not *me*.

PHOTOGRAPHER
Okay, that's it; just like that now; hold it.

DISSOLVE TO:

THE DON leads CONNIE onto the dance floor. They dance as the guests applaud.

FADE OUT.

MOON OVER NEW YORK: PRACTICAL JOKES ON THE SET OF *THE GODFATHER*

Practical jokes were rampant, but the most legendary was mooning (the exposing of one's naked behind), which became almost tradition on set. In the first such display James Caan and Robert Duvall mooned Coppola, Brando, and Salvatore Corsitto in an effort to break some tension during a rehearsal for the first scene of the film. While their impish antics were predominantly met with disapproving stares and silence, somehow they caught on. James Caan in *Time*, 1972: "My best moon was on Second Avenue. Bob Duvall and I were in one car and Brando was in another, so we drove up beside him and I pulled down my pants and stuck my ass out of the window. Brando fell down in the car with laughter." Richard Bright (Al Neri) said that it got to the point where every time you opened a door you expected to see someone's behind. Even the reserved and uptight Pacino got in on the act, as he reported in *Ladies' Home Journal*, 1972: "In a scene where I sit behind the desk, wardrobe made this big fuss about getting me a shirt with a smaller collar. So while everyone was looking at the shirt, I took off my pants. When I came out from behind the desk, I got a laugh, even though we had to do the scene over." The ultimate moon came during the wedding-photo shot, for which Brando and Duvall mooned 400 cast and crew members. They planned it carefully, and Caan, who overheard their scheming, started to shout, "No, no, not here!" Everyone working on the production, and *most* of the extras crowd roared with delight (some of the older ladies didn't appreciate the view). Caan, who had started the whole mooning fad, tried to distance himself from the embarrassing duo. Eventually, the Don himself—Brando—was crowned best prankster, designated by a heavyweight-style leather belt emblazoned with the title "Moon Champion."

HAGEN

The hospital called. Consigliere Genco, he's not going to last out the night.

DON CORLEONE

Santino, go tell your brothers that I want them to come with me to visit Genco; pay their respects. Tell Fredo to drive the big car.

SONNY

Pop, uh, Michael?

DON CORLEONE

All my sons.

EXT DAY: MALL

Silence.

HIGH ANGLE ON THE MALL, late day. The GUESTS are gone. A single black car is in the courtyard.

MED SHOT: THE DON looks at MICHAEL outside the car.

DON CORLEONE

Will your American girlfriend get back to the city all right?

MICHAEL

Tom said he'd take her in.

They get into the car.

INT DAY: HOSPITAL CORRIDOR

A long, white hospital corridor, at the end of which we can see a group of FIVE WOMEN, some old and some young, but all plump and dressed in black.

DON CORLEONE, his SONS, and JOHNNY FONTANE move toward the end. But then MICHAEL stops to take a drink from a drinking fountain, and THE DON slows. The two look at each other, and THE DON gestures toward MICHAEL's uniform.

DON CORLEONE

What are all these Christmas ribbons for?

MICHAEL

For bravery.

DON CORLEONE

What miracles you do for strangers.

ANATOMY OF A SCENE: GENCO ABBANDANDO'S DEATHBED

On April 21, at the New York Eye and Ear Infirmary, the production filmed a significant scene that was written into the shooting script prior to production, but does not appear in the 1972 movie. After the wedding, Vito Corleone, along with his sons and Johnny Fontane, visit the Don's ailing wartime consigliere Genco Abbandando, played by Franco Corsaro. In the novel, young Vito boarded with the Abbandando family on their way to America. He worked in their grocery store in Hell's Kitchen before being ousted by the nephew of a neighborhood Mafioso.

At the end of the scene, the Don stays with Genco, as Puzo writes, "holding his hand and whispering things we cannot hear, as they wait for death." According to the novel, Genco dies in the middle of the night. The Don tells Hagen he is the new consigliere. This is a tremendous break in tradition, for the adopted Tom Hagen is not a full-blooded Sicilian. The scene was included in *The Godfather Trilogy: 1901–1980*.

(DELETED SCENE CONTINUED)

MICHAEL starts to leave.

DON CORLEONE

Just a minute, Michael, I want to talk to you. What are your plans when you get out?

MICHAEL

Finish school.

DON CORLEONE

That's fine. I approve of that. Michael, you never come to me as a son should. You know that, don't you? But when you finish school I want you to come and talk to me, because I have plans for you. You understand?

Slaps face gently.

MICHAEL

Sure.

INT DAY: HOSPITAL ROOM

DON CORLEONE enters the hospital room and moves closest to OUR VIEW. He is followed by his SONS and JOHNNY.

DON CORLEONE

(whispered)

Genco, Genco, I've brought all my boys to pay their respects—even Johnny from Hollywood.

GENCO is a tiny, wasted skeleton of a man. DON CORLEONE takes his bony hand.

GENCO

Godfather, Godfather, it is your daughter's wedding day, you cannot refuse me. Cure me, you have the power.

DON CORLEONE

Genco, I have no such power. Don't be afraid of death.

GENCO

It has been arranged then?

DON CORLEONE

You blaspheme. Resign yourself.

GENCO

You need your old consigliere. Who will replace me?

(suddenly)

Stay, stay with me, Godfather. Help me to meet death. If he sees you, he will be frightened and leave me in peace. You can say a word, pull a few strings, eh? Stay with me, Godfather. Don't betray me.

THE DON motions all the others to leave the room. They do.

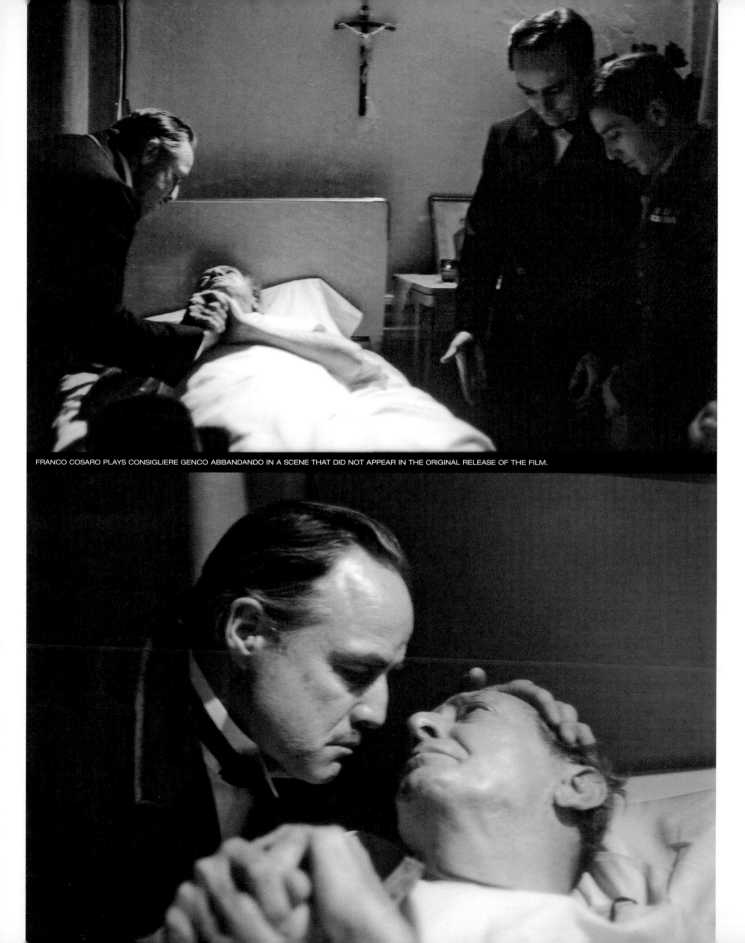

FRANCO COSARO PLAYS CONSIGLIERE GENCO ABBANDANDO IN A SCENE THAT DID NOT APPEAR IN THE ORIGINAL RELEASE OF THE FILM.

ADAPTATION AND THE CUTTING ROOM FLOOR

At this juncture in the narrative, there are many minor interludes that were written into the pre-film shooting script. Some scenes and shots that do not appear in the 1972 film:

- Tom Hagen on the airplane to California
- Carlo and Connie's wedding night
- Sonny visiting Lucy Mancini's apartment
- A close-up of Don Corleone thinking
- Michael and Kay on a train to New Hampshire
- Luca Brasi taking the subway to his meeting with Tattaglia
- Don Corleone embracing Hagen as his new consigliere

 ## THE NUTS AND BOLTS: PRODUCTION DETAIL

The Woltz International Pictures lot is actually Paramount's lot on Marathon Street at Bronson Avenue in Hollywood. This was not production designer Dean Tavoularis's choice—he detested the look of it, and had even suggested the Warner Bros. lot as an alternative—but it was used for budgetary reasons. It was also the location for the Paramount backlot scenes in *Sunset Boulevard*.

COPPOLA'S NOTES ON THE WOLTZ SCENES, IN "THE GODFATHER NOTEBOOK."

SCENE FOUR: WOLTZ'S OFFICE (2:30)

SYNOPSIS:

Hagen puts the Don's proposal to Woltz. He says he is an emissary of a friend of Johnny Fontane's, who would very much appreciate it if Mr. Woltz would give him the part in the picture. Hagan puts forth a couple of possibilities, and Woltz absolutely rejects them, telling Hagen that if the so-called friend is some sort of Mafia heavy, that he is a friend of the BBI in high places and not at all going to be pressured into anything. Hagan is very cool, using lawyer's language, making it clear that he is not making a threat; he is just asking a favor. Woltz turns down the proposal, and Hagen decides to leave. As he passes through the garrish outer office, Woltzs' secretary runs after Hagen, and tells him that Mr. Woltz would like him to have dinner with him that night at his home. A car is sent for Hagen, and he is taken to the Woltz Estate.

THE TIMES:

Clothes of course, and however I can get that Hollywood of the late Forties texture. Actually, the Paramount lot has that feeling, part of it could be used. The furniture in Woltzs' office.
Few servicemen; "Good Citizenship with Good Picture Making" kinds of slogans; bronze lists of those of the studio who gave their lives in the war. Perhaps in the waiting room, would be some large photos of the studio's biggest stars, hopefully, Gable in his uniform, etc.

IMAGERY AND TONE:

Woltz must come over as truly powerful, wealthy man. The more he does, the more powerful the Don will seem when he defeats him, and the more powerful the suspense will be throughout. The more we see and learn of Woltz, the more impossible Hagen's task must seem. Therefore, just as the Don's home and surroundings are not especially impressive, Woltz's must be. His office is a ballroom, his home a mansion. Security guards are important; he is a King and has his own police force. I don't think however, despite this great show of wealth and power, that Woltz should be gauche. He has travelled and been with great people, and in a way is quite sophisticated. He loves and appreciates truly beautiful things. Like Hy Brown, probably owns a few nice Masterpieces, could even have them in his office.
So that, I feel, Woltzs' office should be truly impressive, and with great taste.

FADE IN:

EXT DAY: AIRFIELD

A plane touches down for landing.

DISSOLVE TO:

Overhead shot of Hollywood.

DISSOLVE TO:

EXT DAY: WOLTZ STUDIOS

Studio front gate displays: "WOLTZ INTERNATIONAL PICTURES."

Cab pulls up, HAGEN exits.

DISSOLVE TO:

EXT DAY: STUDIO LOT

HAGEN, carrying a briefcase, walks across the lot.

DISSOLVE TO:

EXT DAY: LOT ALLEYWAY

HAGEN walks through an alleyway and enters sound stage.

DISSOLVE TO:

INT DAY: Stage 7

MAN

You need a little more heat on that arc.

JACK WOLTZ kisses a young starlet in front of a group as flashbulbs pop, then turns his attention to HAGEN, standing in the background. An ASSISTANT holds papers for WOLTZ to sign while they talk.

WOLTZ

All right, start talking.

HAGEN

I was sent by a friend of Johnny Fontane. This friend is my client—he would give his undying friendship to Mr. Woltz if Mr. Woltz would grant us a small . . . favor.

WOLTZ

(not looking up)

Woltz is listening.

HAGEN

Give Johnny the part in that new war film you're starting next week.

WOLTZ looks at the ASSISTANT with raised eyebrows and chuckles. He finishes signing papers and takes HAGEN by the arm, leading him on a walk through the sound stage toward the exit.

WOLTZ

Huh! And what favor would your friend grant Mr. Woltz?

HAGEN

You're gonna have some union problems; my client could make them disappear. Also one o' your top stars has just moved from marijuana to heroin.

They reach the door. WOLTZ turns to face HAGEN suddenly.

WOLTZ

Are you trying to muscle me?

HAGEN

Absolutely not. I've come to ask a service for a friend.

WOLTZ

(interrupts)

Now you listen to me, you smooth-talkin' son of a bitch! Let me lay it on the line for you and your boss, whoever he is. Johnny Fontane will never get that movie! I don't care how many dago, guinea, wop, grease-ball goombahs come out of the woodwork.

HAGEN

(calmly)

I'm German-Irish.

 ADAPTATION AND THE CUTTING ROOM FLOOR

One line in the novel was so beloved by Puzo he used it twice—first as "A lawyer with his briefcase can steal more than a hundred men with guns" and second as "Lawyers can steal more money with a briefcase than a thousand men with guns and masks." He was adamant about its inclusion in the film, but it is never uttered. It did appear in the shooting script, in a scene where the Don embraces Tom Hagen as his new consigliere, but Brando considered it preachy and dissuaded Coppola from using it. Puzo was so annoyed by its exclusion that he used the quote on the frontis page of his book *The Godfather Papers: and Other Confessions.*

"I like the idea of Tom with a big shot, where you can't even sit down with him. You have to catch him between his other things. Talk-to-me-while-I-am-taking-a-walk kind of thing. And that really puts Tom in second place."

—Coppola, in a preproduction crew meeting

 ADAPTATION AND THE CUTTING ROOM FLOOR

Puzo's novel doesn't pull any punches with Woltz's dialogue. He yells: "I don't care how many guinea *Mafia* goombahs come out of the woodwork," and "That's the *Mafia* style," and "if that *Mafia* goombah tries any rough stuff . . ." (italics added). The term *Mafia* doesn't appear in the film.

THE NUTS AND BOLTS: PRODUCTION DETAIL

The Hollywood scenes demonstrate the tightness of the film's budget. For the long exterior shots of Tom Hagen entering the studio lot, and of Hagen and Woltz walking around the grounds, the second unit filmed extras with wigs and hats to avoid having to pay actors Robert Duvall and John Marley. The actual backstage of the Corleone house set served as the set for the backstage of Woltz International Pictures. The horse stable scenes were also shot on a studio set with the second unit filming.

WOLTZ

Well, let me tell ya something, my Kraut-Mick friend. I'm gonna make so much trouble for you, you won't know what hit you.

HAGEN

Mr. Woltz, I'm a lawyer. I have not threatened you.

WOLTZ

I know almost every big lawyer in New York; who the hell are *you*?

HAGEN

I have a special practice. I handle one client. Now, you have my number; I'll wait for your call.

HAGEN moves to shake WOLTZ's hand.

HAGEN

By the way, I admire your pictures very much.

HAGEN exits. The ASSISTANT moves to WOLTZ's side.

WOLTZ

Check 'im out.

DISSOLVE TO:

EXT DAY: JACK WOLTZ ESTATE

A car drives up a winding road and enters an opulent estate. Overhead shot of the car approaching the house. It stops, and HAGEN exits.

DISSOLVE TO:

EXT DAY: WOLTZ GARDENS

HAGEN and WOLTZ comfortably stroll along beautiful formal gardens, martinis in hand.

HAGEN

It's really beautiful.

WOLTZ

Well, look at this. It used to decorate the palace of a king.

HAGEN

Yeah. Very nice.

WOLTZ

Why didn't you say you work for Corleone, Tom? I thought you were just some cheap, two-bit hustler Johnny was running in tryin' to bluff me.

HAGEN

I don't like to use his name unless it's really necessary.

WOLTZ

How's your drink, Tom?

HAGEN

Fine.

They cross the garden and head toward the stables.

WOLTZ

Hey, come on over here with me, I want to show you something really beautiful. You do appreciate beauty, don't you?

DISSOLVE TO:

INT DAY: STABLES

They come to rest by a stall. Two GROOMS lead out a horse.

WOLTZ

There you are—six hundred thousand dollars on four hoofs. I'll bet Russian czars never paid that kinda dough for a single horse.

The animal is truly beautiful. WOLTZ whispers to him with true love in his voice, stroking his face.

⬡ THE NUTS AND BOLTS: PRODUCTION DETAIL

Exterior shots of the Woltz estate are actually Greenacres, the Beverly Hills estate of silent film star Harold Lloyd. Interior scenes were shot at the Guggenheim estate on Sands Point Preserve in Long Island. Guards had to be hired for the priceless art. And, needless to say, the bed was a rental.

> "Woltz must be plausible; as Hitcho said, good villains make good movies. He is bigger than life, but we believe him, and see that he has other areas to him. His love for Khartoum, real love . . ."
>
> —Coppola's notebook

BEHIND THE SCENES

In 1885, General Charles Gordon, British commander of Khartoum (the capital of Sudan), was attempting to evacuate Egyptian forces from the area when rebels beheaded him. The Mahdi Mohammed Ahmed's soldiers hoisted his decapitated head on a pike as a declaration of victory.

GOOFS, GAFFES, AND BLOOPERS

In the dinner scene, the waiter fills Tom's empty glass twice in rapid succession, from two different angles.

ADAPTATION AND THE CUTTING ROOM FLOOR

In the novel, when pleading his case to the Don, Johnny explicitly explains why Woltz doesn't like him. Coppola changed this, preferring to have the explanation come from Woltz's tirade. This adjustment underscores the key line of the scene: "A man in my position can't afford to look ridiculous." Don Corleone makes him look exactly that in the next scene where Woltz discovers Khartoum's head in his bed.

WOLTZ

Khartoum . . . Khartoum. I'm not gonna race him, though. I'm gonna put him out to stud.

    (to GROOM)

Thanks, Tony.

GROOM

Welcome. Come on.

WOLTZ

Let's get somethin' to eat, huh?

HAGEN and WOLTZ exit.

                      DISSOLVE TO:

INT NIGHT: WOLTZ DINING ROOM

HAGEN and WOLTZ sit at an enormous dining room table, attended by SEVERAL SERVANTS. Great paintings hang on the walls. The meal is elaborate and sumptuous. A bowl of oranges is a centerpiece.

HAGEN

. . . Corleone is Johnny's godfather. To the Italian people, that's a very religious, sacred, close relationship.

WOLTZ

I respect it. Just tell him he should ask me anything else. But this is one favor I can't give 'im.

HAGEN

He never asks a second favor when he's been refused the first.
Understood?

WOLTZ

You don't understand. Johnny Fontane never gets that movie. That
part is perfect for 'im. It'll make him a big star. I'm gonna run him
outta the business! And let me tell you why.

WOLTZ stands up and walks over to HAGEN, leaning on the table as he speaks. HAGEN
continues to eat.

Johnny Fontane ruined one of Woltz International's most valuable
protégées. For five years we had her under training—singing lessons,
acting lessons, dancing lessons; I spent hundreds of thousands of
dollars on 'er—

(gesturing emphatically)

I was gonna make 'er a big star. And let me be even *more* frank—just to
show you that I'm not a hard-hearted man, that it's not all dollars and
cents. She was beautiful! She was young; she was innocent! She was the
greatest piece of ass I ever had, and I've had 'em all over the world!
And then Johnny Fontane comes along with his olive-oil voice and
guinea charm, and she runs off. She threw it all away just to make
me look ridiculous! AND A MAN IN MY POSITION CAN'T AFFORD
TO BE MADE TO LOOK RIDICULOUS!! Now you get the hell outta
here! And if that goombah tries any rough stuff, you tell him I ain't
no bandleader.

HAGEN reacts.

WOLTZ

Yeah. I heard that story.

HAGEN

Thank you for the dinner and a very pleasant evening.

HAGEN stands up to leave.

HAGEN

Maybe your car could take me to the airport. Mr. Corleone is a man
who insists on hearing bad news immediately.

HAGEN exits.

DISSOLVE TO:

EXT DAWN: WOLTZ ESTATE

LONG SHOT of the house and pool.

DISSOLVE TO:

Pan over house and courtyard and up to a second-story window.

DISSOLVE TO:

KHARTOUM'S DEMISE

"That horse's head thing was strictly from Sicilian
folklore, only they nailed the head of your favorite
dog to your door as the first warning if you didn't
pay the money. They were great believers in collect-
ing money before doing the job."
—Mario Puzo, in an interview with Terry Gross,
   National Public Radio, 1996

Coppola did not appreciate the novel's gruesome
horse-head scene but recognized that it was too
famous to delete—the audience would be disappointed
if it wasn't done, and done *right*. However, animal
rights activists protested the scene's inclusion. The
crew first tried to use a stuffed horse's head, but it
looked fake and dusty. So they eventually procured
one from a pet food slaughterhouse in New Jersey.
Coppola contemptuously shrugged off the concerns,
afterward saying in a *Variety* interview: "There were
many people killed in that movie, but everyone worries about the horse. It was the same on the set.
When the head arrived, it upset crew members who
are animal lovers, who like little doggies. What they
didn't know is that we got the head from a pet food
manufacturer who slaughters two hundred horses a
day just to feed those little doggies."

The blood effect was created using Karo corn syrup
mixed with red food coloring. By the end of the four-
hour shoot, the bed was a sea of blood. Months after
production ended, John Marley admitted in *Variety*:
"I still see it."

Coppola recognized the importance of Woltz's
scream in this scene. He wrote in his notebook that it
should be LOUD (underlined four times), and edited
an abrupt cut from the scream to a calm shot of Don
Corleone—very effectively illustrating the Don's cold-
bloodedness. In an effort to tone down the scene's
violent impact, when the film was broadcast on television, the network cut out Woltz's slow awakening,
although not the head or the scream.

The construction of this scene in the film was different from both the book and shooting script written
prior to production. As with many violent scenes in
The Godfather, the episode was originally structured
as a flashback—in other words, the audience sees
the impact of a situation before the situation itself is
described. The book begins the scene with a frenzied
and frantic Woltz phoning Hagen and piling on verbal
abuse (e.g., "guinea fuck"). The horse-head-in-the-
bed scene occurs subsequently. Similarly, the shooting
script first has the scene of the Don receiving flowers
from Johnny, announcing he got the movie part,
which is followed by the scene in Woltz's bed.
Throughout Coppola's notebook, he repeatedly
comes back to this issue of overlaps and how to
most effectively and coherently incorporate them into
the film. The finished film, without these flashbacks,
has a more direct, linear route to the denouement,
which allows the tension to build systematically.

> "If the audience does not jump out of their seat on this one, you have failed. Too much in the Corman horror film tradition would also be a mistake. One must find the perfect balance of horror without losing the thread of the overall film. Deliver it and get out."
>
> —Coppola's notebook

 BEHIND THE SCENES

The Academy Award® on Woltz's bedside table: merely a prop, or Coppola's Best Screenplay Oscar®, awarded for *Patton* a month before the scene was shot?

 GOOFS, GAFFES, AND BLOOPERS

Some viewers of *The Godfather* have assumed there is a continuity mistake in Woltz's bedroom, as the white patch on the horse's forehead is not clearly visible. However, this is more likely due to the amount of prop blood. There do seem to be a few continuity blunders, as patches of blood inexplicably appear in long shots. Coppola has admitted to misreading this scene in the book, and thought the head was right with Woltz in the bed. Actually, in the book Puzo had it written as "far down at the foot of his bed." Coppola wanted to create the effect of Woltz (and the viewers) being unsure at first if it is Woltz himself who is injured.

INT DAY: WOLTZ'S BEDROOM

It is a large bedroom, dominated by a huge bed, in which a man, presumably WOLTZ, is sleeping. Soft light bathes the room from the large windows. We move closer to him until we see his face, and recognize JACK WOLTZ. He turns uncomfortably, mutters, feels something strange in his bedsheets. Something wet.

He wakens, feels the sheets with displeasure; they are wet. He looks at his hand; the wetness is blood. He is frightened, pulls aside the covers, and sees fresh blood on his sheets and pajamas. He grunts, pulls the sheets off further, and is terrified to see a great puddle of blood in his bed. He feels his own body frantically, moving down, following the blood, until he is face-to-face with the great, severed head of Khartoum lying at the foot of his bed. The blood comes from the hacked neck. White, reedy tendons show. He struggles up to his elbows in the puddle of blood to see more clearly. Froth covers the muzzle, and the enormous eyes of the animal are yellowed and covered with blood.

Finally, and suddenly, an ear-splitting scream of pure terror escapes from WOLTZ, who is rocking on his hands and knees in an uncontrolled fit, blood all over him.

WOLTZ

Oh God . . .

EXT DAY: WOLTZ ESTATE

DISSOLVE TO:

A REAL HORSE HEAD AND LOTS OF KARO SYRUP MADE FOR A FRIGHTENING AND MEMORABLE SCENE.

INT NIGHT: DON'S LIVING ROOM

CLOSE VIEW on THE DON, who raises his eyebrow and nods.

> DON CORLEONE
>
> You're not too tired, are you, Tom?

HAGEN and SONNY sit on the couch. SONNY munches on nuts throughout.

> HAGEN
>
> Ah, no. I slept on the plane.

> DON CORLEONE
>
> Yeah?

> HAGEN
>
> I have the Sollozzo notes here. Now, Sollozzo is known as The Turk.
> He's supposed to be very good with a knife . . .

EXT DAY: GENCO OLIVE OIL CO.

An unimposing little building on Mott Street in New York City, with a large old sign: "GENCO," across from an open-faced fruit market.

A dark Buick pulls up and a single small man, who we cannot see well because of the distance, gets out and enters the building. This is VIRGIL SOLLOZZO.

> HAGEN'S VOICE
>
> . . . but only in matters of business, with some sort of reasonable complaint.
> His business is narcotics.

INT DAY: OLIVE OIL OFFICES

Looking toward the staircase, we can hear SOLLOZZO's FOOTSTEPS before he actually comes into view. He is very dark, with black hair. But he's wiry, and tight and hard, and obviously very dangerous. He is greeted at the head of the stairs by SONNY, who takes his hand and shakes it, introducing himself.

> HAGEN'S VOICE
>
> He has fields in Turkey where they grow the poppy. In Sicily he has the
> plants to process them into heroin. He needs cash—he needs protec-
> tion from the police for which he gives a piece of the action. I couldn't
> find out how much. The Tattaglia Family is behind him here in New
> York. Now, they have to be in it for something.

> SONNY
> *(introducing himself to SOLLOZZO)*
>
> Santino Corleone.

ADAPTATION AND THE CUTTING ROOM FLOOR

A brief scene that was filmed but does not appear in the 1972 movie concerns Woltz deflowering a young starlet. The scene where Woltz presents the girl with a pony was included in *The Godfather Trilogy: 1901–1980*. The change meant that a subsequent scene referencing it, in which Hagen reports back to the Don about the Woltz episode, also had to be trimmed. The edited portion included dialogue about what it means to be a Sicilian. In Puzo's novel, when Vito asks Hagen if Woltz "has real balls," Hagen ponders what he means: "Did Jack Woltz have the balls to risk everything, to run the chance of losing *all* on a matter of principle, on a matter of honor; for revenge?" Hagen translates the question: "You're asking if he is a Sicilian. No."

A brief episode of Connie weeping, with Mama Corleone reporting that she and her spouse have had another fight, also doesn't appear.

THE NUTS AND BOLTS: PRODUCTION DETAIL

The Genco Olive Oil Company set was built at Filmways Studios, and then mounted on the fourth floor of an old loft building on Mott Street in Little Italy (now Chinatown).

ROBERT DUVALL POSITIONS MARLON BRANDO'S CUE CARDS FOR THE SCENE.

CAST AND CREW:
BRANDO ON CUE

Brando didn't want to memorize his oft-changing lines. He would often get rewrites the day of the shoot, and Coppola would come to the set armed with cue cards. In his autobiography, *Songs My Mother Taught Me,* Brando discusses how he used to memorize lines early in his career, but stopped when he found that overrehearsing spoiled his effectiveness as an actor. So, rather than memorizing a line, he concentrated on its meaning. After *The Godfather* was released, Brando and Coppola appeared on *The Mike Douglas Show.* Brando said, "I found it helpful not to know one single line and to have lines written on the boards—"

"And on the pocket and the body of another actor," interrupted Coppola. On one occasion, Coppola added, he wondered why Brando was handling a melon in such a strange way. Then he noticed that the fruit actually had some dialogue written on it.

INT NIGHT: DON'S LIVING ROOM

DON CORLEONE
How about his prison record?

HAGEN
Two terms: one in Italy, one here. He's known as a top narcotics man.

DON CORLEONE
Santino, what do you think?

SONNY
There's a lot of money in that white powder.

DON CORLEONE
Tom?

INT DAY: OLIVE OIL OFFICES

SOLLOZZO enters, followed by SONNY. He is introduced all around—first shaking hands with HAGEN. They enter THE DON's glass-paneled office, where CLEMENZA, TESSIO, and FREDO formally shake SOLLOZZO's hand.

HAGEN'S VOICE
Well, I say yes. There's more money potential in narcotics than anything else we're looking at. Now if we don't get into it, somebody else will—maybe one of the Five Families, maybe all of them. Now, with the money they earn . . .

INT NIGHT: DON'S LIVING ROOM

HAGEN
. . . they can buy more police and political power. Then they come after us. Now we have the unions, we have the gambling—and they're the best things to have—but narcotics is the thing of the future. Now if we don't get a piece of that action, we risk everything we have, I mean, not *now*, but in ten years from now.

SONNY
So? What's your answer gonna be, Pop?

INT DAY: OLIVE OIL OFFICES

Sitting around in a circle: THE DON, SOLLOZZO, SONNY, HAGEN, FREDO, CLEMENZA, and TESSIO. THE DON is the slightest bit foolish with all his compatriots, whereas SOLLOZZO has brought no one. Throughout all that transpires, however, it is clear that this scene is between two men: SOLLOZZO and DON CORLEONE.

SOLLOZZO
There, Don Corleone, I need a man who has powerful friends. I need a million dollars in cash. I need, Don Corleone, those politicians that you carry in your pocket—like so many nickels and dimes.

DON CORLEONE

What is the interest for my Family?

SOLLOZZO

Thirty percent. In the first year your end should be three, four million dollars, and then it would go up.

DON CORLEONE

(*sipping anisette*)

And what is the interest for the Tattaglia Family?

SOLLOZZO nods toward HAGEN, who nods back.

SOLLOZZO

(*to HAGEN*)

My compliments.

(*to THE DON*)

I'll take care of the Tattaglias. Outta my share.

DON CORLEONE

So, I receive thirty percent for finance, political influence, and legal protection. That's what you're telling me?

"THIS SCENE SHOULD PLAY LIKE A POKER GAME BETWEEEN THE CINCINNATI KID AND THE OLD MAN."

—Coppola's notebook, setting up this scene to play to the audience's fascination with being on the "inside" of a big deal

ITALIANISMS

The anisette appearing in this scene was made by Francis Ford Coppola. In his childhood, his father made similar such bottles, and Coppola knew it had to be homemade because, to look authentic, it had to appear cloudy—this is what happens to anisette if a little water gets into it.

SOLLOZZO

That's right.

DON CORLEONE

(shrugging his shoulders)

Why do you come to me? Why do I deserve this . . . generosity?

SOLLOZZO

If you consider a million dollars in cash just finance, *te salud*, Don Corleone.

SOLLOZZO raises his glass, smiling.

There is a long silence, in which each person present feels the tension. THE DON is about to give his answer.

THE DON rises and pours SOLLOZZO another glass of anisette, hands the bottle to SONNY, and sits back down.

DON CORLEONE

I said that I would see you because I heard that you were a serious man, to be treated with respect.

(sits down)

But I must say no to you.

We feel this around the room.

DON CORLEONE

And I'll give you my reasons: It's true, I have a lot of friends in politics, but they wouldn't be friendly very long if they knew my business was drugs instead of gambling, which they regard as a—a harmless vice; but drugs is a dirty business.

SOLLOZZO

Oh, Don Corleone . . .

DON CORLEONE

(interrupting)

It makes—it doesn't make any difference to me what a man does for a living, understand. But your business is . . . a little dangerous.

SOLLOZZO

If you're worried about security for your million, the Tattaglias'll guarantee it.

This startles SONNY.

SONNY

(blurting out)

Oh, are you tellin' me that the Tattaglias guarantee our invest—

THE DON raises his hand to stop SONNY.

DON CORLEONE

(interrupting)

Wait a minute.

Everyone in the room knows that SONNY has stepped out of line. THE DON gives him a withering glance. CLEMENZA, HAGEN, and SOLLOZZO's eyes flicker.

DON CORLEONE

I have a sentimental weakness for my children and I've spoiled them, as you can see. They talk when they should listen. But, anyway, Signore Sollozzo, my no is final. And I wish to congratulate you on your new business; I know you'll do very well. And good luck to me, especially since your interests don't conflict with mine. Thank you.

SOLLOZZO nods, understands that this is the dismissal. He rises, as do the others. He bows to THE DON, shakes his hand, and formally takes his leave. As everyone else exits, THE DON turns to SONNY.

DON CORLEONE

Santino, come here. What's the matter with you? I think your brain is goin' soft from all that comedy you're playin' with that young girl. Never tell anybody outside the Family what you're thinking again. Go on.

An enormous floral display is carried in.

DON CORLEONE

Tom, what—what is this nonsense?

HAGEN

It's from Johnny—he's starring in that new film.

DON CORLEONE

Ah. Take it away.

HAGEN

(to SOMEONE offscreen)

Take it over there.

The flowers are removed.

DON CORLEONE

And tell Luca Brasi to come in.

LUCA enters and sits down.

DON CORLEONE

I'm a little worried about this Sollozzo fellow. I want you to find out what he's got under his fingernails, y'know? Go to the Tattaglias, make them think that you're not too happy with our Family, and well, find out what you can.

LUCA nods and exits.

FADE OUT.

ADAPTATION AND THE CUTTING ROOM FLOOR

A scene was shot on June 28 at the St. Regis Hotel that doesn't appear in the 1972 movie. Kay and Michael are in a hotel bed together; they call Hagen, pretending to still be in New Hampshire. The scene was included in *The Godfather 1902–1959: The Complete Epic* and *The Godfather Trilogy: 1901–1980*. In the shooting script written prior to filming, this scene includes a discussion of their impending wedding, a contrast to Connie's lavish and traditional one: "quiet, civil ceremony at City Hall, no big fuss, no family, just a couple of friends as witnesses." Michael also tells Tom that there's something important he wants to tell his father before Christmas.

"I left the movie stunned, I mean, I floated out of the theater. Maybe it was fiction, but for me, then, that was our life . . . And not only the mob end, not just the mobsters and the killing and all that bullshit, but that wedding in the beginning, the music and the dancing, it was us, the Italian people!"

—Salvatore Gravano, in *Underboss: Sammy the Bull Gravano's Story of Life in the Mafia*

JOSEPH ANTHONY COLUMBO SR., HEAD OF THE ITALIAN-AMERICAN CIVIL RIGHTS LEAGUE, IN 1971.

THE LEAGUE

Soon after an Italian-American Unity Day rally at Columbus Circle in New York protested the representations of Italians as mobsters, Attorney General John Mitchell ordered that official Justice Department documents would not use the words *Mafia* or *Cosa Nostra* (translation: "Our Thing"). New York governor Nelson Rockefeller had a similar policy for state releases. Newspapers, movies, and TV often used alternative terminology as well, such as "the organization" or "underworld."

The New York–based Italian-American Civil Rights League (aka the "League") was the fastest-growing Italian-American organization in the United States. Before a *Godfather* director was even hired, the League, as well as other Italian associations, began campaigning against the film. Their concern was the defamation of their entire ethnic group.

In July of 1970, the League held a rally in Madison Square Garden. They raised $600,000 to stop the film and instituted a call to action.

The League, run by Joseph Colombo Sr., a self-titled real estate salesman, threatened Paramount with union trouble, economic boycotts, and pressure on government authorities to not cooperate. The executives—mostly Robert Evans and Charles Bluhdorn—received letters of complaint from the likes of the "Grand Venerable of the Grand Council of the Grand Lodge of New York State's Sons of Italy." Close to one hundred letters of protest came in to Paramount from senators, congressmen, and New York State legislators. The New York offices of Gulf+Western received bomb threats. Al Ruddy, the *Godfather* producer, had the windows of his car blown out by a shotgun blast. It is ironic that such hardball tactics were used in an attempt to steer the studio away from stereotypical gangster images.

The League efforts began hindering production. Long Island's Manhasset community was originally selected for the Corleone Mall location, but the township stonewalled. They refused permission for the property wall, and residents made impossible demands. In essence, the location was sabotaged, and it cost the production $100,000 to change locations, as construction

had already begun. Enough was enough. Al Ruddy initiated a sit-down.

Ruddy met with Anthony Colombo (Joe's son) at La Scala Restaurant on West 54th Street. He explained that the filmmakers were not going to defame Italian Americans, and even suggested Colombo read the script. Several League representatives showed up at his office, but none of them wanted to slog through the long screenplay. In the process of these meetings, the good-natured producer made a positive impression on them, so much so that they decided to go along with him—albeit not before first asking for numerous concessions, including that the film change Italian-sounding names to Americanized ones. Ruddy agreed to two of the demands: that all uses of the terms *Mafia* and *Cosa Nostra* be eliminated from the picture, and that proceeds from the premiere be designated to the League's favorite charity. Ruddy asserts that the word *Mafia* was only in the script once anyway (during Jack Woltz's tirade): "It didn't mitigate the quality of the movie and was an easy thing to give up." Obviously, the film was about the Mafia. As James Caan has said, "Nobody's gonna think it's a picture about the Irish Republican Army, that's for sure."

Ruddy accepted a meeting with Colombo at the Park Sheraton Hotel. He was met by about a thousand waiting League delegates. Ruddy reiterated that the film was going to focus on individuals, not slur an entire ethnic group. He started pointing to members, suggesting they could be extras, and the group broke out into cheers, even affixing a League "Captain" pin to his lapel. While Ruddy later disputed that the meeting had any influence on hiring, some members of the League appeared as extras or did crowd control.

On March 19, 1971, Ruddy held a press conference at League headquarters to make the announcement that the two terms would not be included in the dialogue. The national press jumped on the news, with front-page stories in both *The New York Times* and *Wall Street Journal* scorching Paramount for bending under the pressure.

Paramount issued a statement in *Variety* that the deal was "completely unauthorized," but grudgingly acknowledged that their film would indeed comply with the attorney general's directive on the phrases. Gulf+Western CEO Bluhdorn initially fired Ruddy (who absconded with a dozen cigars from his desk on his way out the door). But the deal was made and the damage was done. In the end, Coppola saved Ruddy's job, convincing Bluhdorn that Ruddy was the only one who could get the film done. And, indeed, after Ruddy and the League reached their understanding, all the production problems disappeared—no more union threats, no boycotts or demonstrations. In an interview with the author, Ruddy sums up the experience: "I'd rather deal with those guys than a Hollywood studio, because once the deal was made, no one would go against their obligation."

On June 28, just as New York principal photography was winding down in New York, Joseph Colombo was shot multiple times in the head. The incident occurred at another Italian-American Unity Day rally—just a stone's throw from the Gulf+Western building. The cast and crew were shocked that the film they were making had such relevance in contemporary America.

Ruddy severed ties with the League, who was not invited to the premiere, much less given the proceeds. When the League threatened to sue Paramount, CEO Frank Yablans suggested they sue Ruddy instead. Clearly, although his attempt to smooth over the production problems was successful, Ruddy was made the fall guy of this public relations nightmare. The crew couldn't resist teasing him: when Ruddy sat down to his first screening of *The Godfather*, he watched footage of Bonasera saying he believed in "the Mafia." The prank nearly gave him a heart attack.

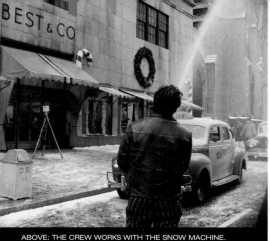

ABOVE: THE CREW WORKS WITH THE SNOW MACHINE.
BELOW: COPPOLA COUNSELS AL PACINO AND DIANE
KEATON ON THE FIRST DAY OF PRODUCTION.

⬡ THE NUTS AND BOLTS: PRODUCTION DETAIL

This was the first scene shot for the picture. It was
filmed in front of Best & Co., on 5th Avenue and 51st
Street. The store had gone out of business, but
reopened for the filming. It was shot earlier than
planned—by the second unit—to take advantage of a
predicted snowfall. Unfortunately, flurries were nonex-
istent. A snow machine was brought in, but it wouldn't
work except under conditions colder than twenty-eight
degrees. By 8 a.m. the weather was too warm, so
wind machines and plastic snow were brought in. In
a preproduction meeting, Coppola discussed that
he wanted to have the snow and winter to indicate
the passing of three months' time, as well as to use
the upbeat concept of Christmas to "mislead" the
audience with its tone—in contrast to the upcoming
frightening and violent scene of the Don's shooting.

⬡ THE NUTS AND BOLTS: PRODUCTION DETAIL

The window displays were designed to show 1945
prices and designs. The scene required 143 extras:
soldiers, sailors, WACs, Christmas shoppers, a Santa,
mothers with children, nuns, and taxi drivers, in addition to 1940s cars. The streetlights were replaced to
match the period at $1,000 a pop, as well as street
signs. Sixty crew members were present for this
twenty-hour first day.

FADE IN:

EXT DAY: 5TH AVENUE (WINTER 1945)

Fifth Avenue in the snow. Christmas week. People are bundled up with rosy faces, rushing
to buy presents. "Have Yourself a Merry Little Christmas" plays over the scene.

KAY and MICHAEL exit a 5th Avenue department store, arm in arm, carrying a stack of
gaily wrapped gifts.

> **KAY**
> I got something for your mother, and for Sonny, and a tie for Freddy,
> and Tom Hagen got the Reynolds pen.

> **MICHAEL**
> And what do *you* want for Christmas?

> **KAY**
> Me? Oh, just you.

They kiss.

INT NIGHT: LUCA'S ROOM

LUCA BRASI's tiny room. The Christmas music continues, on the radio. He is partly
dressed. He reaches under his bed and pulls out a small trunk. He opens it and takes out
a heavy, bulletproof vest. He puts it on over his wool undershirt, and then puts on his
shirt. He takes his gun, quickly disassembles, checks, and then reassembles it.

INT NIGHT: OLIVE OIL OFFICES

FREDO is sitting on a bench in the corner, reading the afternoon paper. THE DON
moves to FREDO and raps his knuckles on his head to take his nose out of the paper.

> **DON CORLEONE**
> *Andiamo*, Fredo. Tell Paulie to get the car; we're going.

> **FREDO**
> Okay, Pop. I'll have to get it myself, Pa. Paulie called in sick this morning.

> **DON CORLEONE**
> Huh?

> **FREDO**
> Paulie's a good kid; I don't mind gettin' the car.

FREDO exits as the OFFICE MANAGER helps THE DON with his coat and hat.

> **DON CORLEONE**
> *Buon Natale . . . Grazie.*

INT NIGHT: BUILDING LOBBY

LUCA walks through an ornate lobby, taking off his coat. He continues through a hallway, approaches the nightclub door, opens it, and enters.

INT NIGHT: NIGHTCLUB

A man moves behind the bar.

> BRUNO
>
> Luca! I'm Bruno Tattaglia.

> LUCA
>
> I know.

> BRUNO
>
> *Sue bequero* Scotch? Prewar.

> LUCA
>
> *Io no bib'.*

Out of the shadows emerges SOLLOZZO.

> SOLLOZZO
>
> You know who I am?

LUCA nods.

BEHIND THE SCENES

When young aspiring actor Marlon Brando first moved to New York in the spring of 1943, he very briefly worked as an elevator operator at Best & Co.

THE NUTS AND BOLTS: PRODUCTION DETAIL

Luca Brasi's room was filmed at the Hotel Edison, West 47th Street and Broadway, near Times Square, Manhattan.

This was also the shooting location of Brasi's murder. To save time and money, the crew used one of the hotel rooms instead of a Mott Street location originally selected.

THE NUTS AND BOLTS: PRODUCTION DETAIL

A fish etching on the front door of the nightclub foreshadows Brasi's sleeps-with-the-fishes demise.

LUCA

(in Italian; subtitled)

I know you.

SOLLOZZO

(in Italian; subtitled)

You have been talking to the Tattaglia Family . . . right? I think you and I can do business.

LUCA listens.

SOLLOZZO

(in Italian; subtitled)

I need someone strong like you. I heard you are not happy with the Corleone Family. Want to join me?

LUCA

(in Italian; subtitled)

What's in it for me?

SOLLOZZO

(in Italian; subtitled)

Fifty thousand to start with.

LUCA looks at him; he had no idea the offer would be so good.

LUCA

(in Italian; subtitled)

Not bad!

SOLLOZZO

(in Italian; subtitled)

Agreed?

SOLLOZZO extends his hand, but LUCA pretends not to see it; rather, he busies himself putting a cigarette in his mouth. BRUNO TATTAGLIA, behind the bar, makes a cigarette lighter magically appear and holds it to LUCA's cigarette. Then he does an odd thing: he drops the lighter on the bar and puts his hand lightly on LUCA's, patting it.

LUCA

Grazie.

Suddenly, TATTAGLIA clamps down as hard as he can, grabbing LUCA's wrist to keep it on the bar. SOLLOZZO stabs a knife into LUCA's hand, pinning it to the bar.

A garrote is thrown around his neck and pulled violently tight. His face begins to turn to purple blotches, right before our eyes; his tongue hangs out; his eyes bulge as he grunts in pain. The STRANGLER slowly forces the gasping LUCA down to the ground.

 ADAPTATION AND THE CUTTING ROOM FLOOR

Puzo's book details a more gruesome passing for Luca Brasi, as well as a very brutal background story on his character. The big-screen visual, though, certainly makes for a vivid death. When the movie was shown on TV, the network eliminated the hand piercing, but the garroting remained.

 THE NUTS AND BOLTS: PRODUCTION DETAIL

In a preproduction special effects memo to the crew, Coppola discusses the strangulation special effect: "This is probably the most difficult effect in the movie. Essentially what I'm after is to see a man strangled before our eyes. Our research tells us that what happens is as follows: The outer veins that return the blood to the body are cut off, but the main artery continues pumping blood into the head. The face bloats and breaks out into dark, purple blotches, and eventually changes to a dark color completely. The eyes bulge; the tongue pushes out, far more than a man could do by voluntarily sticking out his tongue." To make actor Lenny Montana's face turn purple, different makeup methods were tested, such as a purple mist spray. Ultimately, a more realistic effect was achieved by Montana utilizing the muscle-tensing techniques he had learned as a wrestler to bring blood up to his head.

There were so many spectators in front of Polk's Hobby Shop (now defunct) at 5th Avenue and 31st Street that the New York Tactical Patrol Force had to clear the way for filming, and the noise was so loud that dialogue had to be dubbed in later.

POLK'S HOBBIES, THE SECOND LOCATION OF THE FIRST DAY OF SHOOTING. COPPOLA DIRECTS AMIDST THE CROWD IN A SANTA-STYLE HAT.

The exterior of the Genco Olive Oil Company was shot on Mott Street on the Lower East Side of New York, part of Little Italy (now Chinatown). It was actually the outside of the building that held the Genco Olive Oil Company set within.

"Narrow street, unchanged from the turn of the century when it was designed for horse-and-wagon transportation, and its narrow sidewalks are cluttered with stands displaying the wares of local merchants. Windows and fire escapes in the neighborhood were jammed with spectators elbowing each other for a better view."

—Paramount's production notes

EXT DUSK: POLK'S TOY STORE

TOM HAGEN exits carrying a children's sled and a stack of presents, all gift-wrapped. He continues past the windows. As he walks, someone walks right in his way. He looks up. It is SOLLOZZO.

He takes HAGEN by the arm and walks along with him.

> SOLLOZZO
>
> Tom! Tom Hagen. Merry Christmas.

> HAGEN
>
> Thank you.

> SOLLOZZO
>
> Hey, I'm glad I run into ya. I wanna talk to you.

> HAGEN
>
> I haven't got time.

A MAN suddenly appears at his side.

> SOLLOZZO
>
> *(quietly)*
>
> Ah, make time, Consigliere. Get in the car. What're ya worried about? If I wanted to kill you, you'd be dead already. Get in.

HAGEN, sick to his stomach, moves with his ESCORTS, leaving our VIEW on the store windows of a mechanical, gaily spinning Santa and Mrs. Claus.

EXT DUSK: OLIVE OIL CO.

THE DON leaves the building. FREDO leans against a car.

The light outside is very cold and beginning to fail. When FREDO sees his FATHER coming, he moves toward him. THE DON moves to the car, and is about to get in when he hesitates and turns to the long, open fruit stand near the corner.

> DON CORLEONE
>
> Ah, *aspetta*, Fredo. I'm goin' to buy some fruit.

> FREDO
>
> Okay, Pop.

THE DON crosses the street to the fruit stand; FREDO gets into the car.

The PROPRIETOR springs to serve him. THE DON walks among the trays and baskets and merely points to a particular piece of fruit. As he selects oranges, the MAN gingerly picks the pieces of fruit up and puts them into a paper bag.

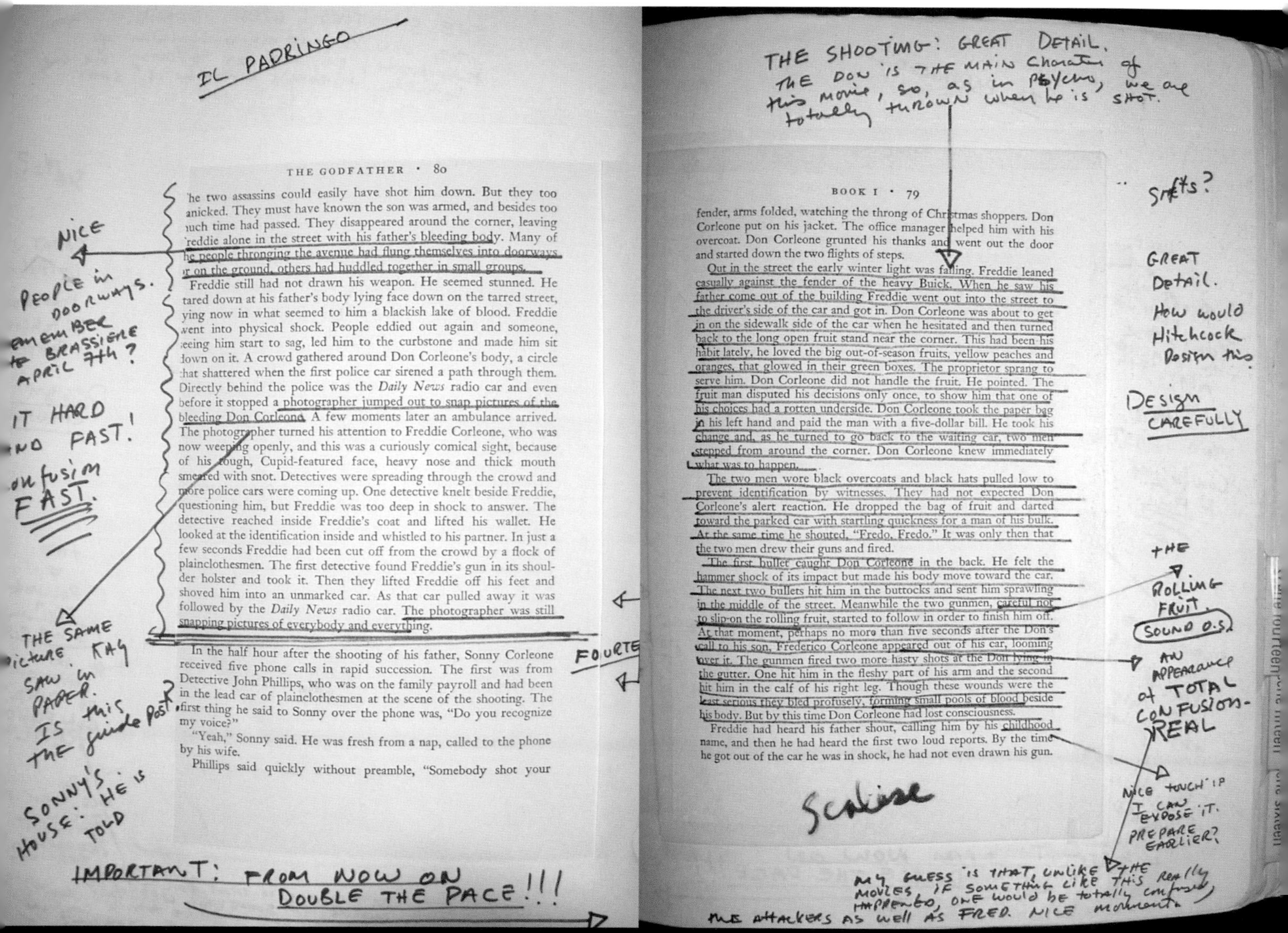

Handwritten annotations:

IL PADRINGO

NICE

PEOPLE in DOORWAYS. remember the BRASSIERE April 7th?

IT HARD NO FAST! confusion FAST.

THE SAME picture KAY SAW in PAPER. IS this THE guide post SONNY'S HOUSE: HE IS TOLD

IMPORTANT: FROM NOW ON DOUBLE THE PACE !!!

FOURTE

THE SHOOTING: GREAT DETAIL. THE DON IS THE MAIN Character of this movie, so, as in PSYCHO, we are totally thrown when he is SHOT.

SFX?

GREAT DETAIL. How would Hitchcock Design this

DESIGN CAREFULLY

THE ROLLING FRUIT (SOUND O.S.)

AN APPEARANCE of TOTAL CONFUSION - REAL

NICE TOUCH if I CAN EXPOSE IT. PREPARE EARLIER?

Scalise

MY GUESS is THAT, UNLIKE THE MOVIES, IF SOMETHING LIKE THIS really HAPPENED, ONE would be totally confused. THE ATTACKERS AS WELL AS FRED. NICE moments.

Left printed page:

THE GODFATHER · 80

he two assassins could easily have shot him down. But they too panicked. They must have known the son was armed, and besides too much time had passed. They disappeared around the corner, leaving Freddie alone in the street with his father's bleeding body. Many of the people thronging the avenue had flung themselves into doorways or on the ground, others had huddled together in small groups.

Freddie still had not drawn his weapon. He seemed stunned. He stared down at his father's body lying face down on the tarred street, lying now in what seemed to him a blackish lake of blood. Freddie went into physical shock. People eddied out again and someone, seeing him start to sag, led him to the curbstone and made him sit down on it. A crowd gathered around Don Corleone's body, a circle that shattered when the first police car sirened a path through them. Directly behind the police was the *Daily News* radio car and even before it stopped a photographer jumped out to snap pictures of the bleeding Don Corleone. A few moments later an ambulance arrived. The photographer turned his attention to Freddie Corleone, who was now weeping openly, and this was a curiously comical sight, because of his rough, Cupid-featured face, heavy nose and thick mouth smeared with snot. Detectives were spreading through the crowd and more police cars were coming up. One detective knelt beside Freddie, questioning him, but Freddie was too deep in shock to answer. The detective reached inside Freddie's coat and lifted his wallet. He looked at the identification inside and whistled to his partner. In just a few seconds Freddie had been cut off from the crowd by a flock of plainclothesmen. The first detective found Freddie's gun in its shoulder holster and took it. Then they lifted Freddie off his feet and shoved him into an unmarked car. As that car pulled away it was followed by the *Daily News* radio car. The photographer was still snapping pictures of everybody and everything.

In the half hour after the shooting of his father, Sonny Corleone received five phone calls in rapid succession. The first was from Detective John Phillips, who was on the family payroll and had been in the lead car of plainclothesmen at the scene of the shooting. The first thing he said to Sonny over the phone was, "Do you recognize my voice?"

"Yeah," Sonny said. He was fresh from a nap, called to the phone by his wife.

Phillips said quickly without preamble, "Somebody shot your

Right printed page:

BOOK I · 79

fender, arms folded, watching the throng of Christmas shoppers. Don Corleone put on his jacket. The office manager helped him with his overcoat. Don Corleone grunted his thanks and went out the door and started down the two flights of steps.

Out in the street the early winter light was falling. Freddie leaned casually against the fender of the heavy Buick. When he saw his father come out of the building Freddie went out into the street to the driver's side of the car and got in. Don Corleone was about to get in on the sidewalk side of the car when he hesitated and then turned back to the long open fruit stand near the corner. This had been his habit lately, he loved the big out-of-season fruits, yellow peaches and oranges, that glowed in their green boxes. The proprietor sprang to serve him. Don Corleone did not handle the fruit. He pointed. The fruit man disputed his decisions only once, to show him that one of his choices had a rotten underside. Don Corleone took the paper bag in his left hand and paid the man with a five-dollar bill. He took his change and, as he turned to go back to the waiting car, two men stepped from around the corner. Don Corleone knew immediately what was to happen.

The two men wore black overcoats and black hats pulled low to prevent identification by witnesses. They had not expected Don Corleone's alert reaction. He dropped the bag of fruit and darted toward the parked car with startling quickness for a man of his bulk. At the same time he shouted, "Fredo, Fredo." It was only then that the two men drew their guns and fired.

The first bullet caught Don Corleone in the back. He felt the hammer shock of its impact but made his body move toward the car. The next two bullets hit him in the buttocks and sent him sprawling in the middle of the street. Meanwhile the two gunmen, careful not to slip on the rolling fruit, started to follow in order to finish him off. At that moment, perhaps no more than five seconds after the Don's call to his son, Frederico Corleone appeared out of his car, looming over it. The gunmen fired two more hasty shots at the Don lying in the gutter. One hit him in the fleshy part of his arm and the second hit him in the calf of his right leg. Though these wounds were the least serious they bled profusely, forming small pools of blood beside his body. But by this time Don Corleone had lost consciousness.

Freddie had heard his father shout, calling him by his childhood name, and then he had heard the first two loud reports. By the time he got out of the car he was in shock, he had not even drawn his gun.

THE NUTS AND BOLTS: PRODUCTION DETAIL

At this juncture, Coppola references Hitchcock in his notebook. He underscores the shooting's impact on the audience in noting: "The Don is the main character of this movie, so, as in *Psycho,* we are totally thrown when he is shot." He also asks, "How would Hitchcock design this?" Coppola does indeed employ the Hitchcockian technique of an overhead shot to suggest a dramatic peak. This sparked debate with Gordon Willis, the cinematographer. The more traditionally inclined Willis questioned whose perspective this overhead viewpoint could possibly be.

BEHIND THE SCENES

According to producer Al Ruddy, Brando "loved the people on Mott Street and they loved him." An enormous crowd gathered to witness the scene of the Don shooting. When he collapsed, those assembled gasped—stunned—and then cheered wildly. Reports suggest the scene had to be reshot numerous times, as the audience couldn't control their applause at Brando's virtuoso performance. When it was completed, Brando bowed to the cheering crowd.

GOOFS, GAFFES, AND BLOOPERS

• The fruit stand contains *cardboard* boxes labeled "Sunkist." According to Sunkist, labels were used on *wooden* citrus boxes until the mid-1950s, only after which they were replaced by cardboard ones with preprinted labels on the box ends.

• There is no sound accompanying the last gunshot.

• After being shot, Vito stops moving while he is lying on his back with his right arm folded on his chest. The camera cuts to a distraught Fredo, and when it returns in a long shot to the Don, he's inexplicably lying on his left side, with his right arm outstretched and his jacket closed.

DON CORLEONE
Ah, Merry Christmas. I want some fruit. . . . Gimme that one.

Two MEN appear and begin walking quickly toward THE DON, their hands in their pockets. THE DON notices them as he takes the bag of fruit. THE MEN begin running. CLOSE-UP on their drawn guns.

Suddenly, THE DON drops the bag of fruit and darts with startling quickness toward the parked car. A fruit basket has hit the ground, and the fruit begins rolling along the sidewalk as we hear GUNSHOTS.

DON CORLEONE
Fredo! Fredo!

OVERHEAD SHOT of multiple bullets catching THE DON in the back; he arches in pain and slumps on the car. The GUNMEN continue to pump bullets into him at close range.

FREDO is hysterical. He tries to get out of the car; he is having difficulty opening the door. He rushes out, a gun trembling in his hand, his mouth open. He actually drops the gun.

The GUNMEN disappear around the corner as quickly as they came. FREDO is in shock. He looks at his FATHER, who slides off the hood of the car and falls into the now empty street.

FREDO falls back on the curb and sits there, saying something we cannot understand. He begins to weep profusely.

FREDO

Papa! PAPA!

EXT NIGHT: RADIO CITY

RADIO CITY MUSIC HALL during the Christmas show. The marquee displays: "IN LEO
MCCAREY'S 'THE BELLS OF ST. MARY'S' AND FAMED CHRISTMAS STAGE SPECTACLE."
KAY and MICHAEL exit, walking arm in arm.

KAY

Mike, would you like me better if I were a nun? Like in the story, you know?

MICHAEL

No.

KAY

Well then would you like me better if I were Ingrid Bergman?

MICHAEL

Now that's a thought.

They have passed a little enclosed newsstand. KAY sees something that terrifies her. She
doesn't know what to do. MICHAEL still walks, thinking about her question.

KAY

(in a little voice)

Michael . . .

KAY stops.

MICHAEL

No, I would not like you better if you were Ingrid Bergman.

KAY

Michael. Michael . . .

**THE NUTS AND BOLTS:
PRODUCTION DETAIL**

The scene between Michael and Kay was filmed
outside Radio City Music Hall, 6th Avenue and 50th
Street, Manhattan. The theater's ushers informed
passersby that the film being shown was not the Bing
Crosby/Ingrid Bergman Paramount production *The
Bells of St. Mary's* as listed on the marquee, but
Paramount's *A New Leaf* with Elaine May and Walter
Matthau, and the 1971 Easter stage show.

ADAPTATION AND THE CUTTING ROOM FLOOR

In the preproduction shooting script, the attempted assassination on Vito Corleone occurs as a flashback: Michael and Kay see the newspaper that announces the shooting, which is followed by the scene of the shooting itself.

THE NUTS AND BOLTS: PRODUCTION DETAIL

The crew constructed both a newsstand and a phone booth, and the newspaper inserts were shot by none other than Coppola's American Zoetrope partner, George Lucas.

MICHAEL

What's the matter?

She cannot answer him. Rather she pulls him by the arm, back to the newsstand, and points. His face goes grave.

The headline reads: "VITO CORLEONE FEARED MURDERED." MICHAEL opens the paper, seeing the interior headline: "ASSASSINS GUN DOWN UNDERWORLD CHIEF," with a photo of his father.

MICHAEL

(desperately)

They don't say if he's dead or alive.

MICHAEL looks around frantically, then races across the street into a phone booth, with KAY following. KAY peers inside as MICHAEL calls SONNY.

MICHAEL

Sonny, Michael.

SONNY'S VOICE

(on phone)

Michael, where you been?

MICHAEL

Is he all right?

SONNY'S VOICE

(on phone)

We don't know yet. There's all kinds o' stories. He was hit bad, Mikey.

MICHAEL

Oh.

SONNY'S VOICE

(on phone)

Are you there?

MICHAEL

Yeah, I'm here.

SONNY'S VOICE

(on phone)

Where you been? I was worried.

MICHAEL

Didn't Tom tell you I called?

SONNY'S VOICE

(on phone)

No. Look, come home, kid. You should be with Mama, d'you hear?

MICHAEL

All right.

CAST AND CREW: JAMES CAAN AS SONNY CORLEONE

As with many roles, the part of Santino "Sonny" Corleone was hotly contested. Carmine Caridi was the original casting choice. Ecstatic, Caridi celebrated with a party for his family and friends. However, for him the role was not meant to be—possibly because of the height differential between him (six feet four inches) and Pacino (five feet seven inches). Caridi went on to appear in another gangster picture, (*The Gang That Couldn't Shoot Straight*), and eventually was cast in *The Godfather: Part II* and *Part III*.

Robert Evans has said he made a deal with Coppola: he would allow Pacino as Michael if James Caan could be Sonny (he actually wanted Caan as Michael). He takes full credit for the casting, remarking in *Maxim*: "I had to fight for Jimmy Caan to be in *The Godfather* more than I had to fight to stay alive." However, Coppola also had Caan in mind from the beginning for the part of Sonny.

James Caan, despite several post-*Godfather* awards for Italian of the Year, was born in the Bronx of German-Jewish descent. He and Coppola were classmates at Hofstra University. His first substantial role was in Paramount's *Lady in a Cage*, and he went on to do work in television and several films, including Coppola's *The Rain People* with Robert Duvall. Caan first received great acclaim as Brian Piccolo in the television production *Brian's Song*. Like Pacino, he signed on to *The Godfather* for a mere $35,000.

Caan clearly relished the role of Sonny, and he acted the part with gusto. He spent time in Brooklyn with "Italian guys" to research their mannerisms and speech—how they carried themselves, with their thumbs in their belts; and how they were great dressers, very clean and neat with their shirts open and ties loose. He enthused in the *Los Angeles Times*: "They've got incredible moves. I watched them with each other and with their girls and wives. It's incredible how affectionate they are to each other. . . . They toast each other—'*centanni,*' '*salute a nostra*'—all of this marvelous old-world stuff from guys who were born here and don't even speak Italian."

INT NIGHT: SONNY'S LIVING ROOM

Sonny hangs up the phone as SANDRA looks on anxiously in the background.

                    SANDRA

  Oh my God.

SONNY moves to comfort SANDRA, when they are startled by a CRASH at the door. A BABY starts crying.

                    SANDRA

    (really frightened)

  Ohhh! Sonny!

SONNY reaches into a cabinet drawer, takes out a gun, and moves quickly to the door as the KNOCKING continues.

                    SONNY

    (to SANDRA)

  Stay back there.

    (to KNOCKER)

  Who is it?

CLEMENZA

Open up, it's Clemenza.

SONNY opens the front door quickly. CLEMENZA enters, and SONNY closes the door.
SANDRA goes to look after the baby.

CLEMENZA

There's more news about your old man.

(turns to SONNY)

The word is, out in the street, he's already dead.

SONNY grabs CLEMENZA by his coat and throws him up against a door.

SONNY

Watch your mouth! What's the matter with you?

CLEMENZA

Jesus Christ, Sonny, take it easy. Take it easy!

SONNY

Where was Paulie?

CLEMENZA

Paulie was out sick. He been a little sick all winter.

SONNY

How many times he been sick?

CLEMENZA

Only maybe three, four times. I mean, I asked Freddy if he wants me to
get a different bodyguard, but he said no.

SONNY

(interrupts)

Listen, do me a favor, pick him up right now. I don't care how sick he
is. If he's breathin', I want you to bring him to my father's house now,
y'understand? Now!

CLEMENZA

Yeah. You want me to send any people over here?

SONNY

No no no, just you and I. Go ahead.

CLEMENZA exits. SANDRA reappears, comforting her crying BABY. SONNY moves
toward her.

SONNY

Look . . . I'm gonna have a couple people come over to the house—a
couple of our people.

A telephone rings. SONNY answers it.

Evans's memoir recounts Caan at the premiere,
yelling: "Hey, you cut my whole fuckin' part out!"
Truly, the role of Sonny Corleone was reduced
from the way it was originally conceived. Caan has
reported—perhaps overstated—that forty-five minutes
of his character was left on the cutting room floor. In
discussing the post-Vito shooting scenes, he
bemoaned how Sonny's sensitive side wasn't shown:
"There were all kinds of nice moments—like Sonny
not being able to bring himself to sit in his father's
chair. I worked hard on those scenes. They meant
something to me as an actor. Little things—showing
Sonny's inability to cry because he thinks it's unmas-
culine, but his voice cracks when he talks to his
mother . . ." Caan was upset the first time he saw the
completed film: "It was like painting a fourteen-foot
canvas and ending up with a three-foot canvas. I felt
like telling everybody they ought to see the other
eleven feet!" Despite the shortened screen time, Caan
was nominated for a Best Supporting Actor Oscar®
for his spirited performance.

GOOFS, GAFFES, AND BLOOPERS

There appears to be a strange continuity error in this
scene: the gun Sonny puts in his belt disappears
when he throws Clemenza against the kitchen counter,
and then reappears when he turns around after talking to his wife. As there is no edit in the scene, it's
unclear what could have happened to the gun, unless
it slipped down Caan's pants.

ADAPTATION AND THE CUTTING ROOM FLOOR

A scene in the shooting script that was shot but doesn't
appear in the 1972 film shows Sonny receiving a call
from an informant letting him know about the attempted
assassination on his father. It was included in *The
Godfather Trilogy: 1901–1980.* The scene where
Michael calls Sonny was an addition made after the
shooting script was written.

ADAPTATION AND THE CUTTING ROOM FLOOR

Several poignant scenes of Sonny were in the shooting script but not in the 1972 movie. Sonny goes to the Corleone Mall, calmly tells his mother about Vito's shooting, calls Tessio to tell him to get more men out on the street—being careful not to sit in his father's chair—and then looks in his phone book:

We follow the names, until the finger stops at one: LUCA BRASI. SONNY dials the number. There is no answer.

> SONNY
>
> Luca.

A similar scene was shot but does not appear in the 1972 film. It was included in *The Godfather Trilogy: 1901–1980*.

SONNY

Hello.

SOLLOZZO'S VOICE

(on phone)

Santino Corleone?

SANDRA moves behind him, anxious to know who it is. SONNY indicates that she be quiet.

SONNY

Yeah.

SOLLOZZO'S VOICE

(on phone)

We have Tom Hagen. In about three hours he'll be released with our proposition. Listen to everything he has to say before you do anything. What's done is done. And don't lose that famous temper of yours, huh, Sonny?

SONNY scribbles the time on a kitchen cabinet door.

SONNY

(quietly)

No, I'll wait.

INT NIGHT: ABANDONED DINER

SOLLOZZO is drinking from a cup; HAGEN sits.

SOLLOZZO

Your boss is dead.

(pauses respectfully)

I know you're not in the muscle end of the Family, Tom, so I don't want you to be scared. I want you to help the Corleones—and I want you to help me.

One of the BUTTON MEN brings a bottle of rye to the table and pours a little into a cup, giving it to HAGEN.

SOLLOZZO

Yeah, we got him outside his office just about an hour after we picked you up. Drink it.

HAGEN drinks gratefully.

SOLLOZZO

So now it's up to you to make the peace between me and Sonny.

HAGEN is still focused on the grief of losing the old man.

SOLLOZZO

Sonny was hot for my deal, wasn't he? And you knew it was the right thing to do.

HAGEN
(*pulling himself together*)

Sonny'll come after you with everything he's got.

SOLLOZZO
That'll be his first reaction, sure. That's why you gotta talk some sense to him. The Tattaglia Family is behind me with all their people. The other New York Families'll go along with anything that'll prevent a full-scale war. Let's face it, Tom, in all due respect, the Don—rest in peace—was slippin'. . . . Ten years ago, could I have gotten to him? Well now he's dead. He's dead, Tom, and nothing can bring him back.

HAGEN is overwhelmed; actual tears spring to his eyes.

SOLLOZZO
So you gotta talk to Sonny. You gotta talk to the Caporegimes: that Tessio, that fat Clemenza. It's good business, Tom.

HAGEN
I'll try. But even Sonny won't be able to call off Luca Brasi.

SOLLOZZO
Yeah. Well . . . let *me* worry about Luca. You just talk to Sonny. And the other two kids.

HAGEN
I'll do my best.

SOLLOZZO
(*lifting his hands in an expression of harmlessness*)

Good. Now, you can go.

SOLLOZZO escorts HAGEN to the door.

SOLLOZZO
I don't like violence, Tom. I'm a businessman. Blood is a big expense.

He opens the door; they step out together.

EXT NIGHT: OUTSIDE ABANDONED DINER

HAGEN and SOLLOZZO exit into a snowstorm.

But a car pulls up, and ONE OF SOLLOZZO'S MEN rushes out. With an air of urgency, he talks to SOLLOZZO in private.

Then SOLLOZZO moves with a grave expression to HAGEN.

SOLLOZZO
He's still alive! They hit 'im with five shots and he's still alive! Well, that's bad luck for me, and bad luck for *you* if you don't make that deal.

 **THE NUTS AND BOLTS: PRODUCTION DETAIL**

The scene between Hagen and Sollozzo was shot in an abandoned diner. The snowstorm when Hagen and Sollozzo exit the diner was real.

ITALIANISMS

Caporegime is a Mafia term for a lieutenant, or second in command.

ADAPTATION AND THE CUTTING ROOM FLOOR

A scene that was shot but doesn't appear in the 1972 film: After Michael arrives at the Mall, he consoles Theresa Hagen, then talks with Sonny about the culprit who "fingered the old man." Sonny has a spy within the phone company, which explains how the Corleones confirm that Paulie is the traitor, not Clemenza. Tom Hagen returns from his abduction. Finally, there is a shot of Paulie Gatto sitting alone in the Don's living room; the clock reads 4:00 a.m. The scene was included in *The Godfather Trilogy: 1901–1980* and is excerpted here.

INT NIGHT: DON'S OFFICE

SONNY and TESSIO are huddled around a yellow pad. They look up, startled.

> SONNY
> Hey, Theresa, sweetheart, don't worry; they're gonna turn Tom loose the minute they get the proposition.

He reassuringly hugs THERESA.

> TESSIO
> *(waving)*
> Hello, Michael.

SONNY embraces MICHAEL.

> SONNY
> Where were you? Hey, kid, you had me worried when I couldn't get in touch with you.

> MICHAEL
> How's Ma taking it?

> SONNY
> She's good. You know, she's been through it before. Me too.

The phone rings. SONNY answers it.

                    SONNY
Yeah.

                    VOICE ON PHONE
Hello, Santino? This is Sam from the company. The number you gave
me? It checked out.

                    SONNY
Hey, listen, thank you very much. You're going to have a very, very
extra-merry Christmas, all right?

                    VOICE
Okay, thanks a lot.

                    SONNY
Thank you.

SONNY hangs up the phone.

                    SONNY
Listen, you two wanna wait outside? I've got some business I want to
finish with Tessio.

THERESA exits.

                    SONNY
          (to MICHAEL)
What are you doing? Hey, you hang around here, you're gonna hear
things you don't wanna hear.

                    MICHAEL
Maybe I can help you out . . .

                    SONNY
No, no you can't, *marone*! The old man'd have my neck if I let you get
mixed up in this. C'mon!

                    MICHAEL
He's my father too, Sonny.

                    SONNY
Oh, you wanna hear? Whose head do we blow off, Clemenza's or
Paulie's?

                    MICHAEL
What do you mean?

                    SONNY
What do I mean? One of them set up the old man.

MICHAEL didn't realize that the men waiting outside were on trial for their lives.

MICHAEL

Not Clemenza. I don't believe it.

SONNY

See? College boy is right. It was Paulie. That was the contact from the phone company. On the three days that Paulie was home sick, he got calls from the pay phone across from the old man's building.

TESSIO

So, it was Paulie.

SONNY

Hey, thank God it was Paulie . . .

TESSIO

That skinny punk.

SONNY

We'll need Clemenza bad.

MICHAEL is just realizing the gravity and extent of the situation.

MICHAEL

Is it going to be all-out war, like the last time?

SONNY

Yeah, until the old man tells me different.

MICHAEL

Wait, Sonny. Talk to Pop.

SONNY

Wait? C'mon! Sollozzo's a dead man—bada bing! Now I don't care what it costs. I mean, we're gonna go after all them families. The Tattaglias are gonna eat dirt.

MICHAEL

(softly)

That's not how Pop would play it.

SONNY

Listen, I'm gonna tell you something and he'd tell you too: when it comes to the action, I'm as good as anybody, and don't forget it.

Outside, we hear THERESA cry out, almost a scream of relief, then open the door and rush ou

Everyone is standing: In the doorway, TOM HAGEN is wrapped in a tight embrace with his WIF

HAGEN

Hey, boy, if I argue against the Supreme Court, I'll never do better than I did against that Turk tonight!

EXT NIGHT: MALL

One of several BUTTON MEN opens a car door and MICHAEL steps out. He walks to the house. A MAN drives the car away, and two other BUTTON MEN hook up a heavy chain across the gateway.

INT NIGHT: HALL

The hallway of the main house is filled with MEN MICHAEL doesn't recognize. They pay little attention to him. Most of them are waiting, sitting uncomfortably; no one is talking.

INT NIGHT: DON'S LIVING ROOM

MICHAEL moves into the living room; there is a Christmas tree, and countless greeting cards taped to the walls.

THERESA HAGEN is sitting stiffly on the sofa, smoking a cigarette; on the coffee table in front of her is a water glass half filled with whiskey. On the other side of the sofa sits CLEMENZA; his face is impassive, but he is sweating. PAULIE GATTO sits, tense and alone, on the other side of the room. CLEMENZA sees MICHAEL. He stands up to shake MICHAEL's hand.

> CLEMENZA
> Your mother's over in the hospital with your father; looks like he's gonna pull t'rough, thank God.

MICHAEL nods his relief.

> DISSOLVE TO:

INT NIGHT: DON'S OFFICE

TESSIO, CLEMENZA, SONNY, HAGEN, and MICHAEL, all exhausted, in shirtsleeves, are about to fall asleep. It is four in the morning. There is evidence of many cups of coffee. They can barely talk anymore.

> SONNY
> What do you think, goombah? Hah?

> CLEMENZA
> (speaks over SONNY and HAGEN)
> That's a lot of bad blood. Sollozzo, Philip Tattaglia, Bruno Tattaglia . . .

CLEMENZA points to a yellow pad containing a hit list.

> HAGEN
> I think it's too much, too far. I think it's too personal. The Don would consider this a purely—

> MICHAEL
> (interrupts)
> You gonna kill all those guys?

> SONNY
> Hey, stay out of it, Mikey. Do me a favor.

HAGEN

Sollozzo's the key. You get rid of him, everything falls into line. Now what about Luca? Sollozzo thinks he . . .

SONNY

I know if Luca sold out, we're in a lotta trouble, believe me, a lotta trouble.

HAGEN

Has anyone been able to get in touch with Luca?

CLEMENZA

We've been tryin' all night. He might be shacked up.

SONNY

Hey, Mikey, do me a favor—try . . . ringing Luca's number.

MICHAEL gets up to light a cigarette and then, very tired, picks up the phone and dials a number.

HAGEN

Luca never sleeps over with a broad. He always goes home when he's through.

SONNY

Well, Tom—you're consigliere. What do we do if the old man dies, God forbid?

HAGEN

If we lose the old man—

CLEMENZA

(in background)

. . . Sollozzo, Philip Tattaglia . . .

HAGEN

—we lose the political contacts and half our strength. The other New York Families might wind up supporting Sollozzo just to avoid a long, destructive war. This is almost 1946. Nobody wants bloodshed anymore. If your father dies . . . you make the deal, Sonny.

SONNY

(angry)

You know, that's easy for you to say, Tom; he's not your father.

HAGEN

(quietly)

I was as much a son to him as you or Mike.

There is a timid knock on the door.

SONNY

What is it?

PAULIE GATTO looks in.

CLEMENZA

Hey, Paulie, I thought I tol' you to stay put.

PAULIE

Well, the guy at the gate they—they say they got a package.

SONNY

Yeah? Well, all right. Tessio, go see what it is.

PAULIE

(coughs)

You want me to hang around?

TESSIO gets up, leaves.

SONNY

Yeah, hang around. You all right?

PAULIE

Yeah, I'm fine.

SONNY

Yeah? There's some food in the icebox. You hungry or anything?

PAULIE

No, 'at's all right.

SONNY

How about a drink? Have a little brandy—it's good, that'll sweat it out.

PAULIE

All right . . .

SONNY

Go ahead, baby.

PAULIE

. . . that might be a good idea.

SONNY

Yeah, right.

PAULIE closes the door.

SONNY

I want you to take care of that sonofabitch right away. Paulie sold out the old man, that *strunz*. I don't wanna see him again. Make that first thing on your list, understand?

CLEMENZA

Understood.

"When you make a movie, there isn't a human being on that set that doesn't think they can make it better than you. Any movie, any set—even the electricians."

—Coppola, 2007

ITALIANISMS

The epithet *strunz* is derived from the Italian word *stronzo,* the vulgar translation for which is "piece of shit." It's also slang for numerous profane insults, such as "asshole."

SONNY

Hey, Mikey, tomorrow, get a couple of guys; you go over to Luca's apartment, hang around, wait for 'im to show up.

HAGEN

Maybe we shouldn't get Mike mixed up in this too directly.

SONNY

Yeah. Listen, hang around the house on the phone and be a big help, huh? Try Luca again, go ahead.

MICHAEL is embarrassed to be so protected. He picks up the phone again.

TESSIO comes back, carrying a package. He puts it in SONNY's lap. SONNY unwraps it; there are two large dead fish wrapped in LUCA'S bulletproof vest.

SONNY

What the hell is this?

CLEMENZA

That's a Sicilian message. It means Luca Brasi sleeps with the fishes.

MICHAEL hangs up the phone.

EXT DAY: CLEMENZA'S HOUSE

Morning in a simple Brooklyn suburb. There are rows of pleasant houses. ROCCO LAMPONE and CLEMENZA walk from the garage to the front door. MRS. CLEMENZA, in a hairnet, stands by the door and sees them off.

CLEMENZA

I'm goin' now.

MRS. CLEMENZA

What time are you gonna be home tonight?

CLEMENZA

I don't know, probably late.

MRS. CLEMENZA makes a kissing sound. CLEMENZA exits.

MRS. CLEMENZA

Don't forget the cannoli.

CLEMENZA

Yeah yeah, yeah yeah.

The two men enter the car. GATTO is driving. He's a bit nervous, like he doesn't know what is up. LAMPONE gets in the rear seat, CLEMENZA in the front. PAULIE flinches a little when he sees LAMPONE will ride behind him; he half turns.

PAULIE

Rocco, sit on the other side; you block the rearview mirror.

ADAPTATION AND THE CUTTING ROOM FLOOR

In Puzo's novel, it is Hagen who replies, "The fish means that Luca Brasi is sleeping on the bottom of the ocean. It's an old Sicilian message."

ADAPTATION AND THE CUTTING ROOM FLOOR

In both the preproduction shooting script and the book, the murder of Luca Brasi is structured as a flashback, occurring *after* the Corleones receive the dead fish.

THE NUTS AND BOLTS: PRODUCTION DETAIL

"My idea was that . . . Clemenza's house would have some suburban-Long Island look . . . the kind of neighborhood where these homes, although they're nice, are all in a row. And he says hello to his neighbors every morning when he works in the garage. He's got one of the few postwar cars, which he obviously paid under the table to get. It means a lot to him; he is the American Valacchi, the American successful man, who has a nice house and money and everything, and is a 'good guy.'"

—Coppola, in a preproduction meeting

CLEMENZA

That Sonny's runnin' wild. He's thinking of goin' to the mattresses already. We gotta find a spot over on the West Side. You try Three-Oh-Nine West Forty-third Street. You know any good spots on the West Side?

CLEMENZA takes out a notebook and glances at it.

PAULIE

Yeah, I'll think about it.

PAULIE relaxes a bit; he thinks he's off any possible hook he was on. Also, there's the money he can make by selling SOLLOZZO a secret location.

CLEMENZA

Well, think about it while you're drivin', will ya? I wanna hit New York sometime this month. And watch out for the kids when you're backin' out.

The car pulls out.

DISSOLVE TO:

EXT DAY: STREET UNDER EL TRACKS

The car turns onto a street under the El tracks.

CAST AND CREW

Richard Castellano's (Clemenza's) real-life wife, Ardell Sheridan, played Mrs. Clemenza.

 ITALIANISMS

"Whenever a war between the Families became bitterly intense, the opponents would set up headquarters in secret apartments where the 'soldiers' could sleep on mattresses scattered through the rooms. This was not so much to keep their families out of danger, their wives and little children, since any attack on noncombatants was undreamed of. All parties were too vulnerable to similar retaliation. But it was always smarter to live in some secret place where your everyday movements could not be charted either by your opponents or by some police who might arbitrarily decide to meddle."

—Mario Puzo's *The Godfather,* defining "going to the mattresses"

 THE NUTS AND BOLTS: PRODUCTION DETAIL

For the exterior shot of the car driving through the city, the crew examined stock 1940s footage. They settled on footage of a car going under the 3rd Avenue El (elevated train), and then located a car to match it.

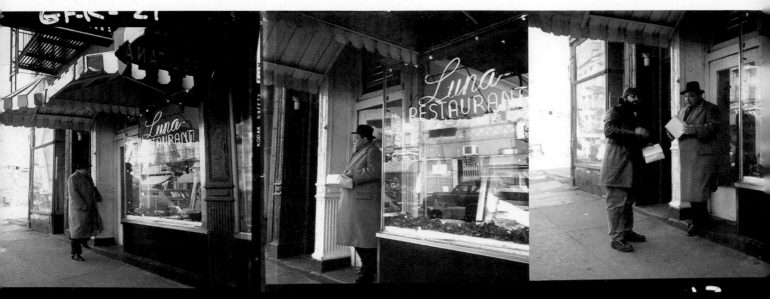

A DELETED SCENE OF CLEMENZA BUYING THE FAMED CANNOLIS.

 ## ADAPTATION AND THE CUTTING ROOM FLOOR

Several scenes leading up to Paulie's murder were filmed but don't appear in the 1972 film: Clemenza gives Rocco Lampone a .22 soft-nosed load for the job and tells him he will "make his bones on Paulie." In the car, Clemenza tells Paulie and Rocco he has to call Sonny, and then proceeds to enjoy a meal in a restaurant and pick up the cannoli. These scenes were included in *The Godfather Trilogy: 1901–1980*.

CLEMENZA'S VOICE

Hey, Paulie, I want you to go down Thirty-ninth Street—Carlo Santos—you pick up eighteen mattresses for the guys to sleep on while you bring me the bill.

PAULIE'S VOICE

Uh-huh. Yeah, all right.

CLEMENZA'S VOICE

Now make sure that they're clean because those guys are gonna be stuck up in there for a long time, you know.

DISSOLVE TO:

EXT DAY: PAULIE'S CAR ON NEW YORK STREET

PAULIE'S VOICE

They're clean. They told me they exterminate them.

CLEMENZA'S VOICE

(laughs)

Exterminate, that's a bad word to use! Exterminate, get this guy!

LAMPONE'S VOICE

(chuckles)

Yeah.

CLEMENZA'S VOICE

Watch out we don't exterminate you!

ABOVE: FILMING PAULIE GATTO'S ASSASSINATION SCENE.

LAMPONE'S VOICE

That's funny, all right.

DISSOLVE TO:

EXT DAY: PAULIE'S CAR ON TURNPIKE

CLEMENZA'S VOICE

Hey, Paulie. (SPEAKS ITALIAN)

PAULIE'S VOICE

(SPEAKS ITALIAN)

CLEMENZA'S VOICE

Hey, pull over, will ya? I gotta take a leak.

EXT DAY: PAULIE'S CAR ON CAUSEWAY

The car moves along the reedy beach area of the causeway (with the Statue of Liberty in the background) and stops. CLEMENZA steps out of the car, OUR VIEW MOVING with him. He turns his back three-quarters from us (we can no longer see the car), unzips, and we hear the SOUND OF URINE HITTING THE GROUND.

In the car, LAMPONE raises his gun to PAULIE's head, and then there are two GUN-SHOTS. CLEMENZA, reacting slightly to the sound, finishes his leak, zips up, and turns, moving back toward the car. PAULIE is dead—his head on the steering wheel, bleeding from the forehead. The windshield is shattered.

⬡ THE NUTS AND BOLTS:
PRODUCTION DETAIL
An "A" coupon for gas rationing from World War II is displayed in the car window.

ADAPTATION AND THE CUTTING ROOM FLOOR

No cannolis are mentioned in the book or shooting script, but Coppola included the detail from his memories of the particular white boxes of cannolis his own father would bring home after work. Richard Castellano, as Clemenza, made movie history by improvising the now famous utterance: "Take the cannolis." The line is cited as a favorite from many cast and crew, such as Michael Chapman, a camera operator on *The Godfather* who went on to become a cinematographer on many great films, including Martin Scorsese's *Taxi Driver* and *Raging Bull*.

ADAPTATION AND THE CUTTING ROOM FLOOR

In Puzo's book, it is clear that Clemenza and Lampone leave Paulie in the car to make his murder more exposed—to frighten would-be traitors and prove that the Corleone Family had not gone soft.

> CLEMENZA
>
> Leave the gun. Take the cannolis.

LAMPONE retrieves the box from the backseat, hands it to CLEMENZA. CLEMENZA shuts the back door and they exit.

> DISSOLVE TO:

EXT DAY: MALL / THE DON'S YARD

MICHAEL sits alone on a bench in the rear yard. He is bundled in a warm marine coat. Then, a shout from the house.

> CLEMENZA'S VOICE
>
> Hey, Mike. Hey, Mikey!

> MICHAEL
>
> Yeah.

> CLEMENZA'S VOICE
>
> You're wanted on the telephone.

INT DAY: DON'S KITCHEN

CLEMENZA is in the kitchen, cooking over an enormous pot. Five BUTTON MEN are seated around the table. MICHAEL enters the kitchen.

> MICHAEL
>
> Who is it?

> CLEMENZA
>
> Some girl.

MICHAEL picks up the phone.

> MICHAEL
>
> Hello, Kay?

> KAY'S VOICE
>
> *(on phone)*
>
> How is your father?

> MICHAEL
>
> He's good; he's gonna make it.

> KAY'S VOICE
>
> *(on phone)*
>
> I love you.

> MICHAEL
>
> Huh?

He glances at the THUGS in the kitchen.

KAY'S VOICE
(on phone)
I LOVE YOU. Michael?

MICHAEL
Yeah, I know.

KAY'S VOICE
(on phone)
Tell me you love me.

MICHAEL
I can't talk.

KAY'S VOICE
(on phone)
Can't you say it?

MICHAEL glances at the HOODS at the kitchen table.

MICHAEL
I'll see you tonight, hmm?

KAY'S VOICE
(on phone)
All right.

MICHAEL hangs up the phone. CLEMENZA is making a tomato sauce for all the
BUTTON MEN stationed around the house.

CLEMENZA
Hey, Mikey, why don't you tell that nice girl you love 'er?

(SINGS) I LOVE YOU WITH ALL-A MY HEART . . . IF I DON'T SEE
YOU AGAIN SOON I'M-A GONNA DIE . . .

(laughs)

Come over here, kid, learn somethin'. You never know, you might have
to cook for twenty guys someday. You see? You start out with a little bit
of oil, and you fry some garlic. Then you t'row in some tomatoes, some
tomato paste. You fry it, you make sure it doesn't stick. You get it to a
boil. You shove in all your sausage and your meatballs. Eh? Add a little
bit o' wine and a little bit o' sugar, and that's my trick.

SONNY enters the kitchen; sees CLEMENZA.

SONNY
Why don't you cut the crap? I got more important things for you to do.
How's Paulie?

CLEMENZA
Aw Paulie, you won't see him no more.

**ADAPTATION AND THE CUTTING
ROOM FLOOR**
Coppola wanted to get an entire recipe in all of his
films. An example of the Puzo/Coppola writing collaboration: when Coppola first wrote "*Brown* some
sausage," Puzo countered with "Gangsters don't
brown, gangsters fry."

MICHAEL starts to leave.

                                        SONNY
            Where you goin'?

                                        MICHAEL
            To the city.

                                        SONNY
            Oh.
                        (to CLEMENZA)
            Well send some bodyguards with him, right?

                                        MICHAEL
            No, I'm just going to the hospital to see—

                                        SONNY
                (overlaps)
            Never mind. Send somebody with him.

                                        CLEMENZA
            Oh, he'll be all right. Sollozzo knows he's a civilian.

                                        SONNY
            Hmm, be careful, huh?

                                        MICHAEL
            Yes, sir.

MICHAEL exits.

                                        SONNY
                (to CLEMENZA as he dips bread into the sauce)
            Send somebody with him anyway.

INT NIGHT: CAR

MICHAEL sits in the rear seat, calmly, as he is being driven into the city. THREE BUT-TON MEN are crowded into the front seat.

                                                        DISSOLVE TO:

INT NIGHT: HOTEL

MICHAEL and KAY eating a quiet dinner at the hotel. He is preoccupied, she's concerned. He rises and puts on his coat.

                                        MICHAEL
            I have to go.

                                        KAY
            Can I go with you?

THE NUTS AND BOLTS: PRODUCTION DETAIL
Michael and Kay's hotel scenes were filmed at the St. Regis Hotel, on East 55th Street at 5th Avenue, Manhattan.

MICHAEL

No, Kay. There's gonna be detectives there—people from the press.

KAY

Well, I'll ride in the cab.

MICHAEL

I don't want you to get involved.

MICHAEL sits down again.

KAY

When will I see you again?

MICHAEL

(pauses)

Go back to New Hampshire, and I'll call you at your parents' house.

KAY

When will I see you again, Michael?

MICHAEL

I don't know.

MICHAEL rises. He leans over her, kisses her. Quietly, he moves out the door.

INT NIGHT: HOTEL LOBBY

MICHAEL crosses the lobby, past lines of servicemen trying to book rooms.

EXT NIGHT: DON'S HOSPITAL

A taxi pulls up in front of a hospital. MICHAEL steps out. He sees the hospital in the night, but it is deserted. He is the only one on the street. There are gay, twinkling Christmas decorations all over the building. He hesitates, looks around. This area is empty. He walks up the steps.

INT NIGHT: HOSPITAL CORRIDOR

MICHAEL walks into an absolutely empty hospital. He looks to the left; there is a long, empty corridor. To the right: the same.

MICHAEL looks into a nurse's station, no one is there. He moves quickly to an open door. He looks onto the desk: there is a half-eaten sandwich and a half-drunk cup of coffee.

Now he knows something is happening. He moves quickly, alertly, running through the hospital corridors.

INT NIGHT: HOSPITAL STAIRS

Now he turns onto a staircase, ever quickening; up a flight.

INT NIGHT: 4TH-FLOOR CORRIDOR

He steps out onto the fourth floor. He looks. There is a special card table set up there with a newspaper—but no detectives, no police, no bodyguards. He proceeds slowly around the corner to a door marked "2" and pauses.

INT NIGHT: DON'S ROOM #2

Slowly he pushes the door open, almost afraid at what he will find. He looks. Lit by a lamp, he can see a FIGURE in the hospital bed, alone in the room. Slowly MICHAEL walks up to it and is relieved to see his FATHER, securely asleep. Tubes hang from a steel gallows beside the bed and run to his nose and mouth.

> **NURSE**
> What are you doing here?!

This startles MICHAEL, who almost jumps around. It is a NURSE.

> **NURSE**
> You're not supposed to be here now.

> **MICHAEL**
> I'm Michael Corleone—this is my father. There's nobody here. What happened to the guards?

The NURSE pushes him out of the way to check on THE DON.

> **NURSE**
> Your father just had too many visitors. They interfered with hospital service. The police made them leave about ten minutes ago.

Quickly MICHAEL moves to a telephone and dials.

MICHAEL

(into phone)

Uh, get me, uh . . . Long Beach four-five-six-two-oh, please.

(to NURSE)

Nurse! Wait a minute. Stay here.

(into phone)

Sonny, Michael. I'm at the hospital.

SONNY'S VOICE

(on phone)

Yeah.

MICHAEL

Listen, I got here late, there's nobody here.

SONNY'S VOICE

(on phone)

What, nobody?

MICHAEL

Nobody. No—no—no Tessio's men, no detectives, nobody. Pop is all alone.

SONNY'S VOICE

(on phone)

Don't panic. We'll send somebody over.

CAST AND CREW:
CASTING THE DON

The casting of the title character from the novel was quite contentious. A plethora of actors were interviewed for the part, including Ernest Borgnine, Anthony Quinn, and Raf Vallone. Every older Italian actor in existence was considered. Two actors who were in contention but then hired for smaller parts in the picture were Richard Conte (Barzini) and John Marley (Woltz), who had appeared in Paramount's extremely successful *Love Story*. Evans had the idea of Sophia Loren's husband, producer Carlo Ponti. Coppola pointed out that he spoke like an Italian, not a New Yorker. Besides, he wasn't well-known enough. George C. Scott was also at the top of the list. Even Frank Sinatra was rumored to want to play him. Of course, Marlon Brando finally got the part, over strenuous Paramount objections. The role garnered him an Academy Award® and a firm place in film history.

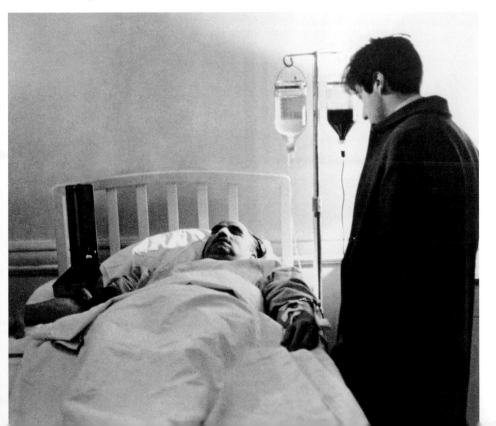

THE NUTS AND BOLTS: PRODUCTION DETAIL

The scene where Michael visits his father in the hospital was scheduled to be Marlon Brando's first—on April 12. Brando missed his plane and arrived on set at 2 p.m., much too late to film a scene, with two to three hours of face-makeup prep alone. According to Robert Evans, when Paramount sent Brando a check for $12,000 for the time he spent looping the movie, Brando called to inform them that they had given him $4,000 too much, because of his missed day, and asked where to send it back.

CAST AND CREW: MARLON BRANDO SPOTLIGHT

 "The scene between Al and Marlon in the hospital was shot at the end of the day. They shot the master and then they shot the reaction on Marlon Brando, who doesn't say anything, but just looks. Then they turn around and the last shot of the day is supposed to be Michael saying, 'Just lie here, Pop . . .' I told Marlon, 'You can get out of makeup if you want, because you're not on camera in this shot.' He replied, 'But I can't do that. I have to be here as Pop for Michael.' He understood what the other actor needs: he needs the actor to respond to him. He wouldn't think of changing clothes when Al had a very serious reaction to do. Marlon was like that. He could be quite selfish, but for people that he was concerned about, liked, or just respected, he did what was needed. He was so good to other actors. When I questioned him about that, he was surprised that I even asked. It was so natural for him to behave like that."

—Dick Smith, makeup artist

ADAPTATION AND THE CUTTING ROOM FLOOR

Puzo's novel includes the Michael dialogue: "Some people want to kill you, understand? But I'm here so don't be afraid." To which Vito replies: "Why should I be afraid now? Strange men have come to kill me ever since I was twelve years old." In Coppola's notebook, he questions how to handle this quote: "Should the Don talk or not? Maybe like in *Five Easy Pieces*—it's a one-way conversation, with just the Don's eyes open."

> MICHAEL
> *(furiously, but kept inside)*
> I won't panic.

MICHAEL hangs up; he inspects the door frame.

> NURSE
> I'm sorry, but you *will* have to leave.

> MICHAEL
> Uhhh . . . you and I are gonna move—move my father to another room. Now can you disconnect those tubes so we can move the bed out?

> NURSE
> That's out of the question!

> MICHAEL
> D'you know my father? Men are coming here to kill 'im. You understand? Now help me, please.

INT NIGHT: 4TH FLOOR HOSPITAL

They roll the bed, the stand, and all the tubes silently down the corridor. We HEAR FOOTSTEPS coming up the stairs, and they push the bed into the first available room. MICHAEL peeks out from the door. We see a montage of the empty hospital corridors. The footsteps are louder; then they emerge. It is a man carrying a bouquet of flowers.

> MICHAEL
> *(stepping out)*
> Who are you?

> ENZO
> I am Enzo—the baker. Do you remember me?

> MICHAEL
> Enzo.

> ENZO
> Yes, Enzo.

> MICHAEL
> You better get out of here, Enzo; there's gonna be trouble.

> ENZO
> If there is trouble, I stay here to 'elp you. For your father. For your father.

MICHAEL thinks. He realizes he needs all the help he can get.

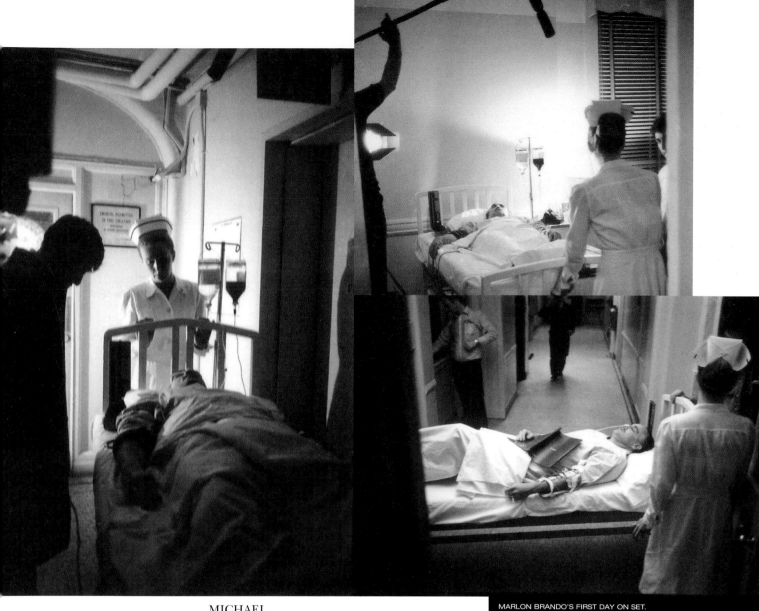

MARLON BRANDO'S FIRST DAY ON SET.

MICHAEL

All right, listen. Wait for me outside, in front of the hospital. All right?
I'll be out in a minute. Go ahead.

ENZO

Okay, okay.

INT NIGHT: DON'S SECOND HOSPITAL ROOM

They part. MICHAEL moves into the hospital room where they put his FATHER.

MICHAEL
        (whispers)

Just lie here, Pop. I'll take care of you now. I'm with you now. I'm with
you.

MICHAEL looks at the OLD MAN; touches his head tenderly. THE DON's eyes are open, though he cannot speak. MICHAEL kisses his hand; THE DON smiles, a tear escaping his eye.

INT NIGHT: HOSPITAL CORRIDOR

MICHAEL walks back through a corridor.

EXT NIGHT: DON'S HOSPITAL STREET

Outside, the hospital is empty save for a nervous ENZO, brandishing the flowers as his only weapon. MICHAEL exits the hospital and moves to him. MICHAEL takes the bouquet of flowers and throws them off the side of the steps.

MICHAEL

Get rid o' these. C'mere. Put your hand in your pocket like you have a gun.

MICHAEL folds up ENZO'S collar, and then his own.

MICHAEL

You'll be all right.

The exterior of the hospital twinkles with Christmas decorations.

MICHAEL

(exhaling)

You'll be okay.

We hear the SOUND OF A SINGLE AUTOMOBILE coming. MICHAEL and ENZO look with fear in their eyes. MICHAEL puts a hand on ENZO's chest to steady him. They stand, hands in their pockets. A long, low black car turns the corner and cruises by them. The car's occupants peer out. MICHAEL's and ENZO's faces are tough, impassive. MICHAEL unbuttons his coat and puts his hand inside. The car seems as though it will stop, and then quickly accelerates. MICHAEL and ENZO are relieved.

MICHAEL

You did good.

ENZO takes out a cigarette. MICHAEL looks down; the BAKER's hands are shaking. MICHAEL lights it; his hands are not.

Another moment goes by and we can hear the distant sound of POLICE SIRENS. They are clearly coming toward the hospital, getting louder and louder. MICHAEL heaves a sigh of relief. A patrol car makes a screaming turn in front of the hospital; then two more squad cars follow, with uniformed POLICE and DETECTIVES. MICHAEL starts toward them. Two huge, burly POLICEMEN suddenly grab his arms while ANOTHER frisks him. A massive POLICE CAPTAIN, spattered with gold braid and scrambled eggs on his hat, with a beefy red face and white hair, seems furious. This is McCLUSKEY.

 GOOFS, GAFFES, AND BLOOPERS

The scene with Enzo was supposed to be filmed at Bellevue Hospital Center, but because Pacino had sprained an ankle ligament and had to go to the hospital, they couldn't finish his scenes for the day. The scene was eventually filmed on a Hollywood lot. Consequently, there is a continuity disruption: the flowers Enzo holds change from pink carnations with baby's breath to plain orange carnations in the exterior shot.

McCLUSKEY

I thought I got all you guinea hoods locked up. What the hell are you doin' here?

MICHAEL studies McCLUSKEY closely.

MICHAEL

What happened to the men who were guarding my father, Captain?

McCLUSKEY

(furious)

Why you little punk! What the hell are you doin', tellin' me my business?! I pulled them guys offa here, eh? Now you get outta here—and stay away from this hospital.

MICHAEL

I'm not moving until you put some guards around my father's room.

McCLUSKEY

Phil, take 'im in!

ANOTHER COP standing nearby.

SONNY GROSSO, SECOND FROM RIGHT.

CAST AND CREW: SONNY GROSSO

Sonny Grosso plays the uncredited role of the police-man with the line "The kid's clean, Captain." In an interview, he reported that with each take his voice rose higher and higher. After about fifteen takes, Coppola took him aside and pointedly said, "You're playing a cop, right?" Grosso was not a professional actor and was under extra stress because he had only taken three hours off from his detective job to be on set. He likened the sensation to getting jumped in a parking lot late at night: "You get to a point where you almost can't scream, and your throat and vocal cords swell up." Through the experience he learned to have respect for actors and what they go through.

Grosso wrangled the police extras for *The Godfather* and got his stint in the movie when William Friedkin introduced him to his friend Francis Ford Coppola. Friedkin was finishing up work on a movie about the life of New York City detective Eddie Egan and his partner, Sonny Grosso: *The French Connection*— another landmark film in the American cinematic renaissance of the seventies. When Grosso mentioned to Friedkin how much more he got paid for *The Godfather* than for *The French Connection*, Friedkin pointed out, "Well, I'm the one who introduced you to Coppola, right?"

DETECTIVE

The kid's clean, Captain. He's a war hero; he's never been mixed up in the rackets.

McCLUSKEY
(overlaps, furious)

Goddamn it! I said take 'im in!

MICHAEL
(deliberately, right to McCLUSKEY's face, as he's being handcuffed)

What's The Turk paying you to set up my father, Captain?

McCLUSKEY

Take a hold of him! Stand 'im up! Stand him up straight!

McCLUSKEY leans back and hits MICHAEL squarely on the jaw with all his weight and strength. MICHAEL groans, and he falls to the ground, just as we see HAGEN and CLEMENZA'S MEN arrive. HAGEN holds MICHAEL up as the CORLEONE MEN rush into the hospital.

HAGEN

I'm attorney for the Corleone Family. These men are private detectives, hired to protect Vito Corleone. They're licensed to carry firearms. If you interfere, you'll have to appear before the judge in the morning and show cause.

McCLUSKEY

All right, let 'im go. Go on.

DISSOLVE TO:

EXT DAY: MALL

HIGH ANGLE VIEW of the CORLEONE MALL. The gateway now has a long black car blocking it. There are BUTTON MEN stationed formally; the houses close to the courtyard have MEN standing by gates. It is clear that the war is escalating. A car pulls up and out get CLEMENZA, LAMPONE, MICHAEL, and HAGEN. MICHAEL's jaw is wired. He looks up at a balcony. We can see MEN holding rifles. They continue walking. TESSIO joins them. The various BODYGUARDS make no acknowledgment.

CLEMENZA

What's with all the new faces?

TESSIO

We'll need 'em now. After the hospital thing, Sonny got mad. We hit Bruno Tattaglia four o'clock this morning.

CLEMENZA

Jesus Christ!

(shakes head)

Looks like a fortress around here.

INT DAY: DON'S OFFICE

SONNY is in THE DON's office; he is excited and exuberant.

SONNY

(to HAGEN)

Tomanuch! Hey, a hundred button men on the street, twenty-four hours a day. That Turk shows one hair on his ass, he's dead, believe me.

SONNY smacks HAGEN on the behind. He sees MICHAEL and examines his swollen face.

SONNY

Hey, Mike, c'mere. Lemme look at you. You're beautiful, beautiful. You're gorgeous.

(pats MICHAEL on his behind)

Hey, listen to this: The Turk he wants to talk. Ye gods, imagine the nerve on that sonofabitch, eh? Craps out last night, he wants a meetin' today.

BOTTOM: GORDON WILLIS AND CREW ON SCAFFOLDING, SETTING UP THE OVERHEAD SHOT OF THE "FORTRESS."

HAGEN

What'd he say?

SONNY

What did he say. Baba beep, baba bap, baba boop, bada beep. He wants us to send Michael to hear the proposition and the promise is that the deal is so good that we can't refuse, hey!

HAGEN

What about Bruno Tattaglia?

SONNY

That's part of the deal, Bruno cancels out what they did to my father.

HAGEN

Sonny, we oughta hear what they have to say.

SONNY

No, no, no! No more! Not this time, Consigliere. No more meetin's, no more discussions, no more Sollozzo tricks. Ya give 'em one message: I want Sollozzo. If not, it's all-out war because we go to the mattresses!

HAGEN

(overlaps)

Sonny! The other Families won't sit still for all-out war!

SONNY

(overlaps)

Then they hand me Sollozzo!

HAGEN

(overlaps)

Your father wouldn't want to hear this! This is business, not personal.

SONNY

(overlaps)

They shot my father—business my ass!

HAGEN

(overlaps)

Even the shooting of your father was business, not personal, Sonny!

SONNY

Well then, business will have to suffer, all right? And listen, do me a favor, Tom. No more advice on how to patch things up. Just help me win, please. All right?

SONNY sits.

HAGEN

I found out about this Captain McCluskey who broke Mike's jaw.

SONNY

What about 'im?

HAGEN

Well, he's definitely on Sollozzo's payroll, and for big money. See? Now McCluskey has agreed to be The Turk's bodyguard. What you have to understand, Sonny, is that while Sollozzo is being guarded like this, he is invulnerable. Now, nobody has ever gunned down a New York police captain. Never. It would be disastrous. All the Five Families would come after you, Sonny; the Corleone Family would be *outcast*! Even the old man's political protection would run for cover! So do me a favor— take this into consideration.

SONNY

(sighs)

All right. We'll wait.

MICHAEL

We can't wait.

"Sh█t these like Ber█man . . . starting on █ne character, keep█ing other dialogue offs█reen, then move to the next, all around the █ircle."

—Coppola's notebook

 BEHIND THE SCENES

The cane in Sonny's hand could be a prop for Vito, but may also be actor Al Pacino's. He was hobbled when he sprained an ankle ligament while shooting the scene where Michael flees Louis' Restaurant after shooting Sollozzo and McCluskey.

                    SONNY
What?

                    MICHAEL
We can't wait.

                    MICHAEL
I don't care what Sollozzo says about a deal, he's gonna kill Pop, that's it. That's the key for 'im. Gotta get Sollozzo.

                    CLEMENZA
Mike is right.

                    SONNY
Lemme ask you somethin' . . . What about this McCluskey? Huh? What do we do with this cop here?

There is a slow camera ZOOM during MICHAEL's speech.

                    MICHAEL
They want to have a meeting with me, right? It will be me, McCluskey, and Sollozzo. Let's set the meeting. Get our informers to find out where it's gonna be held. Now we insist it's a public place—a bar, a restaurant—some place where there's people so I feel safe. They're gonna search me when I first meet them, right? So I can't have a weapon on me then. But if Clemenza can figure a way to have a weapon planted there for me. Then I'll kill 'em both.

Everyone in the room is astonished; they all look at MICHAEL. Silence. CLEMENZA suddenly breaks out in laughter. SONNY and TESSIO join in; only HAGEN is serious.

SONNY walks over to MICHAEL, leaning in.

SONNY

Hey, whatta ya gonna do? Nice college boy, eh? Didn't want to get mixed up in the Family business, huh? Now you wanna gun down a police captain, what, because he slapped ya in the face a little bit? Hah? What do you think this is, the army, where you shoot 'em a mile away? You gotta get up close, like this—bada bing! You blow their brains all over your nice Ivy League suit.

 **ITALIANISMS**

James Caan used his interactions with real Mafia members to craft some of his mannerisms and dialogue. Sonny's parlance here was the inspiration for the name of the strip club featured in *The Sopranos,* the Bada Bing!

Puzo's novel paints a slightly more nuanced portrait of Sonny Corleone, as more than just a hothead. When Michael confronts him for laughing at him, Sonny replies perceptively, "I know you can do it. I wasn't laughing at what you said. I was just laughing at how funny things turn out. I always said you were the toughest one in the Family, tougher than the Don himself. You were the only one who could stand off the old man."

In Puzo's novel, the personal-versus-business dialogue takes on a different tone. Michael more directly asserts himself within the family by challenging the notion that it's just "business": "It's all personal, every bit of business. Every piece of shit every man has to eat every day of his life is personal. They call it business. OK. But it's personal as hell. You know where I learned that from? The Don. My old man. The Godfather. If a bolt of lightning hit a friend of his the old man would take it personal. He took my going into the Marines personal. That's what makes him great. The Great Don. He takes everything personal. Like God."

C'mere.

MICHAEL holds up a hand in defense. SONNY kisses MICHAEL emphatically on his head.

> **MICHAEL**
> *(overlaps)*
> Sonny!

> **SONNY**
> Myah! You're takin' this very personal. Tom, this is business and this man is takin' it very, very personal.

> **MICHAEL**
> Where does it say that you can't kill a cop?

> **HAGEN**
> *(smiling)*
> Come on, Mikey!

> **MICHAEL**
> Tom, wait a minute. I'm talking about a cop that's mixed up in drugs. I'm talking about a—a dishonest cop—a crooked cop who got mixed up in the rackets and got what was coming to him. That's a terrific story. And we have newspaper people on the payroll, don't we, Tom?
> *(HAGEN nods)*
> And they might like a story like that.

> **HAGEN**
> They might, they just might.

> **MICHAEL**
> It's not personal, Sonny. It's strictly business.

INT DAY: CLEMENZA'S CELLAR

CLOSE-UP on a revolver.

> **CLEMENZA**
> It's as cold as they come. Impossible to trace, so you don't worry about prints, Mike; I put a special tape on the trigger and the butt. Here, try it.

He hands the gun to another pair of hands.

"I feel it should be somewhere homey and warm; like being with a favorite uncle in his workshop, and having him explain how to do this or that. Except here, it's how to kill a man."
—Coppola's notebook

**GOOFS, GAFFES, AND
BLOOPERS**

A cigarette jumps from Clemenza's mouth to his hand when he is instructing Michael.

CLEMENZA

Whatsa matter, the trigger too tight?

It fires: very LOUD.

MICHAEL is alone with CLEMENZA in a cellar workshop.

MICHAEL

Marone, my ears.

CLEMENZA

Yeah, I left it noisy, that way it scares any pain-in-the-ass innocent bystanders away. All right, you shot 'em both, now what do you do?

MICHAEL

Sit down, finish my dinner.

CLEMENZA

Come on, kid, don't fool around. Just let your hand drop to your side, and let the gun slip out. Everybody'll still think you got it. They're gonna be starin' at your face, Mike. So walk outta the place real fast, but you don't run. Don't look nobody directly in the eye, but you don't look away either. Hey, they gonna be scared stiff o' you, believe me, so don't worry about nothin'. You know, you're gonna turn out all right. You're takin' a long vacation—nobody knows where—and we're gonna catch the hell.

MICHAEL

How bad do you think it's gonna be?

CLEMENZA

Pretty goddamn bad. Probably all the other Families will line up against us. That's all right. These things gotta happen every five years or so—ten years—helps to get rid of the bad blood. Been ten years since the last one. You know you gotta stop 'em at the beginning, like they shoulda stopped Hitler at Munich. They shoulda never let him get away with that. They were just askin' for big trouble. You know, Mike, we was all proud o' you. Bein' a hero and all. Your father too.

MICHAEL takes back the gun; he practices pulling the trigger.

INT NIGHT: DON'S LIVING ROOM

TESSIO, SONNY, CLEMENZA, and LAMPONE are all eating out of white Chinese food containers around the table. MICHAEL simply smokes. HAGEN enters.

HAGEN

Nothing. Not a hint. Absolutely nothing. Even Sollozzo's people don't know where the meeting's gonna be held.

MICHAEL

How much time do we have?

116 THE ANNOTATED GODFATHER

SONNY

They're gonna pick you up in front of Jack Dempsey's joint in an hour and a half. Exactly an hour and a half.

CLEMENZA

We could put a tail on 'em an' see how it turns out.

SONNY

Sollozzo'd lose our ass goin' around the block!

HAGEN

What about the negotiator?

CLEMENZA

He's over at my place playin' pinochle with a couple o' my men. He's happy; they're lettin' 'im win.

HAGEN

This is too much of a risk for Mike; maybe we oughta call it off, Sonny.

 ADAPTATION AND THE CUTTING ROOM FLOOR

The Godfather novel explains what Hagen means by "the negotiator." The Bocchicchio Family, once a particularly brutal branch of the Mafia in Sicily, became peace brokers in the United States. They utilized their only great assets, honor and ferocity, to serve a unique function. In a time of war, the head of a Family would handle the initial negotiations and arrange for a hostage from the Bocchicchio family. For example, when Michael contacted Sollozzo, a Bocchicchio (paid for by Sollozzo) was left with the Corleones. If Sollozzo were to kill Michael, then the Corleones would in turn kill the Bocchicchio hostage. Consequently, the Bocchicchios would take out their vengeance on Sollozzo as the cause of their clansman's death. They were so primitive, they never let anything dissuade them from their vengeance, so having a Bocchicchio hostage was the ultimate insurance. Later on in the novel, it happens to be a Bocchicchio already on death row who takes the rap for Sollozzo's murder, allowing Michael to return to the country.

CLEMENZA

The negotiator keeps on playing cards until Mike comes back safe and
sound.

SONNY

So why don't he just blast whoever's in the goddamn car?!

CLEMENZA

Too dangerous; they'll be lookin' for that.

HAGEN

Sollozzo might not even be in the car, Sonny!

The phone RINGS.

SONNY

I'll get it.

(hurries to get the phone)

Yeah. Yeah. Well, thanks.

(hangs up the phone and comes back to the table)

Louis' Restaurant in the Bronx.

HAGEN

Well, is it reliable?

SONNY

That's my man in McCluskey's precinct. A police captain's gotta be on
call twenty-four hours a day. He signed out at that number between
eight and ten. Anybody know this joint?

TESSIO

Yeah, sure, I do. It's perfect for us. A small, family place, good food.
Everyone minds his business. It's perfect. Pete, they got an old-fashion
toilet. You know, the box-and-the-chain thing. We might be able to tape
the gun behind it.

CLEMENZA

All right. Mike, you go to the restaurant, ya eat, ya talk for a while, you
relax. You make them relax. Then you get up and you go take a leak.
No, better still, you ask for permission to go. Then, when you come
back, ya come out blastin', and don't take any chances. Two shots in
the head apiece.

SONNY

Listen, I want somebody good, and I mean very good, to plant that
gun. I don't want my brother comin' out of that toilet with just his dick
in his hands, all right?

CLEMENZA

The gun'll be there.

BEHIND THE SCENES

Coppola inserted the detail of the men eating out of
white Chinese takeout containers—a memory from
his childhood.

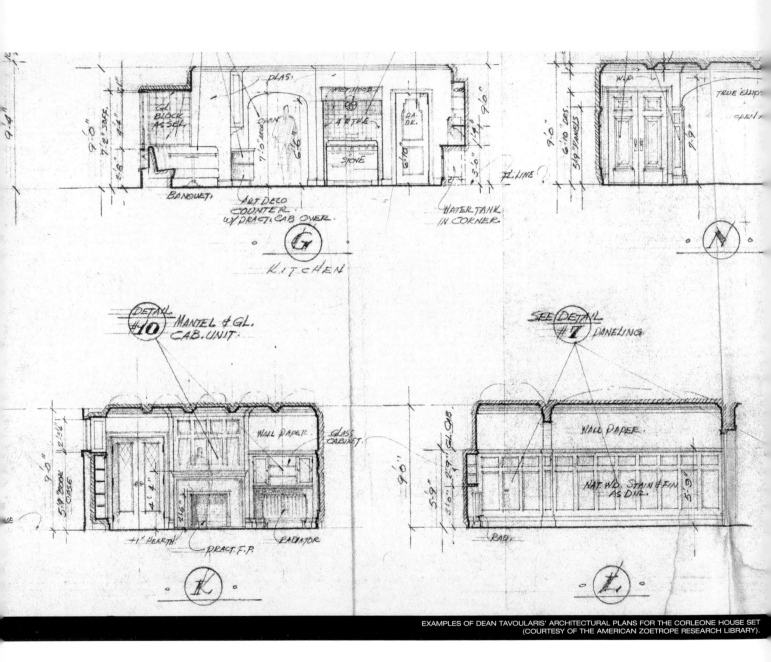

EXAMPLES OF DEAN TAVOULARIS' ARCHITECTURAL PLANS FOR THE CORLEONE HOUSE SET
(COURTESY OF THE AMERICAN ZOETROPE RESEARCH LIBRARY).

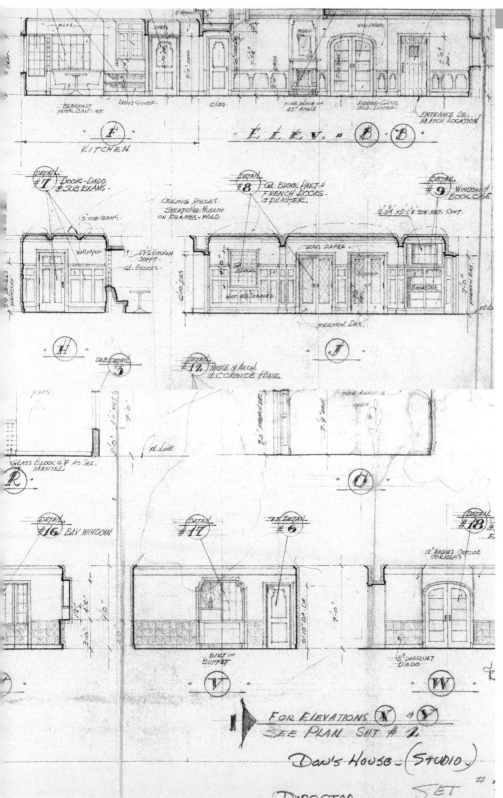

"There is so much invention in that man, it's just incredible."

—Arthur Penn, director of *Bonnie and Clyde,* on Dean Tavoularis, in *Variety,* 1997

The cinematic feel of *Little Big Man* and *Bonnie and Clyde* impressed Coppola, so he chose Dean Tavoularis to do the production design for *The Godfather.* It turned out to be a fantastic collaboration for all. "A film set is a great bouillabaisse of people and taste," cinematographer Gordon Willis said in *Variety.* "I felt very early on when we worked together on *The Godfather* that Dean Tavoularis had a great touch and wonderful taste. He was a very valuable contributor who was hanging these great canvasses for me to shoot."

A production designer is an architect of worlds; he is responsible for creating the visual look of a film—basically everything you see onscreen except for the actors. Tavoularis's work on *The Godfather* was meticulous. He created painstakingly accurate 1940s touches and richly evocative sets. In the opening scene, his set—along with Willis's camera work—created a powerful contrast between the light mood of the wedding and the heavy atmosphere of the Don's study. The study was dark with wood and pink tones, like a church, and he wanted to evoke the feeling of invigoration that comes from leaving a church by making the wedding a contrastingly bright, sunny, and festive affair. Throughout the scenes in the Don's study, one is aware of the other world of the wedding nearby—the shuttered light peeks through the windows, and the energetic music invades the quiet, somber tones.

Tavoularis would go on to be Coppola's trusted production designer on virtually all of his films. He even met his wife on the set of *Apocalypse Now;* she played a role that was edited out of the movie. He has worked with a variety of renowned directors including Michelangelo Antonioni, Wim Wenders, Warren Beatty, and Roman Polanski. He has received Oscar® nominations for five films and won for *The Godfather: Part II,* for which he transformed an entire New York City street into an early-twentieth-century thoroughfare. In 2007, Tavoularis was honored with a lifetime achievement award at the 11th Annual Art Directors Guild Awards.

THE NUTS AND BOLTS: PRODUCTION DETAIL

The pick up scene was shot in front of the now-bygone Jack Dempsey's Restaurant, on Broadway between 49th and 50th streets, Manhattan. An American institution, it was located at the site of the old car barn across from the original Madison Square Garden, and was owned by world heavyweight boxing champion Jack Dempsey. The restaurant was open from 1935 to 1974, and Dempsey himself would often be there to greet patrons. After the scene wrapped, members of the crew stayed behind to drink at the bar.

ADAPTATION AND THE CUTTING ROOM FLOOR

Coppola wanted to film Michael waiting under the Camel cigarettes sign in Times Square but, for budgetary reasons, this idea was scrapped. It would have cost a reported $5,000 to reconstruct the famous sign. In the novel, as in the final film, Michael waits under the Jack Dempsey's Restaurant sign.

BEHIND THE SCENES

The interior of the car scene was shot in an empty sound stage (they're not really moving).

SONNY

All right.

(to TESSIO)

Listen, you drive 'im, and you pick 'im up after the job, okay?

CLEMENZA

Come on. Let's move.

They all stand up and walk to the door. HAGEN helps MICHAEL get his coat on. SONNY puts his arm around MICHAEL.

SONNY

Did he tell you to drop the gun right away?

MICHAEL

Yeah. A million times.

CLEMENZA

You don't forget, two shots apiece in the head, soon as you come out the door, right?

MICHAEL

(to SONNY)

How long do you think it'll be before I can come back?

SONNY

At least a year, Mike.

(warmly)

Listen, I'll square it with Mom—y'know, you're not seeing her before you leave. And I'll get a message to that girlfriend, when I think the time is right.

SONNY and MICHAEL embrace. MICHAEL kisses SONNY.

SONNY

Take care, huh?

MICHAEL and HAGEN embrace.

                              HAGEN

   Take care, Mike.

                             MICHAEL

   Tom . . .

MICHAEL moves out.

                                                    DISSOLVE TO:

EXT NIGHT: JACK DEMPSEY'S RESTAURANT

The enormous "Jack Dempsey's Restaurant" sign. Below it stands MICHAEL, dressed in a
warm overcoat. A long black car pulls up and slows before him. The DRIVER, leaning
over, opens the front door. MICHAEL gets in, and the car drives off.

INT NIGHT: SOLLOZZO'S CAR

Inside the car, SOLLOZZO reaches his hand over the backseat and pats MICHAEL's
shoulder. McCLUSKEY sits next to SOLLOZZO.

                          SOLLOZZO

   I'm glad you came, Mike. I hope we can straighten everything out.
   I mean, this is terrible; it's not the way I wanted things to go at all.
   It should've never happened.

                           MICHAEL

   I'm gonna straighten everything out tonight. I don't want my father
   bothered anymore.

                          SOLLOZZO

   He won't be, Mike; I swear on my children he won't be. But you gotta
   keep an open mind when we talk. I mean, I hope you're not a hothead
   like your brother Sonny. You can't talk business with him. (SPEAKS ITALIAN)

McCLUSKEY reaches his hand over the backseat to shake MICHAEL's hand.

                          McCLUSKEY

   Ah, he's a good kid. I'm sorry about the other night, Mike. I gotta frisk
   ya so turn around, huh? On your knees facing me.

MICHAEL takes off his hat and turns around. McCLUSKEY gives MICHAEL a thorough
frisk.

                          McCLUSKEY

   I guess I'm getting too old for my job. Too grouchy. Can't stand the
   aggravation. You know how it is. He's clean.

MICHAEL puts his hat back on.

 BEHIND THE SCENES

"Most of the scenes involving cops and wiseguys
Francis would discuss with me the night before.
While the scene in the car was being shot, I hear
Sterling [Hayden] say, 'Why don't we ask the
expert?' They wanted to know how to go about
searching Pacino in the car. I wanted to say, 'You
never search a man when he's already *in* the car,'
but I was trying to keep my job as technical advisor,
so I just let it go. I got behind Pacino, who was in
the front seat, Sterling got on the other side of me,
and the driver (a kid from my neighborhood) got
behind the wheel. I wanted to scream, 'I don't know!'
Most of what a cop does is improvise, so I told
Pacino, 'Turn around, on your knees, pull your arms
up.' I searched him on top and down his waist, with
his arms draped over the front seats, and I told the
driver to do his legs and ankles."

—Sonny Grosso, technical advisor, about the somewhat
    awkward frisk of Michael

THE NUTS AND BOLTS: PRODUCTION DETAIL

The scene in Sollozzo's car was shot on the Queensboro Bridge, also known as the 59th Street Bridge, popularized by Simon & Garfunkel's "The 59th Street Bridge Song (Feelin' Groovy)," as well as by many scenes from movies, television series, and books. The 59th Street Bridge spans the East River, connecting Manhattan and Queens. However, the plot indicates that they were originally heading to New Jersey. So, in reality, they would have to be traveling on the George Washington Bridge, which spans the Hudson River and connects Manhattan and New Jersey.

THE NUTS AND BOLTS: PRODUCTION DETAIL

Louis' Restaurant was actually Old Luna Restaurant, on White Plains Road near Gun Hill Road, the Bronx. The restaurant's windows are covered to block out daylight and the crowds. The restaurant owner and his wife play themselves, and Coppola's parents portray diners. With each new take, all of the dinners in the restaurant had to be reset and the floor cleaned of blood. The restaurant was actually situated in close proximity to the elevated train. The El's blast is an effectively jarring and memorable sound effect in the scene. The idea of utilizing this specific sound was mentioned in a preproduction meeting between Coppola, Tavoularis, Willis, and costume designer Johnny Johnstone. However, Tavoularis had originally conceived of using the sound of the Brooklyn El train during the scene where Sonny beats up Carlo. Tavoularis: "The whole idea of the sequence would make this particularly frightening—the slowness of it and the deliberateness, and the professional aspect of it."

INT NIGHT: SOLLOZZO'S CAR, WEST SIDE HIGHWAY

MICHAEL looks at the DRIVER and then ahead to see where they're heading. The car takes the George Washington Bridge. MICHAEL is concerned.

> MICHAEL
>
> Goin' to Jersey?

> SOLLOZZO
>
> *(sly)*
>
> Maybe.

EXT NIGHT: SOLLOZZO'S CAR ON G. W. BRIDGE

The car speeds along the George Washington Bridge on its way to New Jersey. Then suddenly it hits the divider, temporarily lifts into the air, and bounces over into the lanes going back to New York. It then accelerates very fast, on the way back to the city.

INT NIGHT: SOLLOZZO'S CAR

SOLLOZZO leans to the DRIVER.

> SOLLOZZO
>
> Nice work, Lou.

MICHAEL is relieved.

EXT NIGHT: LOUIS' RESTAURANT

The car pulls up in front of a little family restaurant in the Bronx: "LOUIS' ITALIAN-AMERICAN RESTAURANT." There is no one on the street. SOLLOZZO, McCLUSKEY, and MICHAEL get out; the DRIVER remains leaning against the car. They enter the restaurant.

INT NIGHT: LOUIS' RESTAURANT

A very small family restaurant with a mosaic tile floor. SOLLOZZO, MICHAEL, and McCLUSKEY sit at a rather small round table near the center of the room. There are a handful of CUSTOMERS, and ONE or TWO WAITERS. It is very quiet.

> McCLUSKEY
>
> How's the Italian food in this restaurant?

> SOLLOZZO
>
> Good. Try the veal. It's the best in the city.

> McCLUSKEY
>
> I'll have it.

> SOLLOZZO
>
> *(to WAITER)*
>
> *Capit.*

They watch the WAITER silently as he uncorks a bottle of wine and pours three glasses.

SOLLOZZO

(to WAITER)

Right.

(to McCLUSKEY)

I'm gonna speak Italian to Mike.

McCLUSKEY

Go ahead.

SOLLOZZO now begins in rapid Sicilian. MICHAEL listens carefully and nods every so often. Then MICHAEL answers in Sicilian, and SOLLOZZO goes on. The WAITER occasionally brings food, and they hesitate while he is there, then go on. Then MICHAEL, having difficulty expressing himself in Italian, lapses into English.

MICHAEL

Come se diche . . .

(using English for emphasis)

What I want—what's most important to me—is that I have a guarantee: no more attempts on my father's life.

SOLLOZZO

What guarantees can I give you, Mike? I am the hunted one! I missed my chance. You think too much of me, kid. I'm not that clever. All *I* want is a truce.

MICHAEL looks at SOLLOZZO. Then he looks away, with a distressed look on his face.

MICHAEL

I have to go to the bathroom. Is that all right?

CAST AND CREW: STERLING HAYDEN

Sterling Hayden—a seaman at heart—ran away at sixteen to become a mate on a schooner before eventually getting a contract with Paramount, who in 1941 declared him "The Most Beautiful Man in the Movies!" Although he detested film work, before playing Captain McCluskey in *The Godfather,* he appeared in over forty films—mostly Westerns and film noir—including such memorable pictures as *The Asphalt Jungle* and *Dr. Strangelove or: How I Learned to Stop Worrying and Love the Bomb.* According to a production assistant, between takes of this scene the quixotic Hayden snacked on fruit and milk, as he only ate natural foods. He read *Dear Theo*, a collection of Van Gogh's letters to his brother. Then, he mysteriously disappeared. He had taken a stroll, fallen asleep down by the river, and was awakened by boys throwing rocks at him.

CAST AND CREW: AL LETTIERI

Actor Al Lettieri (Sollozzo) was fluent in Sicilian.

 GOOFS, GAFFES, AND BLOOPERS

There's a continuity error in the restaurant scene: the maître d' holds a pipe, but when the camera cuts to another angle, it disappears.

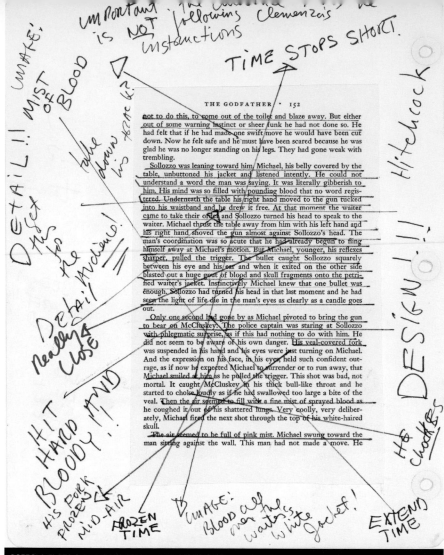

The handwritten annotations on the manuscript page read:

IMPORTANT is NOT following Clemenza's instructions

TIME STOPS SHORT.

Hitchcock

(IMAGE: MIST OF BLOOD)

DETAIL!!!

take down his FORK E?

Detail! really CLOSE

HIT HARD MIND BLOODY!!

his FORK FROZEN

DESIGN!!!

He chokes

FROZEN TIME MID-AIR

(IMAGE: Blood all over waiters white Jacket!)

EXTEND TIME

THE GODFATHER · 152

not to do this, to come out of the toilet and blaze away. But either out of some warning instinct or sheer funk he had not done so. He had felt that if he had made one swift move he would have been cut down. Now he felt safe and he must have been scared because he was glad he was no longer standing on his legs. They had gone weak with trembling.

Sollozzo was leaning toward him, Michael, his belly covered by the table, unbuttoned his jacket and listened intently. He could not understand a word the man was saying. It was literally gibberish to him. His mind was so filled with pounding blood that no word registered. Underneath the table his right hand moved to the gun tucked into his waistband and he drew it free. At that moment the waiter came to take their order and Sollozzo turned his head to speak to the waiter. Michael thrust the table away from him with his left hand and his right hand shoved the gun almost against Sollozzo's head. The man's coordination was so acute that he had already begun to fling himself away at Michael's motion. But Michael, younger, his reflexes sharper, pulled the trigger. The bullet caught Sollozzo squarely between his eye and his ear and when it exited on the other side blasted out a huge gout of blood and skull fragments onto the petrified waiter's jacket. Instinctively Michael knew that one bullet was enough. Sollozzo had turned his head in that last moment and he had seen the light of life die in the man's eyes as clearly as a candle goes out.

Only one second had gone by as Michael pivoted to bring the gun to bear on McCluskey. The police captain was staring at Sollozzo with phlegmatic surprise, as if this had nothing to do with him. He did not seem to be aware of his own danger. His veal-covered fork was suspended in his hand and his eyes were just turning on Michael. And the expression on his face, in his eyes, held such confident outrage, as if now he expected Michael to surrender or to run away, that Michael smiled at him as he pulled the trigger. This shot was bad, not mortal. It caught McCluskey in his thick bull-like throat and he started to choke loudly as if he had swallowed too large a bite of the veal. Then the air seemed to fill with a fine mist of sprayed blood as he coughed it out of his shattered lungs. Very coolly, very deliberately, Michael fired the next shot through the top of his white-haired skull.

The air seemed to be full of pink mist. Michael swung toward the man sitting against the wall. This man had not made a move. He

COPPOLA PLOTS OUT THE INTENSITY OF THE SCENE IN HIS NOTEBOOK.

McCLUSKEY
You gotta go, you gotta go.

SOLLOZZO is intuitively suspicious. He studies MICHAEL with his dark eyes. MICHAEL gets up and SOLLOZZO thrusts his hand onto MICHAEL's thigh, feeling in and around, searching for a weapon.

McCLUSKEY
I frisked 'im; he's clean.

SOLLOZZO
Don't take too long.

MICHAEL calmly walks to the bathroom.

McCLUSKEY
I've frisked a thousand young punks.

INT NIGHT: LOUIS' RESTAURANT TOILET

MICHAEL steps into the small bathroom. Then he moves to the stall, up to the old-fashioned toilet. Slowly he reaches behind the water tank. He panics when he cannot feel the gun.

INT NIGHT: LOUIS' RESTAURANT

SOLLOZZO and McCLUSKEY eating in the restaurant. McCLUSKEY glances back toward the bathrooms.

INT NIGHT: LOUIS' RESTAURANT TOILET

MICHAEL gropes searchingly, finally coming to rest on the gun. He brings it down; the feel of it reassures him.

INT NIGHT: LOUIS' RESTAURANT

SOLLOZZO and McCLUSKEY eating in the restaurant. McCLUSKEY glances back toward the bathrooms.

INT NIGHT: LOUIS' RESTAURANT TOILET

MICHAEL moves to leave the bathroom. He hesitates, his hand on his forehead, and smooths down his hair. Then he goes out. We HEAR the ROAR of the El train.

INT NIGHT: LOUIS' RESTAURANT

MICHAEL hesitates by the bathroom door and looks at his table. McCLUSKEY is eating a plate of spaghetti and veal. SOLLOZZO turns around upon hearing the door and looks directly at MICHAEL. MICHAEL looks back. Then he continues back to the table. He sits down.

SOLLOZZO leans toward MICHAEL, who sits down comfortably. His hands move under the table and unbutton his jacket. SOLLOZZO begins to speak in Sicilian once again, but MICHAEL's heart is pounding so hard he can barely hear him. Slow ZOOM on MICHAEL's face, while we HEAR the SCREECH of the El train's brakes.

"The biggest scene in the movie, effectwise."

—Coppola, in a preproduction special effects memo

Without warning, MICHAEL stands up and points the gun right at SOLLOZZO's head. He pulls the trigger, and we see part of SOLLOZZO's head blown away and a spray of fine mist of blood cover the entire area.

SOLLOZZO seems in a perpetual fall to the floor; he seems to hang in space suspended.

MICHAEL pivots and looks.

There is McCLUSKEY, frozen, the fork with a piece of veal suspended in midair before his gaping mouth.

MICHAEL fires, catching McCLUSKEY in his thick, bulging throat. The air is filled with pink mist. He makes a horrible, gagging, choking sound. Then, coolly and deliberately, MICHAEL fires again—fires right through McCLUSKEY's white-topped skull.

McCLUSKEY finally falls from the chair, knocking over the table. SOLLOZZO is still in his chair, his body propped up by the table.

MICHAEL swings toward a MAN standing by the bathroom wall. The MAN does not make a move, seemingly paralyzed. Then he carefully shows his hands to be empty.

MICHAEL is wildly at a peak. He starts to move out. His hand is frozen by his side, still gripping the gun.

He moves, not letting the gun go.

MICHAEL's face is frozen in its expression.

He walks quickly out of the restaurant. Just before exiting, his hand relaxes; the gun falls to the floor with a dull THUD.

MICHAEL exits.

EXT NIGHT: LOUIS' RESTAURANT

SOLLOZZO's car is still parked outside. Another car drives by and MICHAEL runs to catch it.

INT NIGHT: LOUIS' RESTAURANT

We see a frozen tableau of the murder, as though it had been re-created in wax.

"Once I got the role I was waking up at four or five in the morning and going into my kitchen to brood."
—Al Pacino, in *Life* magazine

AL PACINO

Who to cast in the prime role of Michael Corleone was fiercely debated between Paramount and Francis Ford Coppola. The executives wanted a well-known actor like Warren Beatty, Jack Nicholson, or Robert Redford; all turned it down. Tommy Lee Jones was also considered. Robert Evans liked Ryan O'Neal, who had just starred in Paramount's extraordinarily successful *Love Story* with Evans's then wife, Ali MacGraw. Coppola has speculated that Evans liked O'Neal because he reminded him of himself. Charles Bluhdorn (the head of Gulf+Western, Paramount's parent company) asked for Charles Bronson, who certainly would have brought something different to the character. The rumor mill also held that Dustin Hoffman was interested, and his name was discussed even after the role had been cast.

Among the countless actors Coppola and casting director Fred Roos screen-tested were David Carradine, Dean Stockwell, Martin Sheen, James Caan, and Robert De Niro. It has been widely reported that while watching the Michael Corleone screen tests, Stanley Jaffe, then president of Paramount Pictures, exasperatedly exclaimed: "I think you got the worst bunch of lampshades I've ever seen."

Coppola's true desire was for the unknown thirty-one-year-old theater actor Al Pacino to play the part of Michael Corleone. Alfredo James Pacino, the grandson of genuine Sicilians, was born in East Harlem and moved to the East Bronx at a young age. A wanderer, he dropped out of high school and scraped by, going from job to job, fired often for laziness. Acting piqued his interest, and he enrolled in the Actors Studio in 1966. In 1968 he won the OBIE Award for Best Actor for his work in *The Indian Wants the Bronx,* and followed that up with a Tony-winning performance in *Does a Tiger Wear a Necktie?* At the time of *The Godfather* casting, he had played a substantive role in only one film, the yet-to-be-released *The Panic in Needle Park,* which would be shown at the 1971 Cannes Film Festival.

While reading *The Godfather,* Coppola was haunted by Pacino's face, which he thought exuded an underlying menace integral to the role of Michael. Puzo's novel often cites Michael's ici-ness: "cold chilling anger that was not external-ized in any gesture or change in voice. It was a coldness that came off him like death." . . . "Michael Corleone felt that delicious refreshing chilliness all over his body."

Al's face also had a certain old-Sicilian quality that had become synonymous with Michael Corleone in Coppola's mind. Marcia Lucas, then wife of Coppola's American Zoetrope partner George Lucas, also liked Pacino, saying that he "undresses you with his eyes."

As with many of Coppola's inclinations about *The Godfather,* once he decided what he wanted, he fought for it tooth and nail. Pacino admits that it was Coppola's single-minded tenacity that got him the part. It was a tough fight. With his non–movie star looks, Pacino, Paramount thought, was too Italian, too unattractive, and, at five feet seven inches, too short. He was called a "shrimp" by studio executives—Evans often referred to him as "that midget Pacino." According to producer Al Ruddy, Coppola tried all sorts of tricks to get Pacino hired; for one of the screen tests he instructed the camera be placed on the ground, to make Pacino look taller.

The screen-tested scene was the wedding conversation with Kay about his family—certainly not the most riveting scene in the script. To make matters worse, Pacino tested terribly, repeatedly blowing his lines. Because Pacino knew that Paramount didn't want him, he felt disinclined to invest himself in a role he was certain he'd never get. He said in a *Ladies' Home Journal* interview: "I knew Francis was the only one who wanted me, so I felt, 'What's the sense of learning lines? No mat-ter what I do I won't get the part.'"

Pacino tested for the role no fewer than three times. Reportedly, just seven weeks before filming was to start, Coppola was told to test thirty new actors. Ruddy went to CEO Bluhdorn, asking for a "compromise." Even Marlon Brando put in his two cents, telling Evans that Pacino was a "brooder" like Michael Corleone. Ruddy describes a lunch in which Evans banged on the table, pro-claiming his frustration over the continued Pacino talk: "I'm running the goddamn studio—what the hell do we have to do?" Finally, on March 3, well after every other principal had signed, the deal for Pacino was announced. The Paramount execu-tives saw eight minutes of his impressive turn in the yet-to-be-released *The Panic in Needle Park,* and that, coupled with Coppola's relentlessness, swung the tide in Pacino's favor.

However, the Pacino battles weren't over. While Paramount was hemming and hawing over hiring Pacino, he took another job, in the MGM Mafia picture *The Gang That Couldn't Shoot Straight.* On March 10, just two weeks before shooting began on *The Godfather,* MGM slapped Pacino with a lawsuit to force him to honor their agreement. Eventually, Paramount settled the matter, and Pacino had to pay the court costs and agree to a subsequent MGM film role. A substan-tial chunk of Pacino's $35,000 *Godfather* salary went to MGM for the lawsuit.

As *The Godfather* shooting commenced, there were rumblings that Pacino would be fired. In an interview, he recalled: "It was obvious that some people didn't want me. I remember saying, 'I'll never make it through this picture; it's going to kill me.'" He heard giggling from a merciless crew while on camera. However, he believed that in the initial scenes of the film Michael must appear unsure of himself; as quoted in *Al Pacino: In Conversation with Lawrence Grobel,* Pacino says, "He's caught between his Old World family and the postwar American dream." It wasn't until the fourth day of shooting, in the scene where Michael kills Sollozzo and McCluskey, that Pacino impressed the studio executives enough to quell the rumors.

Coppola's vision to see the unknown Pacino as Michael Corleone, and his gumption to fight for the unpopular choice, was spot-on. Pacino's chilling intensity, and the subtle but inex-orable transformation he works on Michael's soul, are riveting—a pitch-perfect performance to rival any in American cinematic history.

"The Five Families War of 1946 had begun."

—Mario Puzo's, *The Godfather*

MATTRESSES MONTAGE

A sentimental tune plays over the following:

Printing presses turning.

A NEWSBOY dropping a packet of newspapers emblazoned with the headline: "POLICE HUNT COP KILLER."

Another newspaper headline: "CITY CRACKS DOWN: PRESSURE ON ORGANIZED CRIME."

TESSIO sits, doing a crossword puzzle by the light of a lamp.

Spinning newspaper stops. Headline reads: "POLICE CAPTAIN LINKED WITH DRUG RACKETS."

Clemenza prays; starts to lie down on bed.

TEN MEN sit around a crude table, quietly eating. A large bowl of pasta is passed, and the MEN eat heartily. A little distance away, a MAN in his shirtsleeves plays a sentimental tune on an old upright piano, while his cigarette burns on the edge. ANOTHER leans on the piano, listening quietly.

Newspaper scrolls up, headline "MOBSTER BARZINI QUESTIONED IN UNDERWORLD FEUD" over a photo of Barzini and other men (superimposed over CLOSE-UP on a hand cleaning a gun).

A thin, boyish BUTTON MAN writes a letter. Behind him, mattresses are spread out around the otherwise empty living room of an apartment. THREE or FOUR MEN are taking naps, (superimposed over) headline "MOB KILLINGS"—scroll from left to right through this shot and next.

A large bowl of pasta is passed among the BUTTON MEN.

Black-and-white photo: in a restaurant, a man lies in a pool of blood while men stand around the scene.

Black-and-white photo of police, holding guns, kneeling over gunned-down man, (superimposed over) a man cooking food.

Fingers playing the piano, (superimposed over) black-and-white photo of a corpse soaked in blood.

LAMPONE smokes while gazing out a window that has been covered with a heavy mesh, wire grating, then moves away.

Trash is thrown in two or three garbage cans kept in the apartment, (superimposed over) newspaper headline "GANGLAND VIOLENCE" over photo of corpse with head covered by bloody cloth.

Half-naked CLEMENZA lies sleeping on a bed.

THE NUTS AND BOLTS: PRODUCTION DETAIL

The mattresses montage features photos of real gangland assassinations.

BEHIND THE SCENES

The montage music was composed by the piano player in this scene: Coppola's dad, Carmine.

COPPOLA WITH FATHER CARMINE AND JOE SPINELL AS WILLIE CICCI.

LEFT: COPPOLA DIRECTS THE BUTTON MEN.

 THE NUTS AND BOLTS: PRODUCTION DETAIL

The exterior hospital scene was filmed at Lincoln Medical and Mental Health Center, on East 149th Street, the Bronx.

Two nights after this scene was shot, Francis Ford Coppola won an Academy Award® for his original screenplay for *Patton*—but didn't attend the ceremony.

 GOOFS, GAFFES, AND BLOOPERS

In the hospital parking lot, yellow curbing is visible—a practice that didn't occur until several years later.

Newspaper headline: "SYNDICATE BIG SHOT VITO CORLEONE RETURNS HOME."

EXT DAY: DON'S HOSPITAL (SPRING 1946)

A hospital in New York City. POLICE with rifles, teams of PRIVATE DETECTIVES, and BUTTON MEN are guarding the area, and they begin to move toward their cars. Photographer's snap pictures through the windows of an ambulance (presumably carrying THE DON), while orderlies close the back doors. CLEMENZA, carrying a suitcase, walks quickly with OTHER BUTTON MEN toward a car. It speeds off, the ambulance following with flashing lights, and is followed by another dark car. POLICE watch the cars leave.

MAN

Come on, let's go.

The cars exit the hospital lot via a ramp.

EXT DAY: MALL

Equally impressive security stands ready at the CORLEONE MALL—EXTRA BUTTON MEN, as well as SOME POLICE and PRIVATE DETECTIVES.

All is silent. The WOMEN and CHILDREN, dressed in Sunday clothes, wait.

EXT DAY: AMBULANCE

One ambulance, speeding along the Grand Central Parkway.

EXT DAY: MALL

The CORLEONE WOMEN and CHILDREN move toward the gate when they hear the sirens.

INT DAY: DON'S HALL

Inside the main CORLEONE house:

Hospital ORDERLIES carry THE DON on his stretcher carefully, under the watchful eyes of CLEMENZA, TESSIO, HAGEN, and various GUARDS and BUTTON MEN.

All the CORLEONE Family is here today: MAMA, FREDO, SONNY, SANDRA, THERESA, CONNIE, CARLO; the various CORLEONE CHILDREN.

ORDERLY

Okay, you take over.

INT DAY: DON'S BEDROOM

THE DON is made comfortable in his room, which has all but been converted into a hospital room, complete with extensive equipment. The various CHILDREN get a turn to kiss the OLD MAN.

A LITTLE GIRL approaches the bed.

LITTLE GIRL

I love you, Grandpa.

SANDRA approaches the bed with a screaming BABY.

SANDRA

I'm sorry, Pa; he doesn't know you yet.

MAMA kisses the BABY on the head. Then SONNY approaches, carrying a BOY with a piece of paper.

BRANDO JOKES AFTER LOADING HIS STRETCHER WITH SANDBAGS.

BEHIND THE SCENES

Makeup artist Dick Smith recalls the great practical joke from this scene: "They had two actors—pretty strong guys—to play the nurses. When the gurney was brought in with Brando, they wheeled it in just fine, but then they were confronted with those stairs, and they would have to carry him and the gurney up the stairs along a hallway. So these two guys dressed in their white suits tried to carry it up, just with Marlon in it, and it was too heavy for them and they had to stop. Francis Coppola said they had to get someone really strong, and looked over at the stage hands, who promptly brag, 'Yeah, sure, piece of cake.' They get taken off to wardrobe. At this point, Marlon says, 'Hey, let's have a little fun!' He pulls up the gurney mattress and the crew loads in as many sandbags as possible. Once it was well loaded, Marlon got back on, lay down, and pulled the blankets up. Coppola, very businesslike, tells the crew men to pick up the gurney, go up the stairs, and 'remember, don't stop.' 'Yeah, sure,' they say with bravado. We were all watching and holding our breath, while they're exerting all the strength they have. Of course, they're strong and they do it. But when the shot was completed, they yelled, 'What in the hell did you put in here?!' With both Brando and the sandbags, the stretcher weighed over five hundred pounds."

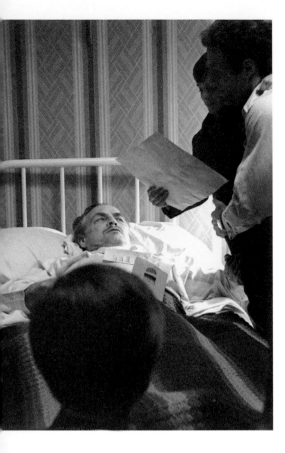

SONNY

All right. Hey, big guy, give it to Grandpa.

FRANKIE

(reading)

Okay. I hope you get well, Grandpa, and I wish I were to see you soon. Love, your grandson, Frank.

FRANKIE

(kisses THE DON)

MAMA

Ohhh! You . . .

SONNY indicates that all the CHILDREN, WOMEN, and CARLO should leave. They do; the door is closed.

SONNY

Go with your mother. Go ahead, take 'em downstairs. Nah. Go on, Carlo, you too. Go on.

INT DAY: DON'S KITCHEN

The mood is quite happy downstairs as the WOMEN prepare the Sunday dinner.

SANDRA

(to CONNIE)

. . . do you want all of that chicken cacciatore for your . . . I know, but how much can you eat?

EXT DAY: MALL

SOME of the CORLEONE GRANDCHILDREN play in the enclosed MALL, in the proximity of the BUTTON MEN stationed liberally by the gate.

ONE CHILD misses a ball and it rolls by the gatehouse. A young BUTTON MAN scoops it up and throws it back, smiling.

INT DAY: DON'S DINING ROOM

CARLO sits alone, a frown on his face. Connie approaches him, eating a piece of bread.

CONNIE

What's the matter with you, Carlo?

CARLO

Shut up and set the table.

INT DAY: DON'S BEDROOM

SONNY, HAGEN, FREDO, TESSIO, and CLEMENZA stand around the hospital bed with grim faces, SONNY and HAGEN closest to the OLD MAN. THE DON holds the children's get-well cards and presents. THE DON does not speak, yet he asks questions with his looks and glances as clearly as if they were verbalized. HAGEN is the spokesman for the family.

> ### HAGEN
> Since McCluskey's killing, the police have been cracking down on most of our operations. And also the other Families. There's been a lot of bad blood.

> ### SONNY
> They hit us, so we hit 'em back.

> ### HAGEN
> Through our contacts in the newspapers, we've been able to put out a lot o' material about McCluskey being linked with Sollozzo in the drug rackets. See, things are startin' to loosen up.

> ### SONNY
> And I'm sending Fredo to Las Vegas, under the protection of Don Francesco of L.A.
>
> *(puts his hand on FREDO's shoulder)*
>
> I want him to rest.

> ### FREDO
> I'm goin' to learn the casino business.

> ### SONNY
> Yeah.

> ### DON CORLEONE
> *(whispers)*
>
> Where's Michael?

HAGEN hesitates, glances at SONNY, and then leans in to THE DON.

> ### HAGEN
> It was Michael who killed Sollozzo. But he's safe. We're starting to work to bring him back now.

THE DON is very angry. He shakes his head, closes his eyes, and then motions with a weak hand that they leave him alone.

The MEN exit.

INT DAY: DON'S STAIRS AND HALL

HAGEN and SONNY come down the stairs. HAGEN seems upset and pensive, SONNY intense and angry.

"...I thought it would be an interesting contrast to play him as a gentle man, unlike Al Capone, who beat up people with baseball bats. . . . I saw him as a man of substance, tradition, dignity, refinement, a man of unerring instinct who just happened to live in a violent world and who had to protect himself and his family in this environment."

—Marlon Brando, on playing Don Corleone, in his autobiography, *Songs My Mother Taught Me*

"I remember when Marlon had been cast, he was doing a movie in England, and for some reason Francis and I had to go talk to him about something. He was on location in the countryside, staying at this house, and as we were walking into the house we started hearing that voice, speaking like the Don—the voice from the movie, with that accent. I don't know if Marlon staged it for us, but he was in the bathtub just practicing his speech delivery. Francis had given him a lot of audio and videotapes of Senate hearings where these Godfather capos had been testifying, so Marlon took an amalgam of them and created his own version of a Mafia don."

—Casting director Fred Roos, in a 2007 interview with the author

SONNY

Did ya ever find out where that old pimp Tattaglia is hidin'? I want his ass now, right now!

HAGEN

(grabbing his hand to stop him)

Sonny—

SONNY

What?

HAGEN

Things are starting to loosen up a little bit. If you go after Tattaglia, all hell's gonna break loose. Let—let the smoke clear. Pop can negotiate.

SONNY

(overlaps)

No, Pop can't do nothing till he's better! I'm gonna decide what's gonna be done . . .

HAGEN

(overlaps)

All right, but your war is costing us a lot of money; nothing's coming in! We can't do business.

SONNY

Well, neither can they! Don't worry about it.

HAGEN

(overlaps)

They don't have our overhead!

SONNY

(overlaps)

Please don't worry about it!

HAGEN

(overlaps; furiously)

We can't afford a stalemate!

SONNY

Well, then there ain't no more stalemate! I'm gonna end it by killin' that old bastard! I'm gonna . . .

HAGEN

Yeah, you're getting a great reputation. I hope you're enjoying it.

SONNY

(overlaps)

Will you just do what I tell you to do?! Goddamn it! If I had a wartime consigliere, a Sicilian, I wouldn't be in this shape! Pop had Genco. Look what I got.

> (exhales)

I'm sorry, I didn't mean that. Ma made a little dinner, it's Sunday . . .

HAGEN storms off. SONNY follows.

INT DAY: DON'S DINING ROOM

The FAMILY—WIVES, CHILDREN, and all—sit around the table over Sunday dinner. SONNY is at the head of the table.

> SONNY

You know the niggers are havin' a good time with our policy banks up there in Harlem—drivin' them new Cadillacs, payin' fifty percent on a bet.

> CARLO

I knew that was gonna happen soon as they started makin' big money.

> SONNY

Yeah . . .

> CONNIE

Well, Papa never talked business at the table in front of the kids.

> CARLO

Hey, shut up, Connie, when Sonny's talkin' . . .

> SONNY

> (overlaps)

Hey! Don't you ever tell her to shut up. You got that?

> CHILD

. . . cake.

> MAMA

> (overlaps, puts a hand up)

Santino, don't interfere.

> CARLO

Look, Sonny, Tom, I'd like to talk to you maybe after dinner. I could be doin' a lot more for the Family.

> SONNY

We don't discuss business at the table.

INT: DON'S BEDROOM

FREDO slowly enters. He sits in a chair next to a fruit basket, watching his FATHER. THE DON still lies in his bed, holding the cards. His eyes move but he doesn't speak.

"I like the idea of starting the movie . . . with, 'I believe in America,' because it's what the whole movie is about. It's saying that our country should be our family in a way, that it should afford us the protection and the honor that, in a strange way, this Mafia Family does; but that we should look to our country in this way."

—Coppola, in a preproduction meeting

"We are in Sicily in the Springtime. We consider the land itself; ancient, with beautiful views of the sea; in part arid, and now, in the Springtime, abundant. Most of all a feeling of its ancient rituals and roots."

—Coppola's notebook

DISSOLVE TO:

EXT DAY: ESTABLISHING SICILY SHOT

LONG SHOT: In the distance are three MEN walking across the Sicilian countryside. Slightly more in the foreground, sheep are herded. A MEDIUM SHOT reveals MICHAEL, with two Sicilian SHEPHERDS, each carrying a shotgun slung over his shoulder—CALO, a squat and husky young man with a simple, honest quality, and FABRIZIO, slender and handsome, likable. A car pulls up and stops. FABRIZIO opens the door for a stout older man, DON TOMMASINO, who exits the car.

The men speak in Italian with SUBTITLES:

FABRIZIO
I kiss your hand, Don Tommasino.

DON TOMMASINO

Why are you so far from the house? You know I'm responsible to your father for your life.

MICHAEL

The bodyguards are here.

DON TOMMASINO

It's still dangerous . . . We've heard from Santino in New York . . . Your enemies know you're here.

MICHAEL

Did Santino say when I can go back?

DON TOMMASINO

Not yet. It's out of the question.

MICHAEL

(pats his shoulder and turns to leave)

Grazie.

DON TOMMASINO

Where are you going now?

MICHAEL

Corleone.

DON TOMMASINO

Take my car.

MICHAEL

No. I want to walk.

DON TOMMASINO

Be careful.

DISSOLVE TO:

EXT DAY: COUNTRYSIDE

MICHAEL, CALO, and FABRIZIO are walking.

DISSOLVE TO:

The THREE walk up a hillside.

SHOOTING IN SICILY

Gray Frederickson, the assistant director for the Italy sequences, had lived on the eastern coast of Sicily and was familiar with Catania. The town of Corleone wasn't picturesque enough, and he recommended Taormina. Production designer Dean Tavoularis looked at Corleone anyway, but it seemed to be somewhat of a gangster town. The locations the production used were Savoca, Forza d'Agro (used for village scenes), Francavilla, and Nunziata (villa scenes). The key personnel went to Sicily on July 22, with the cast following on the 24th. The Sicilian scenes were all shot in a sunny landscape, with different exposure levels and camera filters, meant to convey a gentler, more romantic look than the New York scenes. Although the Sicily scenes were scheduled for a ten-day shoot, with a wrap party at a pizza restaurant on August 5, the shoot took longer than originally planned because it was overcast. The crew had to wait for the sun to come out in order to get the look they needed.

NINO ROTA'S MUSIC FOR
THE GODFATHER

Paramount executive Robert Evans was determined to have Henry Mancini, who had recently scored Paramount's *Darling Lili* and *The Molly Maguires,* score *The Godfather.* Francis Ford Coppola wanted Nino Rota, who had scored some of the greatest Italian films in history, from Luchino Visconti's *The Leopard* to Federico Fellini's *La Dolce Vita* and *8 1/2,* but he was a totally unknown quantity in Hollywood.

Evans relented, but when the Rota score was cut into the film, he loathed it and demanded it be taken out. The snag caused a standoff, and neither party would give in. Over a period of a week or so, Coppola and postproduction consultant Walter Murch would show up at Evans's house, sit by the pool (eating hot dogs served up by Evans's wife, Ali MacGraw), and wait for a break in the impasse. Murch's wife even egged them on, saying if they didn't save their music, then they didn't have a "pair of balls between them." Coppola bluffed—insisting that Paramount would have to fire him and hire a new director in order to take the music out. Finally, he hit upon the idea of a private test screening of the film with a small group of the general public, suggesting that if the audience didn't like the music, he would step back and let Paramount choose the score. Of course, the audience loved it—along with the movie as a whole.

The haunting Rota score was initially nominated for an Academy Award®. However, the Academy discovered that Rota had recycled about seven minutes of music from an obscure Italian film (*Fortunella*) for the love theme. According to producer Al Ruddy, they got a tip from some jealous friends in Italy. Coppola blames the Hollywood establishment, "the Mafia of the Academy," who had it in for Rota. The nomination was thrown out. Rota did, however, win a Grammy for the score.

The theme has been endlessly imitated and embraced. Slash of Guns N' Roses is a big fan and plays his own version of the theme song at his live shows.

DISSOLVE TO:

They continue their long hike. CALO gestures to a grim Sicilian village, almost devoid of people, high on a promontory.

> CALO
>
> Michele, Corleone.

DISSOLVE TO:

EXT DAY: CORLEONE STREET

MICHAEL and his bodyguards move through the empty streets of the village. They move through a very narrow old street. MICHAEL looks at the doorways they pass. Each door has a plaque with a ribbon.

The men speak in Italian with SUBTITLES:

> MICHAEL
>
> Where have all the men gone?

> CALO
>
> They're dead from vendettas.

> CALO
> *(gesturing to a plaque next to a Communist banner)*
>
> There are the names of the dead.

They continue to walk through the barren town square.

DISSOLVE TO:

EXT DAY: ROAD

ADAPTATION AND THE CUTTING ROOM FLOOR

Several Sicily scenes in the shooting script do not appear in the 1972 movie, such as: a procession of communist peasants carrying red banners; Michael looking for his father's boyhood house in Corleone and discovering the place is deserted (both scenes were included in The Godfather Trilogy: 1901–1980); and a scene in which Michael and his bodyguards are eating lunch in an orange grove, and Fabrizio asks Michael about America. This scene was included in *The Godfather 1902–1959: The Complete Epic and The Godfather Trilogy: 1901–1980*. A similar scene appeared in the shooting script, at this juncture in the film.

Note: The men speak in Italian with SUBTITLES.

FABRIZIO

Tell us something about New York.

MICHAEL

How do you know I'm from New York?

FABRIZIO

We heard. Somebody told us you were real important—(*in English*) a big-a shot.

MICHAEL

I'm the son of a big shot.

FABRIZIO

Is America as rich as they say?

CALO

Stop bothering me with this rich America stuff!

FABRIZIO

(*in English*)

Hey, take me to the America! If you need a good *lupara* in America,

(*pats his shotgun*).

take me, I'll be the best man you can got.

(*SINGS*) OH SAY, CAN YOU SEEE...BY DA STARS EARLY LIGHT...

The TRIO continues down a dirt road as an American military convoy speeds by. FABRIZIO waves and calls out to each of the U.S. drivers as they move by.

FABRIZIO

Hey, America! Take me to the America, GI! Hey! . . . Hey, hey, hey! Take me to the America, GI! Clark Gable, hey! America, America, take me to the America, GI! Clark Gable, Rita Hayworth!

(SPEAKS SICILIAN)

DISSOLVE TO:

EXT DAY: SICILIAN COUNTRYSIDE

The MEN cross into a grove. There is a group of young village GIRLS accompanied by two stocky MATRONS, dressed in black. They have been gathering pink sulla and purple wisteria, and mixing them with orange and lemon blossoms. They are singing, off in the distance as they walk down the road.

MICHAEL, CALO, and FABRIZIO watch this fantasy-like scene.

The MEN speak in Italian with SUBTITLES:

FABRIZIO

(referring to the GIRL in front)

Mamma mía, what a beauty.

APOLLONIA

(SPEAKS SICILIAN)

Just short of the grove, she stops, startled. Her large, oval-shaped eyes catch the view of the THREE MEN. She stands there on her toes, about to run.

MICHAEL sees her; now face-to-face. He looks. Her face—incredibly beautiful—with olive skin, brown hair, and a rich mouth.

FABRIZIO

(to MICHAEL)

I think you got hit by the thunderbolt.

MICHAEL takes a few steps towards her. Quickly, she turns and walks away.

CALO

Michele, in Sicily, women are more dangerous than shotguns.

The GIRLS continue walking; APOLLONIA looks back toward MICHAEL.

DISSOLVE TO:

🎥 BEHIND THE SCENES

Coppola reports that actor Robert De Niro came in among the hordes of screen tests and gave what would now be considered a typical De Niro/Scorsese–type test: "very thrilling." Coppola definitely wanted him in the picture, so he gave him the role of the secondary character Paulie Gatto. When Pacino dropped out of *The Gang That Couldn't Shoot Straight* to be in *The Godfather,* De Niro approached Coppola; he wanted to try out for it but worried about losing his *Godfather* part. Coppola offered to hold Paulie Gatto for him, but De Niro got the *Gang* part and dropped out of *The Godfather.* The great boon to film lovers from this situation: because DeNiro relinquished the role of Paulie Gatto, he was subsequently able to give his Oscar-winning® performance as the young Vito Corleone in *The Godfather: Part II.*

EXT DAY: BARONIAL VILLAGE

MICHAEL, flanked by his BODYGUARDS, moves into the central square, to an outdoor café.

The proprietor of the café, VITELLI, is a short burly man. He greets them cheerfully.

CALO

(to VITELLI)

(SPEAKS SICILIAN)

VITELLI

(in Sicilian; subtitled)

Did you have a good hunt?

FABRIZIO

(in Sicilian; subtitled)

You know all the girls around here? We saw some real beauties.

VITELLI pulls out a chair and sits down at the table with the THREE MEN.

VITELLI

(SPEAKS SICILIAN)

FABRIZIO points at MICHAEL, who dabs his nose with a handkerchief.

FABRIZIO

(in Sicilian; subtitled)

One of them struck our friend like a thunderbolt.

VITELLI gives a knowing laugh and looks at MICHAEL with new interest. A waiter brings a bottle of wine and three glasses. MICHAEL pours the wine as they talk.

VITELLI

(SPEAKS SICILIAN)

FABRIZIO

(in Sicilian; subtitled)

She would tempt the devil himself.

CALO

(ECHOES IN SICILIAN)

VITELLI

(gesturing)

(SPEAKS SICILIAN)

FABRIZIO

(in Sicilian; subtitled)

Really put together, eh, Calo?

CALO

(ECHOES IN SICILIAN)

VITELLI

(makes an hourglass shape with his hands)

(SPEAKS SICILIAN)

FABRIZIO

(in Sicilian; subtitled)

 ADAPTATION AND THE CUTTING ROOM FLOOR

In the shooting script, Michael participates in the conversation describing Apollonia. As Pacino didn't speak Italian, Coppola adjusted the scene so that only the bodyguards speak. The effect of this change works better in the scene: not only does the Sicilian translation add a nice rhythm to the scene, but it also makes Michael seem classier for not objectifying Apollonia.

THE PRODUCTION: CASTING (OR, NOW WITH REAL ITALIANS!)

At the end of September 1970, Paramount held a *Godfather* press conference with Bob Evans, producer Al Ruddy, and newly hired director Francis Coppola. In it, Evans discussed the film's casting course. *Variety* had already printed his proclamation, "I want this film to be made with real Italians!" and the trade also reported his press conference vow: "We're going to cast real faces, people who are not names, nor are we going 'Hollywood Italian.'"

The statements had numerous repercussions.

Ruddy recalled that anyone with an ounce of Italian in his blood or who had ever eaten spaghetti contacted the production. According to the *Los Angeles Herald-Examiner*, "every Italian singer in the business—except Sinatra—put in a bid on" the part of Johnny Fontane. One Italian actor staged a billboard in San Francisco, which read "Alioto is the Godfather." Another sent his own personal photograph album to verify his Sicilian heritage. Yet another had business cards made up to read "Michael Corleone." Ruddy even got calls to his office asking if they wanted anyone "hurt." Ruddy said in *The Hollywood Reporter* that opportunistic "talent schools" approached people on the street and videotaped them under the auspices of doing screen tests for *The Godfather*. They would then charge a $100 fee.

Casting director Fred Roos recounts that very early in the casting process he and Coppola resolved to make every effort to cast every role in the script that was Italian or Italian-American with a likewise Italian or Italian-American actor. According to Roos, "I set about meeting every Italian or Italian-American actor in Los Angeles and New York. It wasn't hard to meet me. I mean, some people would lie and say they were Italian and get an interview, and I'd figure out that they weren't really. I truly made every effort to meet every Italian actor that had an agent—and even some that didn't have agents. We would spend long days just testing, interviewing actors for all these different parts, and after all the months and months of doing this in both L.A. and New York, and eventually in Italy as well, we did pretty well on our resolve, with the exceptions of Marlon Brando and Jimmy Caan." Once the casting choices were announced, the public's scrutiny of the production's casting intensified. *Variety* derided the studio's choice for the titular character of the film with the headline: "No Stars for 'Godfather' Cast—Just Someone Named Brando." Picketers showed up at Paramount with signs that read "Indians for Indian Roles, Mexicans for Mexican Roles, Italians for Italian roles," and

Such hair, such mouth!

> CALO
>
> *A bocca.*

> VITELLI
> *(in Sicilian; subtitled)*
>
> The girls around here are beautiful . . . but virtuous.

> FABRIZIO
> *(in Sicilian; subtitled)*
>
> This one had a purple dress . . .

As FABRIZIO describes her, VITELLI stops laughing, until he wears a scowl.

> FABRIZIO
> *(in Sicilian; subtitled)*
>
> And a purple ribbon in her hair.

> CALO
>
> (ECHOES IN SICILIAN)

> FABRIZIO
> *(in Sicilian; subtitled)*
>
> A type more Greek than Italian.

> CALO
>
> *Piu Grega che Italiana.*

> FABRIZIO
> *(in Sicilian; subtitled)*
>
> Do you know her?

> VITELLI
>
> No!

Abruptly, VITELLI stands up.

> VITELLI
> *(in Sicilian; subtitled)*
>
> There's no girl like that in this town.

Then he curtly leaves them and walks into the back room.

> FABRIZIO
> *(in Sicilian; subtitled)*
>
> My God, I understand!

FABRIZIO goes into the back room after the innkeeper, amid VITELLI's shouting.

> MICHAEL
> *(in Italian; to CALO; subtitled)*

What's wrong?

CALO shrugs. FABRIZIO returns and gulps down his wine.

FABRIZIO

(in Sicilian; subtitled)

Let's go. It's his daughter.

FABRIZIO starts to leave, but MICHAEL doesn't move. MICHAEL turns to FABRIZIO with his cold authority.

MICHAEL

(in Italian; subtitled)

Tell him to come here.

FABRIZIO

(protesting in SICILIAN)

MICHAEL

(overlaps)

(SPEAKS ITALIAN) No, no, no, no . . .

(subtitled)

Call him.

FABRIZIO shoulders his *lupara* and disappears into the back room. CALO also picks up his *lupara*. In a moment, FABRIZIO returns with the red-faced VITELLI and two young men.

MICHAEL

(in Sicilian; subtitled)

Fabrizio, you translate.

"More Advantages For Italian Actors"

Ultimately, as Roos suggests, Italians and Italian Americans were indeed hired: namely, Al Pacino, who had grandparents from Sicily. Others of Italian heritage in the cast included Salvatore Corsitto (Bonasera), Richard Conte (Barzini), Al Lettieri (Sollozzo), John Cazale (Fredo), Al Martino (Johnny Fontane), Morgana King (Mama Corleone), Vito Scotti (Nazarine), Talia Shire (Connie), and Richard Castellano (Clemenza), who claimed to have relatives in the real Mafia—not to mention the Italian actors hired in Italy for the Sicilian scenes. Gianni Russo and Lenny Montana were rumored to be Mafia-affiliated. Even Alex Rocco (who plays the Jewish Moe Greene) is actually Italian. Roos explains, "It was Francis's theory that being Italian, if you grow up in an Italian-American community or family, there are locked-in, hardwired behavioral things that are just in you that will come out in performance—without even having to be directed—and he was hoping to get that. I think that he did, and it was successful. It's a subtle thing, but it's there. As I like to say about the *Godfather* movies: you can smell the garlic coming off the screen."

 ITALIANISMS

A *lupara* is a double-barreled, sawed-off shotgun that is often homemade. It's a traditional *Cosa Nostra* weapon in Sicily.

"THE GODFATHER"   SCHEDULE   DATE: 7/14/71
SICILIAN SEQUENCE

PRODUCER: AL RUDDY   ASSOC.PROD. G.FREDERICKSON
DIRECTOR: FRANCIS FORD COPPOLA PROD.MGR. V. DEPAOLIS

DAY AND DATE	SET AND LOCATION SCENE NUMBERS	WHERE LOCATED	CAST WORKING
7/19/71 MONDAY AND 7/20/71 AND 7/21/71 WEDNESDAY	PREPARATION IN ROME F. Coppola to see actors and decide cast. Make-up test and camera test. Gordon Willis to select and prepare equipment. Chevalier e Cottone to Sicily to prepare.		
7/22/71 THURSDAY AND 7/23/71 FRIDAY	Coppola, Ruddy, Frederickson, Willis and Tavoularis go to Sicily to see locations. Coppola to see Sicilian actors and make final cast decisions, if not already set. Trucks leave Friday for Sicily.		
7/24/71 SATURDAY	CREW and CAST to SICILY		
71ST DAY 7/26/71 MONDAY	EXT. ESTABLISHING SHOT (DAY) SC. 58 Michael walks with the two Shepards SUMMER 1948 4/8 page PROPS: 2 Shotguns 2 Knapsacks	Savoca	Michael Fabrizio Calo
	EXT. SICILY ROAD (DAY) SC. 59 Michael meets Don Tomassino and tells him he is going to Corleone. SUMMER 1948 1 4/8 pages PROPS: Flock of Sheep, Don Tomassino's car 2 Knapsacks 2 Shotguns	Savoca	Michael Fabrizio Calo Don Tomassino

BOTTOM: ORIGINAL PRODUCTION SCHEDULE FOR SICILY SCENES. INCLEMENT WEATHER MADE FOR A LONGER SHOOT. (COURTESY OF AMERICAN ZOETROPE RESEARCH LIBRARY)

FABRIZIO
Si, signor.

MICHAEL
(to VITELLI)
I apologize if I offended you.

FABRIZIO
(TRANSLATES IN SICILIAN)

MICHAEL
I am a stranger in this country.

FABRIZIO
(TRANSLATES IN SICILIAN)

MICHAEL
And I meant no disrespect to you or your daughter.

FABRIZIO
(TRANSLATES IN SICILIAN)

VITELLI
(SPEAKS SICILIAN)

MICHAEL
I am an American—hiding in Sicily.

FABRIZIO
(TRANSLATES IN SICILIAN)

MICHAEL
My name is Michael Corleone.

FABRIZIO
(TRANSLATES IN SICILIAN)

MICHAEL
There are people who'd pay a lot of money for that information.

FABRIZIO
(TRANSLATES IN SICILIAN)

MICHAEL
But then your daughter would lose a father . . .

FABRIZIO
(TRANSLATES IN SICILIAN)

MICHAEL
. . . instead of gaining a husband.

FABRIZIO pauses a moment, stupefied, and MICHAEL motions him to continue.

FABRIZIO

(TRANSLATES IN SICILIAN)

VITELLI

Ah. (SPEAKS SICILIAN)

MICHAEL

I want to meet your daughter . . .

FABRIZIO

(TRANSLATES IN SICILIAN)

MICHAEL

. . . with your permission . . .

FABRIZIO

(TRANSLATES IN SICILIAN)

MICHAEL

. . . and under the supervision of your family.

FABRIZIO

(TRANSLATES IN SICILIAN)

MICHAEL

With all respect.

FABRIZIO

(TRANSLATES IN SICILIAN)

VITELLI
(pulling up his suspenders formally; in Sicilian; subtitled)

Come to my house Sunday morning. My name is Vitelli.

MICHAEL stands up to shake VITELLI's hand.

MICHAEL

Grazie.

(in Italian; subtitled)

What's her name?

VITELLI

Apollonia.

MICHAEL

(smiling)

Bene.

 ADAPTATION AND THE CUTTING ROOM FLOOR

The novel delves into the roots and history of the Sicilian Mafia: Corleone had the highest murder rate in the world. In Puzo's own first draft of a screenplay (dated August 10, 1970), Apollonia gives Michael a running commentary on the ways of the Sicilian Mafia as they walk through the region.

ADAPTATION AND THE CUTTING ROOM FLOOR

In many of the Sicily scenes, Michael wipes his nose with a handkerchief. The novel explains that McCluskey's punch did damage to Michael's sinuses.

DISSOLVE TO:

EXT DAY: TOMMASINO COURTYARD

MUSIC comes up as MICHAEL, dressed in new clothes from Palermo, carries a stack of wrapped gifts and hands them to FABRIZIO. CALO and FABRIZIO are each dressed in their Sunday best, with their *luparas* on their shoulders.

They all get into an Alfa Romeo.

DON TOMMASINO waves at them as the car drives off, rocking and bouncing on the dirt road.

DISSOLVE TO:

EXT DAY: VITELLI HOUSE

MICHAEL is presented to each of the Vitelli relatives, by the yard of their little hilltop house—the BROTHERS, the MOTHER, who is given a gift, and several UNCLES and AUNTS. Finally APOLLONIA enters, dressed beautifully in appropriate Sunday clothing.

COPPOLA SETS THE SCENE OF MICHAEL'S WOOING OF APOLLONIA.

VITELLI

(introducing them)

Et cuesta mia figlia. Apollonia—cuesto Michele Corleone.

They shake hands. Now he presents the wrapped gift to APOLLONIA. She looks at her MOTHER, who with a nod, gives her permission to open it. She unwraps it. Her eyes light up at the sight of a heavy gold chain, to be worn as a necklace. She looks at him.

APOLLONIA

Grazia.

MICHAEL

(softly)

Prego.

DISSOLVE TO:

EXT DAY: VITELLI CAFE

Now the little Alfa drives into the village near VITELLI's café.

MICHAEL is, as ever, accompanied by his two BODYGUARDS, though they are all dressed differently.

They sit at the café with VITELLI, who is talking and talking.

MICHAEL looks at APOLLONIA, who sits, respectfully quiet. She wears the gold necklace around her neck. She fingers the necklace, and they smile at each other across the table.

DISSOLVE TO:

EXT DAY: HILLTOP NEAR VITELLI HOME

MICHAEL and APOLLONIA are walking through a hilltop path, seemingly alone, although a respectful distance apart.

As the VIEW PANS with them, we notice that her MOTHER and half a dozen AUNTS are twenty paces behind them, and ten paces further behind are CALO and FABRIZIO, their *luparas* on their shoulders.

Further up the hill, APOLLONIA stumbles on a loose stone and falls briefly onto MICHAEL's arm. She modestly regains her balance, and they continue walking.

Behind them, her MOTHER giggles.

EXT DAY: MANCINI BUILDING

Several cars are parked in front of a pleasant New York apartment building. We recognize a couple of SONNY'S BODYGUARDS loafing by the cars, pitching coins against the curb.

 GOOFS, GAFFES, AND BLOOPERS

Check out the same two men (one with a red shirt, one with a white one) passing behind Apollonia two different times.

ADAPTATION AND THE CUTTING ROOM FLOOR

The novel gives a poignant backdrop to the scene on the hilltop. The women giggle because Apollonia has walked these uneven roads her whole life—she obviously does not stumble because she loses her footing, but to brush against Michael.

INT DAY: APARTMENT BUILDING

Inside the building, a BODYGUARD waits quietly by the rows of brass mailboxes; ANOTHER sits at the foot of the interior steps reading a newspaper; ONE stands with his chin resting in his hand; up one flight of stairs, a single MAN sits on the step. They have been there quite a while.

We hear the SOUND OF A DOOR OPENING. SONNY backs out of an apartment, the arms of LUCY MANCINI wrapped around him.

SONNY

I'm gonna knock you dizzy.

He playfully cuffs her and leaves, adjusting his clothes. She smiles after him. He jauntily skips down the steps, trailed by the bodyguards.

SONNY
(to READING BODYGUARD)

Save it for the lib'ary.

SONNY

(to the BODYGUARD by the mailboxes)

Come on, we gotta go pick up my sister, let's go.

INT DAY: CONNIE'S HALL

CONNIE unlocks the front door for SONNY. As SONNY enters, CONNIE quickly moves into the hallway, her back to him.

SONNY

(tenderly)

Whatsa matter? Huh? Whatsa matter?

He turns her around. Her face is swollen and bruised; and we can tell from her rough, red eyes that she has been crying for a long time. As soon as he realizes what's happened, his face goes red and he bites his knuckles with rage. She sees it coming and clings to him, preventing him from running out of the apartment.

CONNIE

(desperately)

It was my fault!

SONNY

Where is he?

CONNIE

Sonny, please, it was my fault. Sonny, it was my fault! I hit 'im; I started a fight with him. Please lemme me . . . I hit him so he hit me. I didn't . . . I . . .

SONNY listens and calms himself. He touches her shoulder; the thin silk robe. Then he kisses her on the top of her head reassuringly.

SONNY

Sh-sh-sh-sh-sh. Okay. I'm—I'm just—I'm just gonna get a doctor to come and take a look at you, right?

He starts to leave.

CONNIE

Sonny, please don't do anything, please don't do anything!

He stops, and then laughs good-naturedly.

SONNY

Okay. What's the matter with you? What'm I gonna do? I'm gonna make that baby an orphan before he's born?

She, half crying, laughs with him, shaking her head.

SONNY

Hah? Hmm? All right?

CAST AND CREW: FRED ROOS

Francis Ford Coppola had a relationship with casting director Fred Roos prior to *The Godfather,* but only by telephone; Coppola would often call Roos to discuss various actors. Roos, who previously had cast such counterculture films as *Five Easy Pieces* and *Two Lane Blacktop,* recalls: "I guess he thought I was his kind of sensibility, so we had this bond on the phone. When he got the movie, he called up and said, 'I just got this big movie.'" When they finally met face-to-face, the chemistry was great, and they embarked on a relationship that would span decades.

In an interview with the author in 2007, Roos reflected on his experience working with Coppola. "*The Godfather* was a longer casting process than most films I've done, but not to my annoyance. I've always believed that all films should take a long time in casting, and that you should be thorough. So, I was all for it. The casting process with Francis is always a lot of fun because we both like actors and therefore enjoy talking with them. These days, so many directors just look at videotape and never even meet the actors—but we like the real people. We would have long conversations with them, and it's a fun time for us. Sometimes we get to talking to the actors for so long that we get backed up, and the other actors have to wait for an hour for their audition. They get all steamed up, but ultimately they get their time to talk as well."

Roos had started his career in film as a producer in the 1960s, and after working as a casting director for several years, he took up the producing mantle once again. Since casting *The Godfather,* Roos has been a producer or consultant on nearly all of Coppola's films, and he has carried on the tradition to the next generation as well, producing all of daughter Sofia Coppola's feature films.

JAMES CAAN AND FRANCIS FORD COPPOLA REHEARSE THE SCENE OF SONNY BATTERING CARLO.

EXT DAY: CONNIE'S STREET

CARLO sits on the railing of the front steps of the 112th Street building with three business associates. The ball game is blaring from the radio, and the kids on the street are playing in water spraying from a fire hydrant.

CARLO
Those fat slobs still betting Yankees pretty heavy? Tell 'em to stop taking action, all right? We lost enough money last week on the game.

A car comes screeching up the block and halts in front of the steps. A MAN comes hurtling out of the driver's seat. It is SONNY. As soon as CARLO recognizes him, he takes off running. SONNY hurls a sawed-off wooden broom handle at CARLO.

> SONNY
>
> Carlo, c'mere, c'mere, c'mere!

SONNY chases CARLO across the street. He catches CARLO by the shoulders and throws him over an iron railing. CARLO crashes into trash cans. SONNY picks him up and throws him against a brick wall.

The kids who have been playing in the hydrant move up, watching in fascination. SONNY'S BODYGUARDS push them and other spectators out of the way.

SONNY is pounding the cowered CARLO with all his strength in a continuous monologue of indistinguishable cursing.

> SONNY
>
> You bastard!

As CARLO falls, he reaches out for the iron railing and hangs on, his hands in a lock. He cringes while SONNY repeatedly kicks him. SONNY's tight fists are going down like hammers into CARLO's face and body. CARLO's nose is bleeding profusely, but still he does nothing, other than hang on to the railing. SONNY tries loosening CARLO's locked hands, even biting them. CARLO screams but does not let go.

> CARLO
>
> Ahhhhhh!

SONNY grabs hold of CARLO's leg and tries to drag him off the hold on the railing, his teeth clenched in the effort. It's clear that CARLO is stronger than he is and will not be moved. SONNY picks up a trash can and throws it down on CARLO, then, holding him by the hair, smashes him in the face repeatedly with the lid until CARLO lets go and starts crawling into the street. SONNY kicks him three more times, until CARLO is right under the gushing fire hydrant. Totally out of breath, he stammers haltingly to the bleeding CARLO.

> SONNY
>
> Touch my sister again, I'll kill ya.

SONNY gives CARLO one last kick, and CARLO rolls over on his back into the gutter. SONNY and the BODYGUARDS walk back to the car as the children stand looking at CARLO.

 BEHIND THE SCENES

This scene was filmed at 118th Street and Pleasant Avenue, Manhattan. Caan asked the prop master to cut an industrial broom handle and put it in his car; it was his idea to throw it at Carlo. Caan must have performed the scene with gusto—even though much of it was shot with a stand-in and a stuntman, actor Gianni Russo, who played Carlo, received two cracked ribs and a chipped elbow for his efforts.

 GOOFS, GAFFES, AND BLOOPERS

In the most famous technical mistake of the movie, now known as The Miss, one of Sonny's punches misses Carlo by a mile—despite the clear audio of contact. Coppola laments that the gaffe was due to the film's squeezed budget: "At that point we were just rushing, and it turned out that the best take had this one miss. Today they could fix it with digital effects." The mistake is often parodied: in *The Simpsons* Marge beats up a mugger in the same style and sequence; Jay and Silent Bob do the same to Charles Barkley in an episode of *Clerks: The Animated Series*.

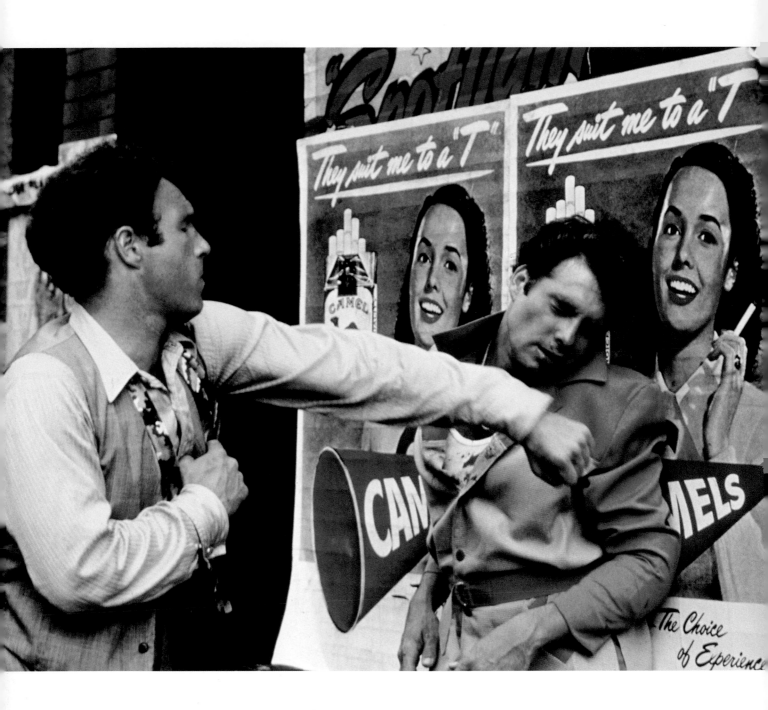

EXT DAY: VITELLI VILLAGE CHURCH

Church bells in an ancient belfry ring out. As the wedding ceremony between MICHAEL and APOLLONIA concludes, MUSIC plays, old and dissonant.

There is a bridal procession in the street of the village, the same in feeling and texture as it might have been five hundred years ago. First, a brass band; followed by FABRIZIO and CALO with their *luparas*; the wedding party, including a child wearing a white confirmation gown; women throwing rice; the men of the family, and DON TOMMASINO in a wheelchair; and countless townspeople. We present the entire bridal procession and ceremony with all the ritual and pageantry, as it has always been, in Sicily.

OVERHEAD SHOT of the procession through the town.

APOLLONIA is radiant as the bride; MICHAEL is handsome despite the grotesque jaw.

EXT DAY: VITELLI VILLAGE SQUARE

MICHAEL and APOLLONIA walk around the wide circle of guests. Then they dance in the great wedding celebration, smiling.

DISSOLVE TO:

THE NUTS AND BOLTS: PRODUCTION DETAIL

Carmine Coppola composed the wedding music.

CAST AND CREW: GORDON WILLIS

According to Coppola, cinematographer Gordon Willis's favorite shot was an overhead shot of the Sicilian countryside.

GF·R· 93

GF·R· 91

ADAPTATION AND THE CUTTING ROOM FLOOR

Scenes that appear in the shooting script, but not in the 1972 movie:

- The morning after the wedding, Michael watches his bride asleep in their bed.

- When Kay visits the Corleone Mall, she encounters a sympathetic Mama Corleone, who accepts her letter. She then tells Kay to give up hope: "You listen to me. You go home to your family, and you find a good young man and get married. Forget about Mikey; he's no good for you anymore." She looks directly into Kay's eyes, and Kay understands what she means. The novel is very explicit as to how Kay interprets this: "She was trying to get used to the fact that the young man she loved was a cold-blooded murderer. And that she had been told by the most unimpeachable source: his mother."

- Scenes involving Kay's parents are in the book, but not the film.

- The fight between Carlo and Connie was edited somewhat, with additional dialogue about the lady caller and dinner cut. A brief part of the scene of Carlo in the shower after Connie gets the call was filmed but not used in the movie. It was included in *The Godfather Trilogy: 1901–1980*.

INT NIGHT: MICHAEL'S ROOM IN VILLA

MICHAEL opens the shutters in his darkened room. He turns and there, in her wedding slip, is APOLLONIA—a little frightened, but lovely. MICHAEL moves to her, and for a moment just stands before her—looking at her incredible face, her lovely hair and body. Slowly and tenderly he kisses her. She lets her bridal slip fall to the floor. They kiss again, embracing.

EXT DAY: MALL

It is a gray, rainy day. Young BUTTON MEN in coats stand in quiet groups of various points around the main house and compound. A taxi arrives; KAY ADAMS steps out, huddled in a bright orange raincoat; she lets the cab go, walks through the gate, and speaks to a BUTTON MAN inside. TOM HAGEN exits the main house and hurries toward her.

> HAGEN
> *(shakes her hand)*
>
> Hey! We weren't expecting you, Kay. You should call.

> KAY
> Yes. Well, I have. I mean I've tried writing and calling. Now, I want to reach Michael.

> HAGEN
> Nobody knows where he is. We know that he's all right, but that's all.

KAY looks in the direction of a car with smashed windows and doors.

> KAY
> Uh, what was that?

> HAGEN
> *(nonchalantly)*
>
> Well, that's an accident, but nobody was hurt.

> KAY
> Tom, will you give this letter to Michael, please? Please.

> HAGEN
> *(refusing the letter)*
>
> Well, if I accepted that, in a court of law they could prove that I have knowledge of his whereabouts. Now just be patient, Kay. He'll get in touch with you, all right?

> KAY
> I let my cab go, so can I come in to call another one, please?

> HAGEN
> Come on, I'm sorry. Come on.

HAGEN takes her by the elbow and leads her into the main house.

FADE OUT.

FADE IN:

INT DAY: CONNIE AND CARLO'S APPARTMENT

A phone rings. CONNIE, pregnant and wearing a slip and bathrobe, answers it.

> CONNIE
>
> Hello. Hello?

> GIRL'S VOICE
> *(on phone)*
>
> Is Carlo there?

> CONNIE
>
> Who's this?

> GIRL'S VOICE
> *(on phone)*
>
> This is a friend of Carlo's. Would you tell him that I can't make it tonight until later.

CONNIE hangs up the phone.

> CONNIE
> *(under her breath)*
>
> . . . Bitch.

CONNIE moves into the bedroom and speaks to CARLO, who is dressing.

> CONNIE
>
> Dinner's on the table.

> CARLO
>
> I'm not hungry yet.

> CONNIE
>
> The food is on the table; it's getting cold.

> CARLO
>
> I'll eat out later.

> CONNIE
>
> You just told me to make you dinner!

> CARLO
>
> Hey, *Ba fa' gul'*, eh?

> CONNIE
>
> Ah, *Ba fa' gul'*, you!

 BEHIND THE SCENES

According to Coppola, Robert Evans had told him to make a real "movie movie." When asked what that meant, Evans explained that it should have a lot of action. At this point in the filming, Evans didn't think the movie was violent enough, and there was a suggestion that an action director would take over. In an effort to work out the logistics of the Connie and Carlo fight scene and pack in as much action as possible, Coppola rehearsed it with Talia Shire and, funnily enough, his nine-year-old son, who played the part of Carlo. In retrospect, Coppola calls the scene "overdone."

 ITALIANISMS

The epithet *ba fa' gul'* translates as "fuck you."

She turns deliberately and runs out into the kitchen. A moment later we begin to hear the sound of DISHES BREAKING.

> CARLO
>
> You filthy little guinea brat.

CARLO slowly walks out, where we see CONNIE systematically smashing all the dishes on the floor.

> CARLO
>
> That's it, break it all, you spoiled guinea brat. Break it all.

CONNIE screams and he follows her into the dining room, where she continues breaking dishes and throwing the dinner on the floor, sobbing.

> CONNIE
>
> Why don't you bring your whore home for dinner?

> CARLO
>
> Maybe I will . . . Now clean it up!

> CONNIE
>
> Aw, like hell I will!

He slides his belt out of his trousers and doubles it in his hand.

> CARLO
>
> Clean it up, you skinny little brat. Clean it up, I say. Clean it up! Clean it up! Clean that up, you . . . Clean it! Clean it up!

He swings the belt against her hips. She runs through the living room, pelting him with knickknacks, and then moves into the kitchen, gets a kitchen knife, and holds it ready.

> CARLO
>
> Yeah, yeah, come on now, kill me. Be a murderer like your father. Come on, all you Corleones are murderers anyway.

> CONNIE
>
> I will! I will! I hate you!

> CARLO
>
> Come on, kill me. Get out here! Get out here!

She makes a sudden thrust at his groin, which he avoids. He pulls the knife away. She breaks away from him and rushes into the bedroom.

> CONNIE
>
> I hate you!

> CARLO
>
> Now go ahead, now I'll kill ya! You guinea brat, you! Get out here!

He pursues her as she runs into the bathroom, slamming the door behind her. CARLO follows, kicking in the door. We hear him beating her as she screams.

**CAST AND CREW:
GIANNI RUSSO**

Gianni Russo had quite an unusual background—although not as an actor—and had held various jobs as a radio personality, an emcee in a Las Vegas nightclub, and a jewelry tycoon. He also had a stint on the Las Vegas TV show *Welcome to My Lifestyle,* for which he interviewed various people on the strip. Russo was determined to get a part in *The Godfather.*

He produced his own thirty-seven-minute screen test and sent it to the producers. According to Russo, he wrote his own script from the book, lost over eighty pounds, and played all the parts he thought would fit his personality: Carlo, Michael, and Sonny.

Months later, he showed up at the studio in a Bentley, chauffeured by a miniskirt-clad driver, demanding a test. For the test, he was asked to beat up an office secretary who had volunteered to stand in for the scene. As he characterized it in *The Hollywood Reporter,* he worked in as much Italian as he could, and really went to town on the terrified woman: "At one point she went flying over a coffee table, and Evans almost had an orgasm and yelled, 'Cut!' Then they said I had the part." Russo reunited with Marlon Brando in a small cameo in *The Freshman* (1991) and with Al Pacino in *Any Given Sunday* (1999).

INT DAY: DON'S KITCHEN

In the kitchen at the MALL, MAMA holds a screaming BABY in one arm, the phone in her other hand.

MAMA

Connie, whatsa matter? I can't hear you. What is it? Connie, talk louder, the baby's crying.

(handing the phone off to SONNY)

Santino, I can't understand . . . I don't know . . . I don't understand.

SONNY

(to BABY)

Shhhh.

(into phone)

Yeah, Connie.

CONNIE'S VOICE

(on phone)

Don't you come . . .

SONNY

Listen, you wait there. No, no, you just wait there.

He hangs up the phone and just stands there for a moment.

SONNY

Sonofabitch!

MAMA

Sonny, what's the matter?

SONNY

Sonofabitch!

MAMA

What's the matter?

SONNY slams his fist against the wall as he runs out.

EXT DAY: MALL

SONNY moves swiftly from the house to a car.

SONNY

(to MAN seated by gatehouse)

Open the goddamn gate. Get off your ass!

HAGEN moves to the outside MALL just as SONNY's car is driving off.

HAGEN

Sonny! Sonny, come on!

SONNY
(to HAGEN)

    Get outta here!

HAGEN moves to a group of BUTTON MEN.

HAGEN

    Go after him, go on!

THREE BUTTON MEN get into a car.

EXT DAY: CAUSEWAY AND TOLLBOOTHS

SONNY's car drives on the Jones Beach Causeway to the tollbooths and pulls up behind another car. SONNY pulls up to the booth and hands the TOLL COLLECTOR a bill. The car in front of him has stopped, trapping SONNY in the booth. SONNY honks at the car.

SONNY

    Sonofabitch! Come on! Come on!

SONNY turns back to the booth. The TOLL COLLECTOR drops his change and bends down to pick it up, sliding the door shut between them. SONNY looks over at the tollbooth on his right. FOUR MEN appear in the windows with machine guns. MEN exit the car in front and an incredible rally of machine-gun fire greets him, coming through and smashing the windows of the tollbooths on both sides of him, and from the MEN in front. The windows of his car are shot out. Bullet holes puncture the doors of his car. His arms and shoulders are riddled by the gunfire, and still it continues, as though the ASSASSINS cannot take a chance that he will survive it.

SONNY actually opens the door and steps out of the car, under fire. He lets out an enormous ROAR, like a bull, and falls to the ground. An ASSASSIN shoots him a few more times at close range, for good measure, and then kicks his face. The ASSASSINS scramble for their cars and make off in the distance.

SONNY'S BODYGUARDS stop their car a safe distance away, realizing they are too late.

JAMES CAAN AND PRODUCER AL RUDDY.

THE NUTS AND BOLTS: PRODUCTION DETAIL
The scene of Sonny's demise was filmed at Floyd Bennett airfield, Brooklyn. The plot indicates that the scene takes place on the Jones Beach Causeway, on the road to Long Beach.

GOOFS, GAFFES, AND BLOOPERS
Although Sonny's windshield is initially shot out by gunfire, when the bodyguard car approaches, you can see a reflection in an intact windshield. A more subtle continuity error is bullet holes visible in the car's roof, which disappear and then reappear.

THE ANATOMY OF A SCENE: THE DEATH OF SONNY CORLEONE

"We blew hell out of that car."

—Producer Al Ruddy, *Ladies' Home Journal*, 1972

In just one take, the vibrant character of Sonny Corleone was obliterated.

The scene, reminiscent of the groundbreaking *Bonnie and Clyde,* was a technical nightmare for the crew.

A beautiful 1941 Lincoln Continental was fitted with breakaway safety glass, as were the tollbooths. Two hundred separate bullet holes were drilled into the car, and then puttied over, painted, and filled with an explosive charge that could be activated by remote control. Everything was electrically wired and rigged.

James Caan became something of a walking time bomb. His clothes were fitted with small brass casings. Each one had a small slit in it, filled with gunpowder and topped with a small plastic sack of fake blood. The casings were wired and attached to a hidden cable behind his back. Casings in his hair and on his face had no gunpowder, just blood. They were attached to nearly invisible wires, which, when pulled by offscreen technicians, caused the sacks to pop and spurt blood. Electrical wires ran from inside Caan's pants to a console, which controlled all the gunpowder charges.

Dangerous if employed incorrectly, the 110 casings that Caan wore was the most ever at that time in movie history. When the assassins started firing, a special-effects crew quickly punched the console buttons, and each one kicked off a little explosion that made it appear as if bullets were ripping into Caan. Simultaneously, other crew members pulled the wires that popped the blood pellets on his face and head. Caan reported in an interview: "I didn't mind the scene too much, but I wouldn't be honest if I said it didn't make me a little nervous."

After the scene, Caan was a little dazed, and kept checking to make sure his face and hair were intact. He wasn't the only one lucky the scene came off without a hitch; at a cost of $100,000, the production couldn't afford another take.

BELOW: JAMES CAAN RELAXES AFTER THE STRESSFUL SHOOT.

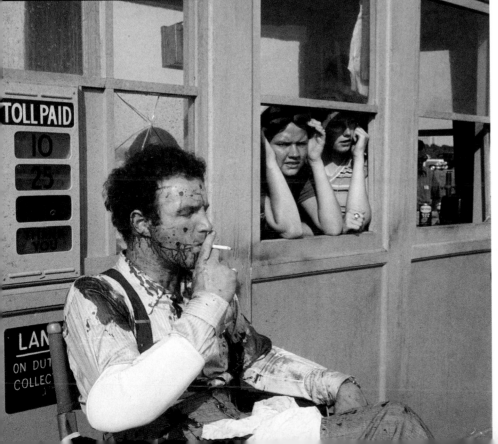

CAST AND CREW: ROBERT DUVALL

Rudy Vallee coveted the part of Tom Hagen, but was much too old to play a thirty-five-year-old. Other potential actors were Peter Donat, Martin Sheen, Roy Thinnes, Barry Primus, Robert Vaughn, Richard Mulligan, Keir Dullea, Dean Stockwell, Jack Nicholson, and James Caan (who seemingly tried out for every part in the film). John Cassavetes and Peter Falk sought the role as well, but there really wasn't any competition—Coppola wanted Robert Duvall.

Duvall began his career in the army and attended the Neighborhood Playhouse School of the Theatre in New York on the GI Bill. He studied under Sanford Meisner (as Caan and Keaton would as well) along with Dustin Hoffman, with whom he shared an apartment. The two struggling actors were also great friends with colleague Gene Hackman. Duvall's film debut was as Boo Radley in *To Kill a Mockingbird*. When he was cast as Tom Hagen, Duvall, an award-winning stage actor who was making a name for himself as a good character film actor, had just finished *M*A*S*H,* and was in George Lucas's *THX 1138*. He had worked with both Brando (*The Chase*) and Caan (in Coppola's *The Rain People*), and was reunited with them for *The Godfather*. Coppola knew from the start that he wanted Duvall and Caan to play the roles of Tom Hagen and Santino Corleone, respectively. He had an early rehearsal with them and bought them lunch. Hundreds of thousands of dollars' worth of screen tests and many months later, Coppola got his original casting choices, which, as Caan put it, he could have had for the price of "four corned beef sandwiches." For his part in *The Godfather*, Duvall made $36,000. Duvall, one of the greatest actors of his generation, refused to appear in *The Godfather: Part III* because, as he claimed on *60 Minutes,* "if they paid Pacino twice what they paid me, that's fine, but not three or four times, which is what they did." Many members of the cast and crew

DISSOLVE TO:

INT NIGHT: THE DON'S OFFICE

HAGEN alone in the office. He is drinking. Behind him, DON CORLEONE slowly enters the room, dressed in a robe and slippers. He walks directly to a chair and sits down. His face is stern as he looks into HAGEN's eyes.

DON CORLEONE
Give me a drop.

HAGEN hands the OLD MAN his glass of anisette. He drinks it.

DON CORLEONE
My wife is crying upstairs. I hear cars comin' to the house. Consigliere of mine, I think you should tell your Don what everyone seems to know.

                              HAGEN

I didn't tell Mama anything. I was about to come up and wake you just
now and tell *you*.

                          DON CORLEONE

But you needed a drink first.

                              HAGEN

Yeah.

                          DON CORLEONE

Well, now you've had your drink.

                              HAGEN

                    (*his voice breaking*)

. . . They shot Sonny on the Causeway. He's dead.

DON CORLEONE sighs and blinks, trying to control his tears.

                          DON CORLEONE

I want no inquiries made. I want no acts of vengeance. I want you to
arrange a meeting with the heads of the Five Families . . . This war
stops now.

THE DON rises unsteadily and pats HAGEN's back.

                          DON CORLEONE

Call Bonasera. I need 'im now.

THE DON leaves the room and walks up the stairs slowly. HAGEN moves to the
phone; dials.

                              HAGEN

This is Tom Hagen. I'm calling for Vito Corleone, at his request. Now
you owe your Don a service.

INT NIGHT: FUNERAL PARLOR EMBALMING ROOM

We see from the PERSPECTIVE BEHIND THE GATE OF AN ELEVATOR, moving down,
with AMERIGO BONASERA on the other side. HAGEN'S VOICE continues.

                          HAGEN'S VOICE

He has no *doubt* that you will repay it. Now, he will be at your funeral
parlor in one hour. Be there to greet him.

The elevator gate opens, and out walk two MEN carrying a stretcher, with a corpse's feet
sticking out from under a gray blanket. HAGEN follows, and then ANOTHER MAN steps
out of the darkness somewhat uncertainly. It is DON CORLEONE. He walks up to
BONASERA, very close, without speaking. His cold eyes look directly at the frightened
UNDERTAKER. Then, after a gaze:

have since credited that film's failure to meet the
expectations of the first two *Godfather*s in part to the
absence of Duvall's Hagen. In 2007, Duvall, assessing
the first film, said, "The brilliance and success of this
film is due wholly to Francis Ford Coppola and
nobody else. It was his vision. He was the only one
that could have done it."

🎞 ADAPTATION AND THE CUTTING ROOM FLOOR

In both the book and the screenplay, Sonny's murder
is structured as a flashback. First Sonny drives out to
the tollbooths, then Tom Hagen calls Bonasera to
reclaim the Don's favor, and only then does Sonny's
assassination occur.

🎞 ADAPTATION AND THE CUTTING ROOM FLOOR

A scene in the preproduction shooting script between
Bonasera and his wife that was not in the 1972
movie: After he receives Hagen's call, Bonasera
sweats profusely and worries he might be made an
accomplice to illegal activities, cursing "the day I ever
went to the Godfather." Also not included was a
scene in which Bonasera opens up the funeral parlor
and waits. When a car drives up and men bring in a
corpse, "BONASERA closes his eyes in fear, but indicates which way the MEN should carry their sinister
burden."

"When I saw *The Godfather*
the first time, it made me
sick; all I could see were my
mistakes and I hated it. But
years later, when I saw it on
television from a different
perspective, I decided it was
a pretty good film."

—Marlon Brando, in his autobiography,
Songs My Mother Taught Me

THE NUTS AND BOLTS: PRODUCTION DETAIL

The scene in the embalming room was filmed at the morgue at Bellevue Hospital Center, 1st Avenue at 29th Street, Manhattan. A freight elevator breakdown meant delays in filming.

BEHIND THE SCENES

While filming in Little Italy, Marlon Brando developed a taste for the spicy squid with hot sauce from Vincent's. When Vito leans over Sonny's dead body here, Brando is holding a carton of the delicacy out of camera range.

DON CORLEONE

Well, my friend, are you ready to do me this service?

BONASERA

Yes. What do you want me to do?

THE DON moves to the CORPSE on the embalming table.

DON CORLEONE

I want you to use all your powers, and all your skills. I don't want his mother to see him this way.

He draws down the gray blanket. BONASERA sees the bullet-smashed face of SONNY CORLEONE.

DON CORLEONE

(with emotion)

Look how they massacred my boy.

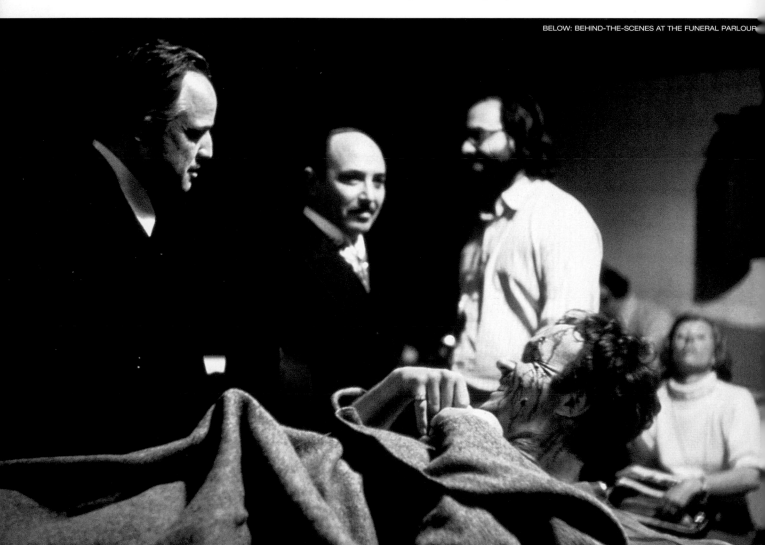

BELOW: BEHIND-THE-SCENES AT THE FUNERAL PARLOUR

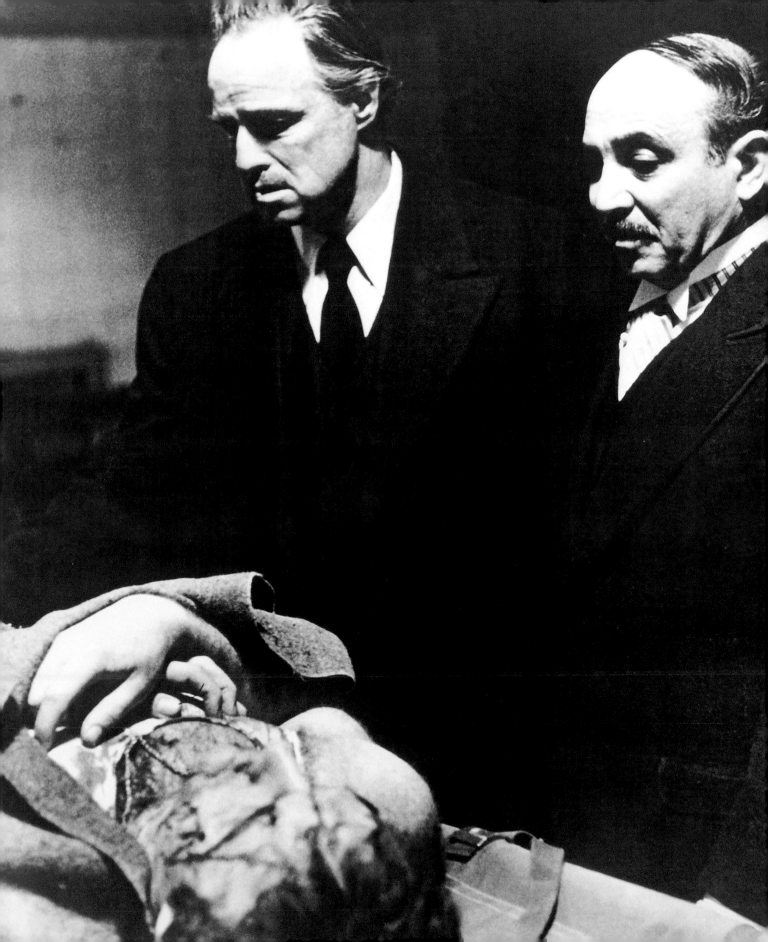

EXT DAY: TOMMASINO COURTYARD

APOLLONIA is laughing, driving the little Alfa. MICHAEL pretends to be frightened as he teaches her to drive. She drives erratically, knocking down an occasional garden chair. At the gate, we notice SHEPHERDS with *luparas,* walking guard duty. The car stops, and MICHAEL gets out.

They speak in Italian with SUBTITLES:

MICHAEL

It's safer to teach you English!

APOLLONIA

I know English . . .

    (says in English)

Monday, Tuesday, Thursday, Wednesday, Friday, Sunday, Saturday.

MICHAEL

Aie, bravo!

APOLLONIA

(SPEAKS ITALIAN)

A car honks and enters the courtyard. MICHAEL helps DON TOMMASINO out of the car.

MICHAEL

Greetings, Don Tommasino.

DON TOMMASINO

(SPEAKS ITALIAN)

MICHAEL

How are things in Palermo?

APOLLONIA kisses DON TOMMASINO.

APOLLONIA

Michael is teaching me to drive . . . watch, I'll show you.

APOLLONIA returns to the car.

MICHAEL

How are things in Palermo?

DON TOMMASINO seems tired and concerned.

DON TOMMASINO

Young people don't respect anything anymore . . . Times are changing for the worse. This place has become too dangerous for you. I want you to move to a villa near Siracusa . . . right now.

MICHAEL

What's wrong?

DON TOMMASINO

Bad news from America. Your brother, Santino, they killed him.

For a moment, the whole world of New York, Sollozzo, the Five Family War, all comes back to MICHAEL. A car horn interrupts his thoughts.

APOLLONIA

(petulantly)

Let's go . . . you promised.

DISSOLVE TO:

EXT DAY: VILLA COURTYARD

Morning. MICHAEL leans out of the bedroom window. Below, FABRIZIO is sitting in one of the garden chairs, combing his thick hair. MICHAEL calls and FABRIZIO looks up to his window.

MICHAEL

Fabrizio!

FABRIZIO

Yes, sir.

MICHAEL

(in Italian; subtitled)

Get the car.

"Marlon Brando is the envy of all the real Godfathers on the island. They all wish they were that good-looking and suave."

—Palermo newspaper editor, after *The Godfather*'s release in Italy, according to *The Hollywood Reporter*

**CAST AND CREW:
SIMONETTA STEFANELLI**

For the role of Apollonia, casting director Fred Roos considered several famous young actresses, such as Olivia Hussey (from Zeffirelli's *Romeo and Juliet*). Coppola says sixteen-year-old Simonetta Stefanelli caught his eye because, after doing her screen test, she skipped away like a young girl. Simonetta later characterized her role thusly: "I met him, I married him, I died."

FABRIZIO

Are you driving yourself, Boss?

MICHAEL

Yes.

FABRIZIO

Is your wife coming with you?

MICHAEL

No, I want you to take her to her father's house till I know things are safe.

FABRIZIO

Okay. Anything you say, Boss.

INT DAY: VILLA KITCHEN

MICHAEL, dressed, enters the kitchen. CALO is eating.

MICHAEL

(speaks Italian; subtitled)

Calo, where is Apollonia?

CALO

(speaks Sicilian; subtitled)

She's going to surprise you. She wants to drive. She'll make a good American wife.

MICHAEL smiles and leaves.

CALO

(speaks Sicilian; subtitled)

Wait, I'll get the baggage.

EXT DAY: VILLA COURTYARD

There is the car, with APOLLONIA sitting in the driver's seat, playing with the wheel like a child.

CALO carries the suitcases to the car and puts them in the trunk.

MICHAEL descends a staircase into the courtyard. Over on the other side of the courtyard, he sees FABRIZIO walking toward the gate.

MICHAEL

(speaks Sicilian; subtitled)

Fabrizio! Where are you going?

The car horn sounds, and MICHAEL turns back.

APOLLONIA
(speaks Italian; subtitled)

Michele! Wait there! I'll drive to you.

Then MICHAEL seems disturbed. He looks at FABRIZIO, who turns, looks back at MICHAEL once more, and runs out of the gate. MICHAEL steps forward and holds out his hand.

MICHAEL

No! No, Apollonia!

His shout is drowned in the roar of a tremendous EXPLOSION as she switches on the ignition. MICHAEL is thrown backward. The car is enveloped in smoke and flames.

FADE OUT.

THE ITALIAN EFFECTS MAN BLEW THE CAR UP WITH DANGEROUS HIGH EXPLOSIVES.

ADAPTATION AND THE CUTTING ROOM FLOOR

This juncture in the film differs from both the novel and the preproduction shooting script in several areas:

• Michael's Revenge

In the novel, Michael, delirious with grief, pointedly says that he wishes now to be his father's son and go home. In the shooting script, Michael, in mourning, vows: "Fabrizio. Let your shepherds know that the one who gives me Fabrizio will own the finest pastures in Sicily." A scene was shot, but doesn't appear in the 1972 movie, with the simple line "Get me Fabrizio." It was included in *The Godfather 1902–1959: The Complete Epic* and *The Godfather Trilogy: 1901–1980*.

• Sicily Sequence and the Meeting of the Five Families

The Sicily scenes in the shooting script ran as one continuous sequence, so the entire episode unfolded at once *after* the Meeting of the Five Families. Had this order been maintained, it may have proven somewhat jarring, as the meeting had supposedly brokered a peace between the Families. The script had a rather weak explanation: the Don postulates that it may have been difficult to call off the hit once put in motion. The 1972 film cuts directly from the scene of Apollonia's death (after Sonny's) right to the meeting. Thus, the completed film directly links the scene of Michael's violence to the call for peace, as well as connects the two heretofore-contrasting worlds of Sicily and New York.

• Michael and The Don's Reunion

Two consecutive scenes that existed in the shooting script (following Apollonia's death) that do not appear in the 1972 movie concern Michael reuniting with his father; they appear here.

FADE IN:

EXT DAY: MALL (SPRING 1951)

Easter.

A HIGH VIEW ON THE CORLEONE MALL in the springtime. Hordes of little CHILDREN, including many of the Corleone children and grandchildren, rush about carrying little Easter baskets, searching here and there for candy treasures and hidden Easter eggs.

THE DON himself, much older, much smaller in size, wearing baggy pants, a plaid shirt, and an old hat, moves around his garden, tending rows and rows of rich tomato plants.

Suddenly, he stops and looks.

MICHAEL stands there, still holding his suitcase.

Great emotion comes over THE DON, who takes a few steps in MICHAEL's direction.

MICHAEL leaves his suitcase, walks to THE DON, and embraces him.

> DON CORLEONE
>
> Be my son . . .

INT DAY: THE OLIVE OIL FACTORY

DON CORLEONE leads MICHAEL through the corridors of the building.

> DON CORLEONE
>
> This old building has seen its day. No way to do business . . . too small, too old.

They enter THE DON's glass-paneled office.

> DON CORLEONE
>
> Have you thought about a wife? A family?

> MICHAEL
>
> *(pained)*

No.

> DON CORLEONE
>
> I understand, Michael. But you must make a family, you know.

> MICHAEL
>
> I want children, I want a family. But I don't know when.

> DON CORLEONE
>
> Accept what's happened, Michael.

> MICHAEL
>
> I could accept everything that's happened; I could accept it, but that I never had a choice. From the time I was born, you had laid this all out for me.

DON CORLEONE

No, I wanted other things for you.

MICHAEL

You wanted me to be your son.

DON CORLEONE

Yes, but sons who would be professors, scientists, musicians . . . and grandchildren who could be, who knows, a governor, a president even, nothing's impossible here in America.

MICHAEL

Then why have I become a man like you?

DON CORLEONE

You are like me; we refuse to be fools, to be puppets dancing on a string pulled by other men. I hoped the time for guns and killing and massacres was over. That was my misfortune. That was your misfortune. I was hunted on the streets of Corleone when I was twelve years old because of who my father was. I had no choice.

MICHAEL

A man has to choose what he will be. I believe that.

DON CORLEONE

What else do you believe in?

MICHAEL doesn't answer.

DON CORLEONE

Believe in a family. Can you believe in your country? Those *pezzono-vante* of the state who decide what we shall do with our lives? Who declare wars they wish us to fight in to protect what they own? Do you put your fate in the hands of men whose only talent is that they tricked a bloc of people to vote for them? Michael, in five years the Corleone family can be completely legitimate. Very difficult things have to happen to make that possible. I can't do them anymore, but you can, if you choose to.

MICHAEL listens.

DON CORLEONE

Believe in a family; believe in a code of honor, older and higher. Believe in roots that go back thousands of years into your race. Make a family, Michael, and protect it. These are our affairs, *sono cosa nostra*. Governments only protect men who have their own individual power. Be one of those men . . . you have the choice.

FADE OUT.

 GOOFS, GAFFES, AND BLOOPERS

Eagle-eyed *Godfather* fanatics have noticed that the flag on the exterior of the bank building displays fifty stars, instead of the correct number for the time period: forty-eight (Alaska and Hawaii were added as states in 1959).

 THE NUTS AND BOLTS: PRODUCTION DETAIL

The exterior of the bank was filmed at the Federal Reserve Bank of New York. The interior shooting location was the boardroom of the Penn Central Railroad in Grand Central Terminal, 32nd floor.

CAST AND CREW: RUDY BOND

Rudy Bond (Ottilio Cuneo) had appeared with Marlon Brando in two of his most famous films: *A Streetcar Named Desire* (1951) and *On the Waterfront* (1954).

Speculation is that the character of Vito Corleone was really a combination of Vito Genovese and Joe Profaci.

EXT DAY: BANK BUILDING

An impressive bank building in the financial center of New York.

INT DAY: BOARDROOM

The boardroom of a bank, daylight shines in the windows. EMILIO BARZINI sits at a conference table. We HEAR:

> DON CORLEONE
> Don Barzini, I want to thank you for helping me organize this meeting here today.

The VIEW PASSES to the impressive array of MEN seated around the table, on which there are bottles of wine, cigars, and bowls of nuts and fruit.

> DON CORLEONE
> And also the other heads of the Five Families, from New York, New Jersey. Carmine Cuneo from the Bronx, and from Brooklyn—Philip Tattaglia—and from Staten Island, we have with us Victor Stracci. And all the other associates that came as far as from California, Kansas City, and all the other territories of the country. Thank you.

HAGEN seats DON CORLEONE at the table, pours him a glass of water, and then sits in the background.

THE SYMBOLISM OF ORANGES IN *THE GODFATHER*

Many *Godfather* aficionados believe the orange fruit symbolizes or foreshadows death in the film—and with good reason. Consider the following scenes and the end result of the characters depicted within:

- The traitor Tessio is introduced in the film as he throws an orange into the air at the wedding.

- At the wedding, when wife Sandra mentions Sonny's unmentionables, a bowl of oranges is on the table in front of her.

- A bowl of oranges is prominently displayed on Woltz's dinner table.

- Don Corleone buys a bag of oranges before he is shot, and then knocks over some oranges as he falls down.

- Fredo stands next to a basket of oranges when visiting his father on his sick bed.

- At the Meeting of the Five Families, there are oranges in the bowls of fruit in front of Tattaglia and Barzini.

- Vito has an orange peel in his mouth when he has a heart attack and dies.

Coppola says that he gravitated toward the orange because it's a versatile prop and reminded him of Sicily, but that the symbolism of the orange wasn't in the foreground of his mind. The production designer, Dean Tavoularis, has also explained it away. As the set consists primarily of somber and ochre tones, orange is a nice color contrast. It also complements the low-lighting cinematography of Gordon Willis. Still, speculation continues . . .

 **ITALIANISMS**

Pezzonovante means someone who is powerful, a big shot.

DON CORLEONE

How did things ever get so far? I don't know. It was so unfortunate, so unnecessary. Tattaglia lost a son. And I lost a son. We're quits. And if Tattaglia agrees, then I'm willing to let things go on the way they were before.

BARZINI

We're all grateful to Don Corleone for calling this meeting. We all know him as a man of his word—a modest man, he'll always listen to reason.

TATTAGLIA

Yes, Don Barzini. He's *too* modest. He had all the judges and politicians in his pocket. He refused to share them.

DON CORLEONE

When? When did I ever refuse an accommodation? All of you know me here. When did I ever refuse, except one time? And why? Because I believe this drug business is gonna destroy us in the years to come. I mean, it's not like gambling or liquor. Even women, which is something that most people want nowadays and is, too, forbidden to them by the *pezzonovante* of the Church. Even the police departments, that've helped us in the past with, uh, gambling and other things, are gonna refuse to help us when it comes to narcotics. And I believed that *then*, and I believe that *now*.

BARZINI

Times have changed. It's not like the old days when we can do any-thing we want. A refusal is not the act of a friend. If Don Corleone had all the judges and the politicians in New York, then he *must* share them or let others use them. He must let us draw the water from the well. Certainly he can present a bill for such services; after all, we are not Communists.

Everyone laughs. ZALUCHI stands up.

ZALUCHI

I also don't believe in drugs. For years, I paid my people extra so they wouldn't do that kind of business. Somebody comes to them and says "I have powder; if you put up three, four-thousand-dollar investment, we can make fifty thousand distributing." So they can't resist. I want to control it as a business, to keep it respectable.

(his hand strikes the table)

I don't want it near schools. I don't want it sold to children. That's an *infamia.* In my city we would keep the traffic in the dark people, the colored. They're animals anyway so let them lose their souls.

General agreement from THE DONS. DON CORLEONE has listened and assessed.

DON CORLEONE

I hoped that we could come here and reason together. And as a rea-sonable man, I'm willing to do whatever's necessary to find a peaceful solution to these problems.

BARZINI

Then we are agreed. The traffic in drugs will be permitted, but con-trolled, and Don Corleone will give us protection in the east, and there will be the peace.

TATTAGLIA

But I must have strict assurance from Corleone. As time goes by and his position becomes stronger, will he attempt any individual vendetta?

BARZINI

Look, we are all reasonable men here; we don't have to give assurances as if we were lawyers.

DON CORLEONE

You talk about vengeance. Is vengeance gonna bring your son back to you? Or my boy to me? I forgo the vengeance of my son. But I have selfish reasons. My youngest son was forced to leave this country because of this Sollozzo business.

DON CORLEONE stands.

All right, and I have to make arrangements to bring him back in safety, cleared of all these false charges. But I'm a superstitious man, and if some unlucky accident should befall him—if he should get shot in the

head by a police officer, or if he should hang himself in his jail cell, or if he's struck by a bolt of lightning, then I'm going to blame some of the people in this room. And that I do not forgive.

(pauses)

But, that aside, let me say that I swear—on the souls of my grandchildren—that I will not be the one to break the peace we've made here today.

TATTAGLIA stands, nodding, and he and DON CORLEONE embrace at the head of the table, in front of BARZINI. The MEN applaud.

"[Marlon Brando] was a very shrewd guy in terms of quickly sizing people up. He hated phonies, particularly people who tried to pull the wool over his eyes. He would cut the phonies to dead."
—Makeup artist Dick Smith

"Brando was the kind of guy who could spot bullshit immediately."
—Producer Al Ruddy

ADAPTATION AND THE CUTTING ROOM FLOOR

The novel stipulates that a man on death row, Felix Bocchicchio, confesses to the murders of Sollozzo and McCluskey, allowing Michael to return home.

INT NIGHT: THE DON'S LIMO

THE DON's black limousine. He sits quietly in the padded rear seat; HAGEN is next to him. It is night. Lights flash by them every so often.

> HAGEN
>
> When I meet with the Tattaglia people, should I insist that all his drug middlemen have clean records?

> DON CORLEONE
>
> Mention it, don't insist. Barzini is a man who'll know that without bein' told.

> HAGEN
>
> You mean Tattaglia.

> DON CORLEONE
>
> Tattaglia's a pimp. He never could've outfought Santino.
>
> *(pauses)*
>
> But I didn't know it till this day that it was Barzini all along.

EXT NIGHT: STREET

THE DON's car drives off through the night.

DISSOLVE TO:

EXT DAY: NEW ENGLAND ELEMENTARY SCHOOL (FALL 1950)

We hear CHILDREN LAUGHING and SHOUTING, and see a group of them following their teacher: KAY ADAMS. She seems older, different, but quietly happy with her work and her life.

She leads the children across the street, past a black limousine parked in the shade.

> KAY
>
> Come on, Nancy. Keep together, everyone. Ryan? Okay, all right.

KAY notices MICHAEL stepping out of the rear of the limousine. He wears an austere tailored overcoat and a homburg, and has apparently been waiting for her. We watch her closely; it's clear she is surprised; she doesn't know whether to rush into his arms or break out into tears.

> KAY
>
> How long have you been back?

> MICHAEL
>
> I've been back a year. Longer than that, I think. It's good to see you, Kay.

DISSOLVE TO:

DELETED SCENE

EXTERIOR MALL

MICHAEL and DON CORLEONE walk through the garden.

DON CORLEONE

(gesturing)

Lettuce, tomatoes, peppers . . .

MICHAEL

Papa, what about Sonny? What about Sicily?

DON CORLEONE

I swore that I would never break the peace.

MICHAEL

But won't they take that as a sign of weakness?

DON CORLEONE

It *is* a sign of weakness.

MICHAEL

You gave your word that you wouldn't break the peace. I didn't give
mine. You don't have to have any part of it. I'll take all responsibility.

DON CORLEONE

(smiling)

We have a lot of time to talk about it now.

They move on through the garden.

MICHAEL AND VITO WALK AMONGST THE EXPENSIVE
TOMATO PLANTS.

✪ ADAPTATION AND THE CUTTING ROOM FLOOR

In Puzo's book, Kay keeps in touch with Mama
Corleone, who tells her when Michael has returned
home. The scene of Michael and Kay reuniting in New
Hampshire was shot in Mill Valley, California, and was
added to the film long after principal photography
had finished. It is how the movie shows Michael is
back in America. The shooting script, however,
included this brief scene in which Michael reunites
with his father, followed by Michael and his father
walking in the garden, discussing the "peace" brokered between the Five Families. The scene was shot
but does not appear in the original 1972 release of
the film.

EXT DAY: NEW HAMPSHIRE ROAD

MICHAEL and KAY move slowly down a leaf-cluttered road. A black limo moves behind them, keeping a respectful distance, but always following them as they walk.

> MICHAEL
>
> I'm working for my father now, Kay. He's been sick. Very sick.

> KAY
>
> But you're not like him, Michael. I thought you weren't going to become a man like your father. That's what you told me.

> MICHAEL
>
> My father's no different than any other powerful man.

> KAY
>
> *(blinking back tears)*
>
> Hah.

> MICHAEL
>
> Any man who's responsible for other people—like a senator or president.

> KAY
>
> You know how naive you sound?

> MICHAEL
>
> Why?

> KAY
>
> Senators and presidents don't have men killed.

They stop walking.

> MICHAEL
>
> Oh, who's being naive, Kay? Kay, my father's way of doing things is over, it's finished. Even he knows that. I mean, in five years the Corleone Family is gonna be completely legitimate. Trust me. That's all I can tell you about my business. Kay . . .

> KAY
>
> *(very moved)*
>
> Michael, why did you come here? Why? What do you want with me after all this time? Without even calling and writing.

> MICHAEL
>
> I came here because I need you. Because I care for you.

> KAY
>
> *(crying)*
>
> Please stop it, Michael.

MICHAEL

Because I want you to marry me.

KAY

(shakes her head)

It's too late, it's too late.

MICHAEL

Please, Kay . . . I'll do anything you ask, anything to make up for what's
happened to us. Because that's important, Kay. Because what's important is that we have each other. That we have a life together. That we
have children. Our children. Kay . . . I need you. And I love you.

MICHAEL motions for the car and they get in.

FADE OUT.

FADE IN:

INT DAY: DON'S OFFICE (1955)

VIEW ON DON CORLEONE, much older, much smaller in size. He wears baggy pants
and a warm plaid shirt. He feeds fish while TESSIO, MICHAEL, and CLEMENZA talk
offscreen around the desk.

 **THE NUTS AND BOLTS:
PRODUCTION DETAIL**

The office in this scene is the same room as the
opening scene, with the same desk—with an updated
remodel for the new Don. According to specifications
in a preproduction memo, the wallpaper was replaced
by paint, and added were an air conditioner, new
sofa, small TV set, and wall-to-wall carpeting.

TESSIO

Barzini's people chisel my territory and we do nothin' about it. Pretty soon there won't be one place in Brooklyn I can hang my hat!

MICHAEL

Just be patient.

TESSIO

I'm not askin' you for help, Mike; just take off the handcuffs.

MICHAEL

Be patient.

TESSIO

We gotta protect ourselves. Uh, gimme a chance to recruit some new men.

MICHAEL

No. I don't want to give Barzini an excuse to start fighting.

TESSIO

Mike, you're wrong.

CLEMENZA enters the VIEW.

CLEMENZA

Don Corleone, you once said that the day would come when Tessio and me could form our own Family. Till today, I would never think of it. I must ask your permission.

The VIEW widens, and we see the men in the room also include HAGEN and AL NERI.

DON CORLEONE

Michael is now head of the Family and if he gives his permission, then you have my blessing.

MICHAEL

After we make the move to Nevada, you can break off from the Corleone Family and go on your own. After we make the move to Nevada.

CLEMENZA

How long will that be?

MICHAEL

Six months.

TESSIO

Forgive me, Godfather, but with you gone, me and Pete'll come under Barzini's thumb sooner or later.

CLEMENZA

And I hate that goddamn Barzini! In six months' time, there won't be nothing left to build on.

"Before I used it, no Mafia man ever used the word 'Godfather' in that sense. Nobody used it. In Italian family culture, when you're a little kid, you called all the friends of your parents 'godfather' and 'godmother' the way in American culture you called all family friends 'aunt' and 'uncle,' even though they're not your aunt and uncle . . . Now the Mafia uses it. Everybody uses it."

—Mario Puzo, interviewed by Terry Gross of National Public Radio, on the term "Godfather", 1996

DON CORLEONE

Do you have faith in my judgment?

CLEMENZA

Yes.

DON CORLEONE

Do I have your loyalty?

CLEMENZA

Yes, always, Godfather.

DON CORLEONE

Then be a friend to Michael, and do as he says.

MICHAEL

There are things being negotiated now that are gonna solve all your problems and answer all your questions. That's all I can tell you now.

(addressing CARLO on the couch)

Carlo, you grew up in Nevada. When we make our move there, you're
gonna be my right-hand man. Tom Hagen's no longer consigliere.
He's gonna be our lawyer in Vegas. That's no reflection on Tom, but
that's the way I want it. Besides, if I ever need help, who's a better
consigliere than my father? Well, that's it.

MICHAEL sits behind the desk. NERI opens the door; TESSIO, CLEMENZA, and CARLO
leave. TESSIO shakes MICHAEL's hand. As CARLO leaves, THE DON pinches his cheeks
affectionately.

> CLEMENZA
> *(shakes THE DON's hand)*

Godfather.

> CARLO

Thank you, Papa.

> DON CORLEONE

I'm happy for you, Carlo.

DELETED SCENE

> HAGEN

Michael, why are you cutting me out of the action?

> MICHAEL

We're going to be legitimate all the way, Tom. You're the legal man—
what's more important than that?

> HAGEN

I'm not talking about that. I'm talking about Rocco Lampone building
a secret regime. Now, why does Neri report directly to you instead of
through me, or the Caporegimes?

> MICHAEL

How did you find that out?

> HAGEN

Rocco's men are a little too good for their jobs! I mean, they're getting
more money than the job's worth.

> DON CORLEONE

I told you this wouldn't escape his eye.

> HAGEN

Mike, why am I out?

 ADAPTATION AND THE CUTTING ROOM FLOOR

Some extra footage before and after Hagen asks
Michael why he is "out," concerning Michael's bodyguard Al Neri, was shot but doesn't appear in the
1972 film. The footage appears in *The Godfather
Trilogy: 1901–1980.*

MICHAEL

You're not a wartime consigliere, Tom. Things may get rough with the move we're trying.

DON CORLEONE

Tom, I advised Michael. I never thought you were a bad consigliere. I thought Santino was a bad Don, rest in peace. Michael has all my confidence just as you do. But there are reasons why you must have no part in what is going to happen.

HAGEN

Maybe I could help.

MICHAEL

(coldly)

You're out, Tom.

THE DON pats HAGEN's shoulder. TOM pauses, then exits. MICHAEL loosens his tie, and THE DON pats him reassuringly.

DISSOLVE TO:

THE LAS VEGAS STRIP.

EXT DAY: LAS VEGAS (1955)

A MOVING VIEW: driving up the Las Vegas Strip of 1955.

DISSOLVE TO:

EXT DAY: FLAMINGO HOTEL

A car pulls up to the Flamingo Hotel. MICHAEL, FREDO, and another MAN exit the car.

INT DAY: FLAMINGO HOTEL HALLWAY

FREDO walks with his arm around MICHAEL. HAGEN, NERI, and two BELLHOPS follow.

FREDO

I can't get over the way your face looks. It really looks good. This doctor did some job. Who talked you into it, Kay?

(to the BELLHOPS)

Hey, hey, hey, hey, hey, wait! Hey. Leave them out here; we'll deal with them later. He's tired; he wants to clean up. All right, now lemme open the door, all right?

INT DAY: FLAMINGO HOTEL SUITE

A magnificent, circular table has been set up in his suite; a lavish table setting for eight. Standing by the table are JOHNNY FONTANE, looking wonderful—a little heavier, beautifully dressed—and FOUR LAS VEGAS GIRLS. A polka band plays a festive tune.

> JOHNNY
>
> Welcome to Las Vegas.

> FREDO
>
> It's all for you, kid. Huh?
>
> *(moves to JOHNNY)*
>
> It's all his idea, right? Didn't ya?

> JOHNNY
>
> Well, your brother Freddy . . .

> FREDO
>
> Well, it was . . . Girls?

FREDO and JOHNNY chuckle. MICHAEL motions his head to FREDO.

> FREDO
>
> Hah? I'll be right back.

> JOHNNY
>
> All right, okay.

> FREDO
>
> You keep 'em occupied, huh?
>
> *(to MICHAEL)*
>
> Anything you want, kid. Anything. Huh?

> MICHAEL
>
> *(serious)*
>
> Who are the girls?

> FREDO
>
> *(jokingly)*
>
> That's for you to find out.

> MICHAEL
>
> Get rid of them, Fredo.

> FREDO
>
> Hey, Mike, uh . . .

> MICHAEL
>
> Fredo, I'm here on business. I leave tomorrow. Now get rid of them. I'm tired. Get rid of the band too.

> FREDO
>
> *(to GIRLS, then BAND)*

THE NUTS AND BOLTS: PRODUCTION DETAIL

The exterior shots of the Las Vegas strip were taken from stock footage. The Vegas interiors were filmed in Manhattan at the Americana Suite of the Americana Hotel. Coppola had hoped to film everything on location, but budgetary considerations did not allow for this.

GOOFS, GAFFES, AND BLUNDERS

In the lobby of the Flamingo Hotel are two hippie types, obviously not appropriate for the time period. It also doesn't appear to be actor John Cazale getting out of the car, but presumably someone less expensive for the tight budget.

Hey, take off, huh? Let's go. Hey . . . Angelo.

> ### JOHNNY
> Come on, let's go.

> ### FREDO
> Hey, come on, SCRAM!

> ### JOHNNY
> Come on, honey, let's go.

> ### FREDO
> I don't know, Johnny. I don't know what the hell's the matter with him. Sorry, babe, come on. Ah, I dunno, he's tired . . . he's . . .

The BAND and GIRLS leave.

> ### MICHAEL
> What happened to Moe Greene?

> ### FREDO
> He said he had some business. He said give him a call when the party started.

> ### MICHAEL
> Well, give him a call.

MICHAEL pats FREDO on the back, and then moves to JOHNNY, who shakes his hand.

> ### MICHAEL
> Johnny, how are you?

> ### JOHNNY
> Hello, Mike. Nice to see you again.

> ### MICHAEL
> We're all proud a' you.

> ### JOHNNY
> Thanks, Mike.

> ### MICHAEL
> Sit down, Johnny; I want to talk to you. The Don's proud a' you too, Johnny.

MICHAEL and JOHNNY sit.

> ### JOHNNY
> Well, I owe it all to him.

> ### MICHAEL
> Well, he knows how grateful you are. That's why he'd like to ask a favor of you.

> ### JOHNNY
> Mike, what can I do?

CAST AND CREW: THE LEGACY OF JOHN CAZALE

The casting for the role of Fredo was uniquely undisputed. Gifted theater actor John Cazale had won two OBIEs—one in a production of *The Indian Wants the Bronx,* with his childhood friend Pacino. Casting director Fred Roos was invited by actor Richard Dreyfuss to see his performance in the off-Broadway play *Line,* by Israel Horovitz, which also starred Cazale. According to Roos, "We were looking for a Fredo at that time, and I had no idea who John Cazale was. He knocked me out. First chance I got, I brought him in and I said, 'Francis, this is Fredo, we don't need to look any further, this is him.' We loved John, who was with us on both *Godfather* films. A terrific guy." After *The Godfather,* Cazale went on to appear in four more feature films: *The Conversation, The Godfather: Part II, Dog Day Afternoon,* and *The Deer Hunter.* Not only were every one of his films nominated for Best Picture Academy Awards®, but they also have all held up over time and are today considered classics. Cazale was stricken with bone cancer during the shooting of *The Deer Hunter* and died shortly after filming was completed.

MICHAEL

The Corleone Family is thinking of giving up all its interests in the olive-oil business; settling out here.

JOHNNY

(nodding)

Mm-hmm.

MICHAEL

Now, Moe Greene will sell us his share of the casino and the hotel so it could be completely owned by the Family. Tom—

FREDO joins them at the table. MICHAEL gestures to HAGEN.

FREDO

(anxious)

Hey, Mike, are you sure about that? Moe loves the business—he never said nothin' to me about sellin'.

MICHAEL

Yeah, well, I'll make him an offer he can't refuse.

HAGEN hands contracts to MICHAEL.

MICHAEL

See, Johnny, see we figure that entertainment will be a big factor in drawing gamblers to the casino. Now, we hope you'll sign a contract to appear five times a year. Perhaps convince some of your friends in the movies to do the same. We're counting on you.

JOHNNY

(smiling)

Sure, Mike, I'll do anything for my Godfather, you know that.

MICHAEL

Good.

MOE GREENE enters, followed by TWO BODYGUARDS. He is a handsome hood, dressed in the Hollywood style. His BODYGUARDS are more West Coast–style.

MOE

Hey, Mike! Hello, fellas. Everybody's here. Freddy, Tom. Good to see you, Mike.

CAST AND CREW: ALEX ROCCO

"The Godfather is what made me go from hamburgers to steaks." —Alex Rocco, 2007

Alex Rocco was born Alexander Federico Petricone Jr. in Massachusetts in 1936. Early in life, he had some brushes with the law. Rocco admits he was a suspect in the murder of a gangster, "which I had nothing to do with," and spent a year in jail for bookmaking. After his release, he vowed he would never be locked up again. Petricone changed his name and headed for California. He recalls that he stole his first TV job (as a thug on *Batman*) from a fellow bartender, who was in the bathroom when the call came in.

He describes his *Godfather* audition: "For the screen test, you had to tell Coppola what part you wanted. Before the test, I was a nervous wreck. I got to Paramount and had to give myself a pep talk: 'You're going to make an ass of yourself. Be a man and grow up!' I said a prayer in my Volkswagen: 'Dear God, please, let me just get out of here. I don't care about the job. I just don't want to sound stupid!'

"I walked in and immediately Coppola said to Fred Roos (casting director), 'Ah, looks like I got my Jew!' I replied, 'I wouldn't know how to play a Jew!' They said that the key to playing an Italian is the gesture of pinching your fingers together, with your palm up, and bobbing your wrist up and down, whereas the key to playing a Jew is placing your palms together and moving your hands up and down [Editor's note: Rocco (Moe Greene) uses the gesture in this scene]. Ever since then, I've been playing a lot of Jews."

During his forty-two-year career, Rocco has played a variety of characters, from Jo's dad on *The Facts of Life* to his Emmy-winning performance in *The Famous Teddy Z*, but he is most remembered for his short role as the Bugsy Siegel–inspired Moe Greene in *The Godfather*. He says that directors often hire him because of their love for the Greene character. He is regaled in elevators by college kids reciting, "I made

> **MICHAEL**
> How are you, Moe?

> **MOE**
> All right. Ya got everything you want? The chef cooked for you special, the dancers will kick your tongue out, and your credit is good.
>
> *(to his BODYGUARDS)*
>
> Draw chips for everybody in the room so they can play on the house. Well.

MOE sits.

> **MICHAEL**
> My credit good enough to buy you out?

MOE and FREDO laugh.

> **MOE**
> Buy me out . . .?

> **MICHAEL**
> The casino, the hotel. The Corleone Family wants to buy you out.

MOE stops laughing. The room becomes tense.

> **MOE**
> The Corleone Family wants to buy me out? No, I buy *you* out, you don't buy *me* out.

> **MICHAEL**
> Your casino loses money. Maybe we can do better.

> **MOE**
> You think I'm skimming off the top, Mike?

> **MICHAEL**
> *(the worst insult)*
> You're unlucky.

MOE laughs and stands up, shaking hands up and down, palms together.

> **MOE**
> You goddamn guineas really make me laugh. I do you a favor and take Freddie in when you're having a bad time, and then you try to push me out!

> **MICHAEL**
> Wait a minute. You took Freddie in because the Corleone Family bankrolled your casino; because the Molinari Family on the coast guaranteed his safety. Now we're talkin' business, let's talk business.

> **MOE**
> Yeah, let's talk business, Mike. First of all, you're all done. The Corleone Family don't even have that kind of muscle anymore. The Godfather's

sick, right? You're getting chased out of New York by Barzini and the other Families. What do you think is going on here? You think you can come to my hotel and take over? I talked to Barzini. I can make a deal with him and still keep my hotel!

MICHAEL

Is that why you slapped my brother around in public?

FREDO

Aw, now that—that was nothin', Mike. Now, now, Moe didn't mean nothin' by that. Sure, he flies off the handle once in a while, but—but Moe and me, we're good friends, right, Moe? Huh?

FREDO moves to MOE and pats him on the back.

MOE

I got a business to run. I gotta kick asses sometimes to make it run right. We had a little argument, Freddy and I, so I had to straighten him out.

MICHAEL

(quietly, deadly)

You straightened my brother out?

MOE

He was banging cocktail waitresses two at a time! Players couldn't get a drink at the table. What's wrong with you?

FREDO looks away, embarrassed.

MICHAEL

(in a tone of dismissal)

I leave for New York tomorrow. Think about a price.

MICHAEL rises from his chair. MOE also gets up, upsetting a drink.

MOE

Do you know who I am? I'm Moe Greene. I made my bones when you were goin' out with cheerleaders!

FREDO

(frightened)

Wait a minute, Moe. Moe, I got an idea. Tom—Tom, you're the consigliere and you can talk to the Don; you can explain . . .

HAGEN

Just a minute now. Don is semiretired, and Mike is in charge of the Family business now. If you have anything to say, say it to Michael.

MOE exits angrily.

FREDO

Mike! You don't come to Las Vegas and talk to a man like Moe Greene like *that*!

my bones when you were goin' out with cheerleaders!" and he still gets residuals from shows and movies parodying the character. "Moe Greene broke me out the best I could ever imagine," Rocco reflected in 2007. "I am so blessed and lucky."

 BEHIND THE SCENES

Alex Rocco came to the production midshoot, so he wasn't included in the camaraderie that had formed among the other actors early in the production. Part of Rocco's intensity for this scene was, as he calls it, "a bit of a frig you" to the other cast members because he felt so out of the loop. Pacino's acting technique also gave him a boost. "Al Pacino was either very bright, or he played a trick on me. In rehearsal, Al played really low, and I had much more volume. So when we rolled camera, I lowered my volume, to match him punch for punch. It was very effective. To this day, I thank him."—Alex Rocco, in an interview with the author, 2007

GOOFS, GAFFES, AND BLOOPERS

Fredo removes his sunglasses not once but twice in quick succession.

Similarly, Michael twice takes out his cigarettes and lighter.

CAST AND CREW: DIANE KEATON

For the part of Kay Adams, Jill Clayburgh, Susan Blakely, and Michelle Phillips all tested. Coppola and casting director Fred Roos also considered Geneviève Bujold, Jennifer Salt, and Blythe Danner, among others. Coppola was worried that the part had the potential to be "bland," and he found actress Diane Keaton to be quirky enough to make Kay a little more interesting. She was commonly known as "that kooky actress." She was also, according to Coppola, a "real WASP."

Diane Keaton had been mostly known for her portrayal of a housewife in deodorant commercials. She had had a few roles on Broadway, including *Lovers and Other Strangers* (with Richard Castellano), which Coppola saw. *The Godfather* was her first significant film role.

> MICHAEL
>
> Fredo. You're my older brother and I love you. But don't ever take sides with anyone against the Family again. Ever.

EXT DAY: MALL

A limo pulls through the gate of the MALL and stops.

INT DAY: LIMO

KAY, MICHAEL, and their young son, ANTHONY, are in the backseat.

> MICHAEL
>
> I have to see my father and his people, so have dinner without me.

> KAY
>
> Oh, Michael.

> MICHAEL
>
> This weekend we'll go out.

> KAY
>
> Mmm.

> MICHAEL
>
> We'll go to the city, we'll see a show and we'll have dinner, I promise.

MICHAEL and KAY kiss. The driver, NERI, carries the little boy out. MICHAEL exits. KAY wants to talk just a little more.

> KAY
>
> Oh, Michael, Michael, your sister wants to ask you something.

> MICHAEL
>
> Well, let her ask.

> KAY
>
> No, she's afraid to. Connie and Carlo want you to be Godfather to their little boy.

> MICHAEL
>
> Well, we'll see.

> KAY
>
> Will you?

> MICHAEL
>
> Lemme think about it. We'll see. Come on.

KAY exits the car.

DISSOLVE TO:

EXT DAY: THE GARDEN

THE DON, older and frailer, and MICHAEL are seated in the garden, talking and eating.

DON CORLEONE

So, Barzini will move against you first. He'll set up a meeting with someone that you absolutely trust, guaranteeing your safety. And at that meeting, you'll be assassinated.

THE DON picks up a glass of wine and drinks.

DON CORLEONE

I like to drink wine more than I used to. Anyway, I'm drinkin' more.

MICHAEL

It's good for you, Pop.

DON CORLEONE

I don't know. Your wife and children, are you happy with them?

MICHAEL

Very happy.

DON CORLEONE

That's good. I hope you don't mind the way I—I keep goin' over this Barzini business.

MICHAEL

No, not at all.

DON CORLEONE

It's an old habit. I spend my life tryin' not to be careless. Women and children can be careless, but not men . . . How's your boy?

ANATOMY OF A SCENE:

DANCING ON A STRING

During the time of the *Godfather* production, Robert Towne had a reputation for being a great script doctor. He eventually became an accomplished screenwriter in his own right, winning the Academy Award® for Best Screenplay for *Chinatown* (and beating out *The Godfather: Part II* in the process). In this excerpt of a 2007 interview, he recalls writing the scene that takes place in the garden of the Corleone Mall between Vito and Michael:

"My first recollection of Francis is rowing around in a rowboat in a lake in Belgium around the Gulf Hotel. I saw him briefly in Ireland during the making of *Dementia 13,* and we had been in touch with each other over the years.

"In June 1971, Fred [Roos] called me and said that Francis had been going over the script and had realized that there were no scenes in the film between father and son. In fact, Mario [Puzo] had not written a scene in which the Don ceded power to Michael. Fred told me that Francis didn't have time to stop and figure it out, and asked if I would help. As I recall, Francis also called me, and he felt that there should be a scene where the father and son expressed their feelings for each other. I felt that I had to be careful about that—they couldn't just outwardly declare their love for each other. He suggested that I fly to New York to look at footage.

"I remember speaking to several Paramount executives, Jack Ballard in particular, who said that the movie was 'a fucking disaster.' I told him 'I'm going to contribute to the disaster.' I was met by Fred, and we went up into the Gulf+Western building at Paramount and looked at close to an hour of assembled footage, to give me an idea of what had been shot.

"I was not prepared for it. I was absolutely stunned by what I'd seen. It may be the best dailies I'd ever seen. I told that to Francis, and I could see a look of alarm on his face, like he had asked for the advice of a friend who was a little crazy—because it wasn't what he had been hearing from everyone else.

"From there we went and had a couple of meetings. I had one brief meeting with Marlon, and at that meeting I remember him saying: 'Just once, I would like Vito Corleone not to be inarticulate.' I responded, 'In other words, you want him to talk?'

"I had one night to write the scene because they were going to lose Marlon that day, and he either got a scene he wanted to shoot or they weren't going to have him. Buck Henry had loaned me his apartment and I wrote the scene all that night, finishing it around four in the morning—I had a hard time with it, as you can imagine. I had the book with me, and on the cover was the hand of a puppeteer, with strings dangling from it—that was my inspiration for the scene. In the scene, Don Corleone says 'I refuse to be a fool dancing on a string.' I felt that this was a scene that had to be about the transfer of power from older to younger generation, the difficulty of giving up that power, and the guilt of giving it to someone he never thought would have to have such power in the underworld. So I bookended the scene, paying attention to what Marlon wanted (and, incidentally, what I thought was right)—for him to talk. I started the scene with the Barzini exposition, and all the kinds of concerns of a guy who has been in charge for so long. When the Don says that his hope for Michael was that he would be able to hold the strings, it's an apology and an expression of love and a passing of the old order. Marlon finishes the scene with 'Just remember, the one on our side is the guy who's going to betray you.' So, in other words, I deliberately kept that plot point so the audience would have to wait for the other shoe to drop, and yet they could have this discursive conversation about their lives.

"Francis came by to pick me up in the morning and drive out to the set. I remember we drove about halfway there without him saying a word to me. After about thirty minutes, he turned and said, 'Any luck?' He read the scene, and he nodded and said, 'Good. Let's go show it to Al.' Al liked it. Then Francis said, 'So *you* go show it to Marlon.' Marlon could be kind of prickly. He was getting his makeup done and he looked at me and said, 'Why don't you read the scene to me?' which was very intimidating, of course, because I would be reading *his* part along with Al's. I remember feeling an instant flash of anger, thinking 'son of a bitch!' I made up my mind that I was not going to act the scene; I was simply going to read it. Marlon stopped, and it caught him, and he looked at me and said, 'Read it again,' at which point I knew he was interested. Then he went through an extraordinary dissection, line by line, asking me what I was thinking when I wrote each part. We went through it, and he said, 'Okay. Would you come out on the set while we do the scene?' I asked Francis, and he was obviously relieved and consented.

"The scene was written on huge pieces of cardboard and placed around the set so Marlon could see them. After every take, Marlon actually conferred with me. I don't think I left the garden all that day until the very last shot, and at the end of it, Marlon said something like, 'Gosh, who are you?' and I said, 'I'm a friend of Francis's.' He said, 'I don't know who you are, but I appreciate that you wrote like crazy to get it done.' And then I never saw him again."

MICHAEL

He's good.

DON CORLEONE

You know he looks more like you every day.

MICHAEL

(smiles)

He's smarter than I am. Three years old. He can read the funny papers.

DON CORLEONE

(smiles)

Read the funny papers . . . Yeah, well . . . I want you to arrange to have a telephone man check all the calls that go in and outta here . . .

MICHAEL

(overlaps)

I did already, Pop.

DON CORLEONE

(overlaps)

It could be anyone.

MICHAEL

(overlaps)

Pop, I took care a' that.

DON CORLEONE

Oh, that's right. I forgot.

MICHAEL reaches toward his father.

MICHAEL

What's the matter? What's bothering you?

THE DON doesn't answer.

MICHAEL

I'll handle it. I told you I can handle it, I'll handle it.

THE DON rises to sit closer to MICHAEL.

DON CORLEONE

I knew that Santino was goin' to have to go through all this. And Fredo, well, Fredo was . . . well . . . But I never—I never wanted this for you. I work my whole life, I don't apologize, to take care of my family, and I refused to be a fool dancing on a string held by all those big shots. I don't apologize—that's my life, but I thought that—that when it was your time, that—that *you* would be the one to hold the strings. Senator Corleone, Governor Corleone, somethin'.

"*The Godfather* is about more than the Mafia; it's about conflicts in American culture. It's about a powerful man who builds a dynasty through crime—but he wants his son to be a senator, a governor; it's about the very nature of power. What it does to you. Who survives. I think it's a tragedy."

—Al Pacino, Seventeen magazine

MICHAEL

Another *pezzonovante*.

DON CORLEONE

Well, just wasn't enough time, Michael, wasn't enough time.

MICHAEL

We'll get there, Pop. We'll get there.

THE DON kisses his son.

DON CORLEONE

Well . . . Now listen, whoever comes to you with this Barzini meeting, he's the traitor. Don't forget that.

THE DON rises, and MICHAEL lays back in his chair, thinking.

DISSOLVE TO:

EXT DAY: DON'S GARDEN

DON CORLEONE is in his garden, in the baggy clothes and fedora, tending the tomato plants. Michael's little BOY follows him. THE DON shows him how to use an insect sprayer and then sits down. The sun is very hot. He wipes his brow.

ANTHONY

Can I hold it, please? Yeah, I will take care . . . .

DON CORLEONE

Come here, come here, come here.

ANTHONY

Can I water these?

DON CORLEONE

Yes, go ahead. Over here, over here. Be careful, you're spilling it, you're spilling it. Anthony, come here, come here. Come here.

THE DON motions to the BOY, and then takes the sprayer.

DON CORLEONE

There. That's it. We'll put it right there. *Aie*. Come here. I'll show you something, come here. Now you stand there . . .

ADAPTATION AND THE CUTTING ROOM FLOOR

In the preproduction shooting script, after the scene between Michael and Vito, Mama coaxes Kay into going to church, shows her how to bless herself, and then "with great dignity, she closes her eyes, says a prayer, and then lights twenty candles." This would have foreshadowed the original ending scene of Kay going to church and lighting thirty candles with a silent prayer, which also was not used for the final film. Coppola's "pitfall" warning to himself in his notebook regarding the characterization of Mama: "I warn you now, Francis, the Mama Mia cliché will be devastating."

"There is a sort of bittersweet irony here; the Don has evolved into a lovable old grandpa in his 'baggy gray trousers, a faded blue shirt, battered dirty-brown fedora decorated with a stained gray silk hatband.' He is much heavier now. This scene is evocative of Sicily—a sense of the Don's roots; a primeval feeling, almost on the verge of a fantasy. The light is almost unreal."

—Coppola's notebook, quoting Puzo's novel

ANTHONY

Give me a orange.

THE DON cuts an orange and, hiding his face, inserts the peel into his mouth, like fangs. He grunts like a monster. The BOY cries out. THE DON rises, holding the boy.

DON CORLEONE
(laughing)

Oh no!

THE DON sets him back down, and they play among the tomato plants.

DON CORLEONE

That's a new trick.

ANTHONY

See . . . Where are you? . . . Get down!

They laugh. Then THE DON starts to cough. He collapses among the plants. The BOY thinks he's still playing and squirts him with the watering can.

ANTHONY

Uh-uh-uh-uh-uh-uh-uh-uh-uh ouch!

LONG SHOT of the BOY running away.

DISSOLVE TO:

THE YOUNG ACTOR NATURALLY REACTS TO BRANDO'S ANTICS.

 BEHIND THE SCENES

According to Coppola, Paramount instructed him to eliminate the scene of the Don's death, in order to save money. They suggested that the death scene would be extraneous, as the funeral itself would show that the Don had died.

Coppola had planted some tomato vines in a little garden situated in the same location as the wedding scenes—a controversial move, as the plants had to be imported from Chicago at great expense. On a day that the production was shooting wedding scenes, Coppola instructed the crew, "Let's run real fast and set up Brando sitting by the tomatoes, playing with this little kid." Coppola attempted to shoot the death scene with just two cameras, but it was very nearly lunchtime, and the production was facing an expensive meal penalty if they didn't break soon. According to Coppola, when Jack Ballard (the Paramount representative assigned to watch costs) noticed what was happening, he shouted at the crew that they had to break for lunch right then and there—especially since the scene was no longer in the script. Ballard's histrionics, coupled with an uncooperative child, made for an increasingly pressurized moment.

Camera operator Michael Chapman recalls of the shoot, "I seem to remember that Brando thought up the idea of carving the fangs out of an orange peel." Coppola concurs, saying that Brando announced he wanted to do something he did with his own children to get the kid to cooperate. Under the gun, Coppola assented without even knowing Brando's plan. "Brando cut the orange peel, put the score in it, and put it in his mouth and we said, 'Roll.' Because the little kid wasn't on the spot, he was curious about what Brando was doing and then the kid reacted because he was scared of those teeth. Brando hugged him and laughed, and then the kid laughed." After the scene played out, Coppola said, "Cut!" and Ballard immediately yelled, "Lunch!"

Chapman cites the scene in which Brando "changes from a benign grandfather into a monster who frightens the child, and then dies" as his favorite in the film, and Coppola acknowledges that the scene, "which to some people is one of their favorite scenes, very nearly wasn't in the movie—had Ballard been there ten minutes before and seen what I was doing, or had Brando not done what he did."

"Acting is an empty and useless profession."
—Marlon Brando, *Time* magazine

THE GREAT MARLON BRANDO

Francis Ford Coppola and casting director Fred Roos had thought a lot about what charismatic actor should play the Godfather. According to Roos, "We made every effort to find an Italian-American Don Corleone, and there just wasn't. There were a lot of actors in that age category, but the Don is talked about so much—as well as his power and his strength and his leadership—that when he comes on the screen, he better be something pretty great." Clearly it couldn't be an unknown—any actor worth his salt couldn't have reached the age of fifty without being known. They decided that when in doubt, go with the world's greatest actor—regardless of whether he seemed to fit the part—and trust that, with his talent, he would be able to make the role work. In Coppola's mind, that meant either Lawrence Olivier or Marlon Brando. (Roos also mentioned George C. Scott as someone they considered). Olivier, although British, was the right age, resembled the Mafia don Vito Genovese, and his recent turn as the premier of Russia showed his ability to completely make himself over. Unfortunately, the actor was quite ill at the time. That left Brando, at forty-seven seemingly too young and handsome for the part, and although he was arguably the greatest actor, he was also rumored to be the world's biggest headache for studios.

After beginning his career as a true force of stage and screen—most notably in *A Streetcar Named Desire* and *On the Waterfront,* Brando had recently appeared in a string of failures. His foray into directing, Paramount's *One-Eyed Jacks,* did respectably at the box office, but his production costs doubled the budget. His interloping on the set of *Mutiny on the Bounty* also made for an exorbitant production. His last film, *Burn!,* was a huge flop. He was considered box office poison, and Paramount wanted nothing to do with him.

Mario Puzo had thought of Brando for the role two years earlier and sent him the book, along with a note: "Dear Mr. Brando, I wrote a book called *The Godfather* which has had some success and I think you're the only actor who can play the part. I know this was presumptuous of me, but the best I can do by the book is try. I really think you'd be tremendous." At first, Brando wasn't interested—some reports have suggested that he didn't consider himself a "Mafia godfather," and indeed, in his autobiography, *Songs My Mother Taught Me,* he wrote, "I had never played an Italian before, and I didn't think I could do it successfully. By then I had learned that one of the biggest mistakes an actor can make is to try to play a role for which he is miscast." Film writer and friend Budd Schulberg has said that Brando initially refused because of his unwillingness to glorify the Mafia. Brando's assistant Alice Marchak read the book and tried to talk him into changing his mind. Brando did call Puzo and thanked him for the book and, knowing his own reputation, advised Puzo that he'd have to get a strong director on board before even mentioning the idea of casting Brando to a studio.

Coppola met with strong resistance from the studio executives on the subject of Brando. Not only did they think that he was too young for the part, but they were convinced he would cost them money. In Robert Evans's memoir, *The Kid Stays in the Picture,* he recalls his orders from New York: "Will not finance Brando in title role. Do not respond. Case closed." Coppola cites the direct refusal he received from Stanley Jaffe: "As president of Paramount Pictures, I assure you Marlon Brando will not appear in this motion picture, and furthermore I order you never to bring the subject up again." Ruddy's remembrance is a little more colorful: "As long as I'm president of this fuckin' company, Marlon Brando will never do this movie!"

Still, Coppola persisted, and the studio finally relented. The catch: three seemingly impossible stipulations:

1. Brando would basically do the film for free; no money up front, just a share of the back end, with per diem and expenses.
2. He would have to put up a million-dollar bond that would ensure his behavior would not cost the movie money.
3. He would have to do a screen test—unheard of for an actor of Brando's caliber.

Coppola quickly agreed, as he felt he had nothing to lose, and was able to work out the first two requirements—and somehow Brando got $50,000 up front, plus $10,000 a week expenses for his six weeks of work. He also was granted a percentage of the film's gross. Unfortunately for Brando, he sold the points back to the studio for a mere $100,000 in cash—a move that cost him millions. Needless to say, he fired his agent, lawyer, and anyone else remotely involved in the transaction.

As to the third stipulation, Coppola was unsure how to finesse asking the great Marlon Brando for a screen test. He decided to call Brando and suggest that they do some experimentation, to see if he would feel comfortable playing an Italian. He showed up at Brando's house on Mulholland Drive with a few guys with cameras and some Italian props: provolone cheese, salami, prosciutto, anisette, and cigars. Coppola now says that, in general, in approaching Brando, "my theory was to supply him with the goods, and he'll know what to do." After a short while, Brando emerged from his bedroom in a beautiful robe and set about transforming himself. While nibbling on the food and glancing in a mirror, he pinned up his long blond hair and ran black shoe polish through it. He bent the tips of his shirt collars, stuck Kleenex in his cheeks—saying that he should look like a "bulldog"—penciled in a mustache, added some black under his eyes, and began mumbling in husky tones, noting that the character had been wounded in the throat. He even answered a telephone call in character. Coppola filmed him as discreetly and quietly as possible, as he had heard that Brando didn't like loud noises. Afterward, Coppola hustled his camcorder footage back to New York, straight to the top: the president of Gulf+Western, Charlie Bluhdorn. Bluhdorn, who had been warned by Frank Yablans that casting Brando would actually keep audiences *away* from the film, loudly protested, "No, no, absolutely not!" as soon as he recognized who was on the tape. But as he watched Brando work his transformation, he abruptly changed his tune, expressing in amazement, "That's incredible!"

THE NUTS AND BOLTS: PRODUCTION DETAIL

The funeral was shot at Calvary Cemetery, in Queens. Twenty funeral limos and 150 extras were used, with flowers costing over $10,000. According to his notebook, Coppola wanted the funeral to be a big, extravagant affair, as he considered it to be the "counterpoint" to the lavish wedding that opens the film.

EXT DAY: CEMETERY

The Cemetery. Late day. The hundreds of cars, limousines, and flower cars line the road through this Italian-Catholic cemetery in Queens Village.

Enormous bouquets of flowers are unloaded. A long line of DRIVERS open doors for their PASSENGERS. There is a slow procession toward the grave. A brief shot of the Vito Corleone marker.

MICHAEL sits with his family—his MOTHER and TOM HAGEN at his sides. AL NERI watches over.

One by one, the mourners come by, weeping, or merely with grave expressions; pay their respects and continue on. JOHNNY FONTANE takes his turn. CLEMENZA whispers into the ear of LAMPONE. LAMPONE immediately arranges for the members of the Five New York Families to pay their respects. BARZINI stands a long time, tosses a rose, and glances at MICHAEL.

MICHAEL watches the scene.

As BARZINI leaves, it seems as though everyone is fawning over him. It is clear that he is the new *Capo di Capi*—the place formerly held by DON CORLEONE.

GOOFS, GAFFES, AND BLOOPERS

A famous mistake: a ghostly orange image of Morgana King (Mama Corleone) appears on Michael's suit during the funeral. Years later, film critic Roger Ebert queried Coppola about the mishap, who asked Kim Aubry, producer of *The Godfather* DVDs and Coppola's vice president of postproduction and technology, to look into it. The image comes from a fluke of light, distortion, shadow, and lens peculiarity, as the lens edge had picked up King's appearance from just beyond the frame. What's even more bizarre: Mama is chewing gum at her husband's funeral! She legitimately thought she was out of camera range. Aubry said in Ebert's *Answer Man* column: "We get so much bogus stuff that it was fun to check out a real one, and it turns out not to be an artistic trompe l'oeil, but a GOOF! Love it!"

After Marlon Brando's death, his own annotated script of *The Godfather* fetched a staggering $312,800 at a New York auction—over twenty times its estimated price and the highest amount ever paid for a film manuscript.

TESSIO bends down to speak to MICHAEL.

TESSIO

Mike, could I have a minute?

MICHAEL nods, and they move to a private place.

TESSIO

Barzini wants to arrange a meeting. He says we can straighten any of our problems out.

MICHAEL

You talked to 'im?

TESSIO

Yeah. I can arrange security. On *my* territory. All right?

MICHAEL

All right.

TESSIO

All right.

They return to their places. HAGEN leans over to MICHAEL.

HAGEN

Do you know how they're gonna come at you?

MICHAEL

They're arranging a meeting in Brooklyn. Tessio's ground. Where I'll be safe.

TESSIO moves to speak to BARZINI. They shake hands.

HAGEN

I always thought it would've been Clemenza, not Tessio.

MICHAEL

It's a smart move. Tessio was always smarter.

But, I'm gonna wait. After the baptism. I've decided to be Godfather to Connie's baby. And then I'll meet with Don Barzini and Tattaglia—all the heads of the Five Families.

MONTAGE:

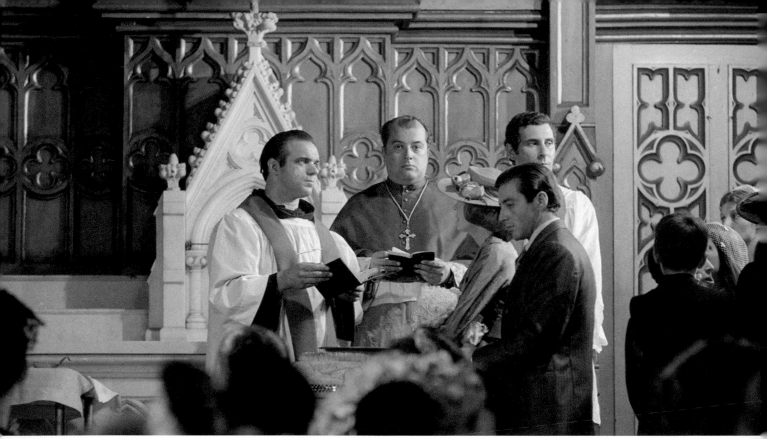

 THE NUTS AND BOLTS: PRODUCTION DETAIL

The exteriors of the baptism scene were filmed at Mount Loretto Church, Staten Island. The church subsequently burned down in 1973.

The interiors were filmed at Old St. Patrick's Cathedral, Mulberry Street, Manhattan.

 BEHIND THE SCENES

Newborn Sofia Coppola plays Michael Rizzo. Diane Keaton appears to not have much experience holding a baby—as infant Sofia's head flops around.

 BEHIND THE SCENES

Puzo couldn't resolve how the climactic scene should unfold on film, but Coppola devised the idea of inter-cutting the baptism with the assassinations, and having the priest's dialogue lay over the murder scenes. During postproduction, something still seemed to be missing from the sequence. Out of desperation, editor Peter Zinner conceived of laying the organ track over the murder scenes, which indeed made the sequence work.

INT DAY: CHURCH

A LONG SHOT of a church interior. An organ plays, a BABY is crying. A medium shot of KAY, MICHAEL, and the PRIEST walking to the altar. KAY holds a BABY. A GROUP views the proceedings from the pews.

> PRIEST
> (SPEAKS LATIN)

MEDIUM CLOSE-UP: the PRIEST breathes on the BABY three times. CLOSE-UP on MICHAEL's. The BABY's bonnet is removed.

> PRIEST
> (SPEAKS LATIN)

INT DAY: MOTEL ROOM

In a Long Island motel, LAMPONE carefully disassembles a revolver, oils it, checks it, and puts it back together.

> PRIEST'S VOICE
> (SPEAKS LATIN)

EXT DAY: CLEMENZA'S HOUSE

PETER CLEMENZA carries a long box and is about to get into his Lincoln. He hesitates, takes a rag, and cleans some dirt off the fender.

> PRIEST'S VOICE
> (SPEAKS LATIN)

INT DAY: CHURCH

CLOSE-UP of MICHAEL being blessed with oils. CLOSE-UP of the PRIEST's fingers as he gently applies oil to the INFANT's face.

> PRIEST
>
> (SPEAKS LATIN)

INT DAY: BARBERSHOP

WILLIE CICCI gets a shave.

> PRIEST'S VOICE
>
> (SPEAKS LATIN)

INT DAY: NERI'S APARTMENT

ALBERT NERI in his small Corona apartment; he opens a small trunk, and we see in it, neatly folded, a New York City policeman's uniform. He takes it out piece by piece, almost reverently.

> PRIEST'S VOICE
>
> (SPEAKS LATIN)

INT DAY: CHURCH

CLOSE-UP on the PRIEST's fingers, blessing the BABY with oil.

> PRIEST
>
> (SPEAKS LATIN)

INT DAY: NERI'S APARTMENT

CLOSE-UP on hands emptying a paper bag. A gun and then a badge drop on the bed. We see NERI in a police uniform. He wipes the sweat from his face.

> PRIEST'S VOICE
>
> (SPEAKS LATIN)

INT DAY: HOTEL STAIRS

CLEMENZA is climbing the back stairs of a large hotel, still carrying the box. He rounds the corner, wipes the sweat from his brow, and then continues upward.

> PRIEST'S VOICE
>
> (SPEAKS LATIN)

INT DAY: CHURCH

MEDIUM SHOT of the PRIEST blessing the BABY, then a CLOSE-UP. CLOSE-UP of MICHAEL. PRIEST continues to bless the BABY.

BEHIND THE SCENES

The shooting location for the barbershop, the revolving doors, and Clemenza's walk up the stairs was the St. Regis Hotel. Richard Castellano's wife alleges that Coppola made him go up the stairs an extra thirty-eight times.

ADAPTATION AND THE CUTTING ROOM FLOOR

Puzo's novel contains extended exposition on the character of Albert Neri, whose first profession was as a cop, which explains how he came to have a badge and uniform.

PRIEST

(SPEAKS LATIN)

CLOSE-UP of MICHAEL.

PRIEST

Michael, do you believe in God, the Father Almighty, Creator of
Heaven and Earth?

MICHAEL

I do.

INT DAY: HALLWAY

BARZINI walks down the hallway of an ornate building. He stubs out a cigarette and continues.

PRIEST'S VOICE

Do you believe in Jesus Christ, His only Son, our Lord?

MICHAEL'S VOICE

I do.

PRIEST'S VOICE

Do you believe in the Holy Ghost, the Holy Catholic Church?

MICHAEL'S VOICE

I do.

EXT DAY: MUNICIPAL BUILDING STEPS

NERI is in front of a municipal building. On his side of the street, he spots a limousine waiting
directly across from the main entrance of the building. He taps on its fender with his night-
stick. The DRIVER waves at him. NERI taps again, motioning for the DRIVER to move on.

PRIEST'S VOICE

(SPEAKS LATIN)

INT DAY: HOTEL STAIRS

CLEMENZA continues up the stairs.

                    PRIEST'S VOICE
    (SPEAKS LATIN)

INT DAY: ROOM

ROCCO LAMPONE and another MAN each take a gun and exit.

                    PRIEST'S VOICE
    (SPEAKS LATIN)

INT DAY: BARBERSHOP

CICCI exits barbershop.

                    PRIEST'S VOICE
    (SPEAKS LATIN)

INT DAY: CHURCH

CLOSE-UP of the BABY. LONG SHOT of the church interior. We hear the BABY
CRYING.

                        PRIEST
    (SPEAKS LATIN)

EXT DAY: GOVERNMENT BUILDING

BARZINI starts to walk down the exterior steps. He motions to his BODYGUARD to see
what is happening with the limousine. At the bottom of the steps, NERI is standing next
to the car with the CHAUFFEUR, writing him a ticket. The BODYGUARD hurries down.

                    PRIEST'S VOICE
    (SPEAKS LATIN)

                    BABY'S VOICE
    (CRYING)

INT DAY: HOTEL

CICCI walks up steps, smoking. He pauses.

                    PRIEST'S VOICE
    (SPEAKS LATIN)

                    BABY'S VOICE
    (CRYING)

INT DAY: HOTEL

CLEMENZA reaches an elevator. He presses the button.

> **PRIEST'S VOICE**
> (SPEAKS LATIN)

> **BABY'S VOICE**
> (CRYING)

INT DAY: MASSAGE ROOM

MOE GREENE lies on a table, getting a massage.

> **PRIEST'S VOICE**
> (SPEAKS LATIN)

> **BABY'S VOICE**
> (CRYING)

INT DAY: CHURCH

CLOSE-UP on PRIEST's fingers, blessing BABY. CLOSE-UP on MICHAEL.

> **PRIEST**
> Michael Francis Rizzi, do you renounce Satan?

INT DAY: HOTEL ELEVATOR

The elevator doors open, revealing three MEN. STRACCI starts to exit. CLEMENZA kicks a DON back into the elevator, pulls a gun from the box, and opens fire.

INT DAY: CHURCH

CLOSE-UP on MICHAEL.

> **MICHAEL**
> I do renounce him.

INT DAY: MASSAGE ROOM

A MAN enters the room. MOE puts on his glasses to see who it is and is shot through the eye. Blood gushes out.

INT DAY: CHURCH

CLOSE-UP on MICHAEL.

> **PRIEST**
> And all his works?

NT DAY: HOTEL

CICCI stubs out his cigarette and continues up the stairs. He comes to a revolving door and locks CUNEO inside. CUNEO turns around to see a gun pointed at him—he mouths "No!" CICCI shoots CUNEO through the glass four times.

NT DAY: CHURCH

CLOSE-UP on MICHAEL.

> MICHAEL
>
> I do renounce them.

NT DAY: MOTEL

LAMPONE and another GUNMAN burst into a room, surprising TATTAGLIA and WOMAN in bed, and pump rounds of bullets into them.

> GIRL
> *(screams)*
>
> God!

NT DAY: CHURCH

CLOSE-UP on MICHAEL.

> PRIEST
>
> And all his pomps?

> MICHAEL
>
> I do renounce them.

BEHIND THE SCENES

"A sequence on Wall Street at 9 a.m. . . . drew a crowd of 15,000 onlookers and brought *The New York Times* comment that the lensing was 'the biggest show in town.'"—*Variety,* March 1972

FILMING BARZINI'S DEATH SCENE AT THE NEW YORK COUNTY SUPREME COURTHOUSE.

THE COMPLETE ANNOTATED SCREENPLAY 227

EXT DAY: GOVERNMENT BUILDING

NERI shoots the BODYGUARD and CHAUFFEUR, and then bends down, steadying his arm, to shoot BARZINI, who attempted to flee up the stairs. NERI shoots him twice in the back, and BARZINI tumbles down the stairs as a car drives by to pick up NERI.

INT DAY: CHURCH

CLOSE-UP on MICHAEL.

> PRIEST
> Michael Rizzi . . . will you be baptized?

> MICHAEL
> I will.

The PRIEST baptizes the BABY with holy water.

> PRIEST
> *In Nomine Patris . . .*

INT DAY: MOTEL

CLOSE-UP on bloody corpse of PHILIP TATTAGLIA.

> PRIEST'S VOICE
> *. . . et Filii . . .*

INT DAY: REVOLVING DOORS

CLOSE-UP on bloody corpse of CUNEO.

> PRIEST'S VOICE
> *. . . et Spiritu Sanctu.*

EXT DAY: GOVERNMENT BUILDING

We see the corpses of BARZINI, the CHAUFFEUR, and the feet of the BODYGUARD from behind BARZINI's car.

> PRIEST'S VOICE
> Michael Rizzi . . .

INT DAY: CHURCH

CLOSE-UP on MICHAEL behind a lit candle.

> PRIEST
> . . . go in peace and may the Lord be with you. Amen.

⬡ **THE NUTS AND BOLTS: PRODUCTION DETAIL**
The courthouse is actually the New York County Supreme Court building on Centre Street, Manhattan.

EXT DAY: CHURCH

The christening party outside the CHURCH.

Four or five limousines have been waiting and now pull up to receive MAMA, CONNIE and the BABY, and the others. Everyone is very happy; only MICHAEL seems aloof and grave. CONNIE holds the BABY up to MICHAEL.

> MICHAEL
>
> Kay, come on.

> CONNIE
>
> Kiss your Godfather.

MICHAEL kisses the BABY. As the fuss is going on, a car pulls up. LAMPONE gets out and works his way to MICHAEL. He whispers in his ear. This is the news MICHAEL has been waiting for. MICHAEL turns to CARLO.

> MICHAEL
>
> Carlo can't go to Vegas. Something's come up. Everybody's gonna leave without us.

> CONNIE
>
> Oh, Mike, it's our first vacation together.

> CARLO
>
> *(overlaps)*
>
> Connie, please.
>
> *(to MICHAEL)*
>
> What do you want?

> MICHAEL
>
> *(overlaps)*
>
> Go back to the house, wait for my call. It's important.

CARLO

Right.

MICHAEL

(to KAY)

I'll only be a couple a' days.

MICHAEL kisses KAY, pats ANTHONY on the head, then walks down and kisses MAMA.

MAMA

(SPEAKS ITALIAN)

LONG SHOT of the PRIEST and MONSIGNOR going up the steps as people find the correct limousines.

INT DAY: DON'S KITCHEN

TESSIO is on the phone in the kitchen of the main house on the MALL. HAGEN stands next to him.

TESSIO

(into phone)

We're on our way to Brooklyn.

(hangs up phone)

I hope Mike can get us a good deal tonight.

HAGEN

I'm sure he will.

EXT DAY: MALL

The TWO MEN walk out onto the MALL, toward a car. On their way, they are stopped by a BODYGUARD.

CICCI

Sal, Tom, the Boss says he'll come in a separate car; he says for you two to go on ahead.

TESSIO

Hell, he can't do that; it screws up all my arrangements.

CICCI

Well, that's what he said.

HAGEN

I can't go either, Sal.

TWO MORE BODYGUARDS appear around him. He flashes at the men surrounding him; for a moment he panics, and then he accepts it.

TESSIO

(after a pause)

Tell Mike it was only business. I always liked 'im.

HAGEN

He understands that.

CICCI

(frisks TESSIO)

Excuse me, Sal.

TESSIO looks at the MEN, and then pauses.

TESSIO

Tom, can you get me off the hook? For old time's sake?

HAGEN

Can't do it, Sally.

HAGEN motions for the MEN to take him away, and then turns and walks away from the group. TESSIO is led off. HAGEN enters the house. He looks back through the window. TESSIO is led into a waiting car. HAGEN looks away and walks off.

INT DAY: CARLO'S LIVING ROOM

MICHAEL, still dressed in a dark suit, enters the house. LAMPONE, NERI, and HAGEN follow. CARLO, sweating, turns to face them. He puts down the phone middial.

MICHAEL

You have to answer for Santino, Carlo.

CARLO pauses, then rises to meet them.

CARLO

Mike, you got it all wrong.

MICHAEL

You fingered Sonny for the Barzini people. Ahhh, that little farce you played with my sister. Did you think that could fool a Corleone?

CARLO

Mike, I'm innocent. I swear on the kids . . . Please, Mike, don't do this to me.

MICHAEL

(overlaps)

Sit down.

CARLO sits. MICHAEL pulls up a chair beside him.

CAST AND CREW: ABE VIGODA

After several years in the theater and a few television roles, namely on the *Dark Shadows* series, Abe Vigoda got the part of Tessio by answering an open casting call and beating out hundreds of other actors. *The Godfather* was his first film. It has been reported that visitors on the set would often assume that the tall, gruff-sounding Vigoda was an actual Mafioso, not a member of the cast.

ADAPTATION AND THE CUTTING ROOM FLOOR

In Puzo's novel, it is Hagen who asks Michael if he could let Tessio "off the hook." In his own first draft of the script, Puzo changed it to Tessio making the request—which is how it occurs in the film.

CARLO

Mike, don't do this to me, please.

MICHAEL

Barzini's dead. So is Philip Tattaglia. Moe Greene, Stracchi, Cuneo.

CARLO puts his face in his hands.

MICHAEL

Today, I settle all Family business, so don't tell me you're innocent, Carlo. Admit what you did.

CARLO is shaken.

MICHAEL

Get 'im a drink. Come on. Don't be afraid, Carlo. Come on, do you think I'd make my sister a widow? I'm Godfather to your son, Carlo.

A drink is brought and CARLO gulps it, weeping silently.

MICHAEL

Go ahead, drink it. Drink. No, Carlo, you're outta the Family business, that's your punishment. You're finished. I'm putting you on a plane to Vegas. Tom?

MICHAEL hands a plane ticket to CARLO.

MICHAEL

I want you to stay there. Understand?

CARLO

Mm-hmm.

MICHAEL

Only, don't tell me you're innocent. Because it insults my intelligence
and makes me very angry.

(long pause)

Now, who approached you? Tattaglia or Barzini?

CARLO

(sees his way out)

It was Barzini.

MICHAEL stares at him for a long moment.

MICHAEL

(softly)

Good.

(rises and puts the chair back)

There's a car waiting for you outside to take you to the airport. I'll call
your wife, tell her what flight you're on.

CARLO

Mike . . .

MICHAEL

Go on, get outta my sight.

LAMPONE helps CARLO with his coat.

EXT DAY: MALL

CARLO moves out to the MALL; the BUTTON MEN are putting his things in the trunk.
ONE opens the front door for him. SOMEONE is sitting in the rear seat, though we
cannot see who. CARLO gets into the car. Out of nervousness, he looks back to see the
other man. It is CLEMENZA, who nods cordially.

CLEMENZA

Hello, Carlo.

EXT DAY: CARLO'S STEPS

MICHAEL and his party watch.

INT DAY: CAR

The motor starts, and as the car pulls away, CLEMENZA suddenly throws a garrote around CARLO's neck. He chokes and leaps up like a fish on a line, kicking his feet. His thrashing feet kick right through the front windshield. Then his body goes slack.

EXT DAY: CARLO'S STEPS

MICHAEL and his grim party watch. Then he turns, and they all walk off, the GRAVEL CRUNCHING under their feet.

DISSOLVE TO:

EXT DAY: MALL

HIGH ANGLE ON THE CORLEONE MALL: Several moving vans are parked on the MALL; one feels that these are the final days; the families are moving out; signs indicating that the property is for sale are evident.

A black limousine pulls up. Just as it stops, the rear door flies open, and CONNIE attempts to run out, restrained by MAMA. She manages to break free and runs across the MALL into MICHAEL's house.

MAMA
Will you . . . moving . . . I'm tryin' to tell you . . .

CONNIE

Aw, Mama, please!

INT DAY: DON'S LIVING ROOM

Inside the CORLEONE house. Big boxes have been packed; furniture prepared for shipping. CONNIE hurries into the living room, where she comes upon KAY.

CONNIE

Michael! Michael!

KAY

What is it?

But CONNIE avoids her and moves directly to THE DON's study, looking for MICHAEL.

CONNIE

Where is he? Michael!

INT DAY: DON'S STUDY

CONNIE bursts in. NERI is watchful.

CONNIE

Michael! Michael, you lousy bastard, you killed my husband. You waited until Papa died so nobody could stop you and then you killed 'im. You blamed him for Sonny, you always did. Everybody did. But you never thought about me, you never gave a damn about me.

> (crying)

Now what am I gonna do?!

KAY

> (comforting)

Connie . . .

CONNIE

Why do you think he kept Carlo at the Mall? All the time he knew he was gonna kill 'im. And you stood Godfather to our baby. You lousy coldhearted bastard.

(to KAY)

Wanna know how many men he had killed with Carlo? Read the papers, read the papers!

She throws down a newspaper.

CONNIE

That's your husband! That's your husband!

She moves toward MICHAEL. NERI restrains her, and MICHAEL waves him off. She tries to spit into MICHAEL's face, but in her hysteria she has no saliva. MICHAEL holds her, but she struggles away.

MICHAEL

Come on . . .

CONNIE

No! No! No!

MICHAEL

(to NERI)

Get her upstairs. Get her a doctor.

NERI and CONNIE exit. MICHAEL sighs.

KAY is shocked, never taking her look of amazement from MICHAEL. He feels her look.

MICHAEL

She's hysterical. Hysterical.

He lights a cigarette, but KAY won't let him avoid her eyes.

KAY

Michael, is it true?

MICHAEL

Don't ask me about my business, Kay.

KAY

Is it true?

MICHAEL

Don't ask me about my business.

KAY

No . . .

MICHAEL

Enough!!

He slaps his hand down on the desk. KAY looks down. He sighs and pushes a chair in frustration. He moves toward her, stubbing out his cigarette.

CAST AND CREW:
TALIA SHIRE

In interviews, Talia "Tally" Shire said her therapist urged her to start asserting herself in the family, which is why she tried out for *The Godfather*. Coppola was understandably nervous that casting his sister would smack of nepotism. Also, he says, "I really thought she was too beautiful to play the part, because my idea was that the character was some dumpy daughter that the guy only wanted to marry because of whose daughter she was." Shire is quoted in *California* magazine as saying: "He was real angry that I accepted without asking him first. Just because you're a genius doesn't mean that you're completely developed emotionally." When Coppola thought Paramount was going to fire him, he relented, thinking that at least somebody in the family should get something out of the experience

MICHAEL

All right. This one time—this one time I'll let you ask me about my affairs.

KAY

(whispers)

Is it true? Is it?

She looks directly into his eyes and he returns the look, so directly that we know he will tell the truth.

MICHAEL

(after a long pause)

No.

KAY is relieved; she throws her arms around him and hugs him.

KAY

I guess we both need a drink, huh?

INT DAY: DON'S KITCHEN

She moves back into the kitchen and begins to prepare the drinks. From her vantage point, as she makes the drinks, she sees CLEMENZA, NERI, and ROCCO LAMPONE enter the house with their BODYGUARDS.

She watches with curiosity as MICHAEL stands to receive them. He stands arrogantly at ease, weight resting on one foot slightly behind the other. One hand on his hip, like a Roman emperor. The CAPOREGIMES stand before him.

CLEMENZA takes MICHAEL's hand, kissing it.

CLEMENZA

Don Corleone.

LAMPONE also kisses his hand. MICHAEL raises a hand to his face. NERI moves to the office door.

VIEW ON KAY's face as she looks at what her husband has become. The door shuts.

THE END

⚙ ADAPTATION AND THE CUTTING ROOM FLOOR

Puzo's story concludes in early autumn of 1955. In the book, Kay leaves Michael the morning after he lies to her about Carlo, but Tom Hagen convinces her to come back.

⚙ ADAPTATION AND THE CUTTING ROOM FLOOR

Both the book and the preproduction shooting script conclude with a dialogue-free scene of Kay in church, taking communion and lighting candles, presumably for Michael's soul. The scene was shot, and although it doesn't appear in the finished film, it showed up in *The Godfather: The Complete Epic*—aka *Mario Puzo's The Godfather: The Complete Novel for Television*.

THE AFTERMATH

"I remember being in Beverly Hills when we were cutting the film, living for free in Jimmy Caan's maid's room because I had no money. There was a nice young man who was an editing assistant and used to ride home on a bicycle. This big, tall young kid is walking his bike and he had just seen *The French Connection*. *The French Connection* was so exciting and dynamic—it was a huge splash in Hollywood at the time I was cutting *The Godfather*. When you're making a movie, you're insecure about it—it's hard to evaluate it because you're so sick of it, and there's no newness, so I said to him, 'I guess after *The French Connection*, everyone is going to just think that *The Godfather* is this long, boring, dark movie.' And the kid said, 'Yeah, I guess you're right.'

"I felt so terrible, going home to my maid's room, that I've fantasized that after he left, Mephistopheles popped out of the bushes and said, 'Francis, how would you like this movie to be the most successful movie ever made?' Something like that must have gone down, because the idea that this disastrous movie would be successful and would be remembered and it would even be in the annals where it would be compared to movies that I thought were among the greatest—is so surprising."

—Coppola, 2007

During filming, Coppola complained about the station wagon that picked him up so he and Evans made a bet that if the film made $50 million, Paramount would spring for a new car. As *The Godfather*'s grosses climbed, Coppola and George Lucas went car shopping and selected a Mercedes-Benz 600 stretch limousine—instructing the salesman to send the bill to Paramount. The car appears in an opening scene of Lucas's *American Graffiti*.

BOX OFFICE BONANZA

On March 15, 1972, five New York theaters screened the world premiere of *The Godfather* for the public. That night, the film took in a record $57,000. In the first week, the take was $465,000, also a record. New York City, which over five days at fifty-six theaters took in an eye-popping $1.9 million, was a hotbed for *Godfather* attendance, with lines regularly stretching around the block. Screenings were held on the hour every hour from nine in the morning to midnight. On opening night, the excess crowds caused the start times to move later and later—the last screening of the night let out at 4 a.m., only two hours before lines began to form for the early showing. Bribes were advanced to get to the head of the line; spouses took turns waiting in line; the *Los Angeles Times* printed a how-to guide entitled "Life-styles for Waiting in Line to See *Godfather*." The scene was not always civilized: a manager of a Loews Theatre was shot in the arm when stickup-men stole the day's receipts, totaling $13,000.

The buzz surrounding the movie was apparent even before it premiered. Going against convention, Paramount prebooked the hotly anticipated *Godfather* in 350 theaters. The film, which cost $6.2 million to make, garnered $13.8 million from these bookings before it even opened.

Paramount Pictures president Frank Yablans ushered in a new distribution model with *The Godfather*. By opening it in multiple theaters at once, rather than one theater at a time, Paramount was able to maximize their advertising dollars. They also mandated cash on the barrelhead. Such new practices opened the financial floodgates for Paramount.

In 1972, the average movie ticket price in the United States was around $1.60. With the soaring demand, Paramount boosted ticket prices for the film to $3.50, then increased the weekend ticket price to $4.00. The value of Gulf+Western stock jumped by a whopping $97 million a month after *The Godfather* opened.

In the film's initial release, Paramount made $85.7 million on it. It was the first movie in screen history to gross an average of $1 million a day. It was the highest-grossing film of all time, until *Jaws* surpassed it in 1975. To date, it has grossed nearly $135 million domestically, and an estimated $250 million worldwide. *The Godfather* not only made moviemaking history, it made moviegoing history.

CRITICAL RESPONSE TO *THE GODFATHER*

A month before *The Godfather*'s release, Ivor Davis of *London Express* sneaked into a private Paramount screening for exhibitors. His review of the much-anticipated film appeared in the *New York Post* two days later, with the headline: "Smuggled into *Godfather* Screening." He raved about Brando's turn as Don Corleone and said that Pacino had "the looks of Alain Delon and the intensity of a young Rod Steiger."

Although the film is now widely lauded, at the time it received some lukewarm reactions. *Variety* damned it with faint praise, saying it was "overlong," and seemed confused by what they termed "some sort of tinting effect." The esteemed Stanley Kauffman of *The New Republic* blasted Brando, characterized Rota's score as "rotten," and called the print "washed out." But raves ruled the day, most noting how the film had an artistic excellence in addition to its broad appeal:

"Francis Ford Coppola has made one of the most brutal and moving chronicles of American life ever designed within the limits of popular entertainment."

—Vincent Canby, *The New York Times*

"An instant classic."
—Charles Champlin, *Los Angeles Times*

"Coppola has found a style and a visual look for all this material so *The Godfather* becomes something of a rarity: a really good movie squeezed from a bestseller."
—Roger Ebert, *Chicago Sun-Times*

"If ever there was a great example of how the best popular movies come out of a merger of commerce and art, *The Godfather* is it. . . . The dark-and-light contrast is so operatic and so openly symbolic that it perfectly expresses the basic nature of the material. . . . *The Godfather* keeps so much in front of us all the time that we're never bored."
—Pauline Kael, *The New Yorker*

THE OSCARS®

The Godfather earned a healthy ten nominations for the 45th Academy Awards®. Only twenty-one films before it had garnered more (and only thirteen received more if you count Nino Rota's initially nominated score). The nominations included Best Picture, Director, Supporting Actor (for Robert Duvall, James Caan, and oddly—considering his screen time—Al Pacino), Adapted Screenplay, Sound Editing, Costume Design, and Best Actor for Marlon Brando's portrayal of Don Vito Corleone.

A woman dressed in full Native American garb and claiming to be Apache Indian Sacheen Littlefeather retrieved Brando's tickets on the day of the ceremony. Panicked about the prospect of a militant acceptance speech, the show's producer considered arresting her, but instead talked her out of reading a five-page speech Brando had prepared on the plight of Native Americans. Littlefeather's abbreviated speech explained

that Brando could not accept the award due to "the treatment of American Indians in the motion picture industry, on TV reruns, and what's happening at Wounded Knee today." The audience reacted with a mixture of applause and boos. Brando, who didn't think highly of awards given to actors anyway, thought it would be a great opportunity for a Native American to speak to sixty million people. Strangely enough, Littlefeather turned out not to be Native American at all, but an aspiring actress named Maria Cruz.

To present the Best Picture category, Clint Eastwood took over for an ailing Charlton Heston. Eastwood and producer Al Ruddy were friends, and Ruddy joked beforehand that Eastwood should just announce "And the winner for Best Picture is . . . Al Ruddy for *The Godfather*!" and then tear up the ballot and swallow it—nobody would know the difference. The night wasn't going as well as everyone had hoped for *The Godfather*—in addition to Brando's no-show, *Cabaret* won many of the awards, including Best Director. When Eastwood got to the podium, he opened the envelope and announced the winner: "Albert S. Ruddy, for *The Godfather*!" A shocked Ruddy thought for a moment that Eastwood was actually doing his friend a favor. According to Ruddy, Eastwood called him an "idiot" and showed him the ballot. *The Godfather* had indeed won. A footnote to the story is that thirty-two years later, Ruddy received his second Best Picture Oscar® alongside none other than Clint Eastwood, for *Million Dollar Baby*. "It was like closing the loop for me," he said in an interview with the author.

Coppola was saddened to not receive the award for Best Director. In his personal journal, he framed the loss in this way: "On Losing the Oscar: Certainly, a sense of disappointment—but more because I wanted it to symbolize the end of a phase of my life; the end of the idyll of possessing a career, success, money—so that I could begin a new phase. Sort of like waiting for your bank account to be exactly seven dollars even. I wanted to walk away the complete winner; so that *The Godfather: Part II* would have been an appendage. Now it becomes my last chance. But NO—give that up. It's over. It will be whatever it will be—and I will go on anyway." (See Appendix III: Notable Awards.)

READY FOR PRIME TIME

With *The Godfather*'s success, it was only a matter of time before television got in on the act. NBC paid a then-record $10 million to air *The Godfather* over two nights in November of 1974. An estimated 42,400,000 households watched a slightly abridged version of the film.

Three years later, NBC broadcast *The Godfather Saga*. The four-part miniseries was a combination of *The Godfather* and *The Godfather: Part II*, edited to tell the Corleone family story in mostly chronological order. It was nine hours long and included about sixty minutes of restored scenes. With 100 million viewers, it became the most-viewed movie on television.

THE GODCHILDREN: FROM FAT TONY TO TONY SOPRANO

The Godfather's legacy is found in legions of allusions in books, movies, and television. The Internet Movie Database lists more than three hundred films and television shows that have referenced *The Godfather,* from Francois Truffaut's *Day for Night* to *You've Got Mail,* and nearly one hundred programs with spoofs, from *Revenge of the Pink Panther* to *Family Guy*. Films as diverse as the comic *Old School* and the tragic *Requiem for a Dream* use *The Godfather*'s trademark orange "death cue."

Some of the more famous spoofs include John Belushi as Vito Corleone in the *Saturday Night Live* skit "Godfather Therapy"; Harry Belafonte as an African-American mob boss in *Uptown Saturday Night*; and the *Seinfeld* episode "The Bris," in which Jerry loses out to Kramer in a bid to become godfather to a newborn. Reminiscent of the film's finale: Jerry watches the infant's parents kissing Kramer's hand as the door on his apartment closes. Marlon Brando reprised his character in the most directly referential film, *The Freshman*.

Several cast members have relished satirizing the film. Billy Crystal's character in *Analyze This* has a nightmare mimicking Vito Corleone's shooting, with the Fredo character played by Robert De Niro (who was in *The Godfather: Part II*). In *Annie Hall*, Woody Allen's character quips that he's "standing out here with the cast of *The Godfather*," while waiting in front of a movie theater with Hall (played by Diane Keaton). On the TV show *Las Vegas*, James Caan's character, Ed, is pulled aside and told to speak with authority, "the way Sonny spoke to his brother in that scene from *The Godfather*." Caan replies, "I've never seen the movie." To which he is admonished: "Are you kidding? That movie is a classic."

Two television programs that have made a business out of *Godfather* references are *The Simpsons* and *The Sopranos*. *The Simpsons* creators have even joked that they could re-create the entire film from snippets of their parodies. In one episode, Bart makes his clubhouse into a bachelor pad à la the Playboy Mansion, complete with actor James Caan. Caan is eventually gunned down at a tollbooth and ruefully says, "That's it! Next time, I fly." The horse-head scene is parodied in the "Lisa's Pony" episode. Mo, the bartender, tells bedtime stories from *The Godfather* (and the real Moe Greene, Alex Rocco, voices the part of Roger Meyer on the show). Mob character Fat Tony (voiced by Joe Mantegna, who appeared in *The Godfather: Part III*) names his son after Michael Corleone. And the "symbolic" oranges are spoofed often, as is the final scene.

The Sopranos often alludes to *The Godfather*, as when mob boss Tony Soprano stops to buy orange juice just before an attempt is made on his life, but it also uses *The Godfather* in a subtler way—to give contextual reference to the characters. Tony, one of the old guard, loves the first two *Godfather*s and laments how he has come into the "business" at a time when the type of respect shown in *The Godfather* is at an end; "the best is over." The young up-and-comer Christopher Moltisanti is partial to the more contemporary gangster flick *Scarface*. To fit in with his colleagues, Christopher quotes *The Godfather*—ineptly: "Lewis Brazi sleeps with the fishes." Big Pussy corrects him exasperatedly: "LUCA Brasi, Luca!" There is a conflict inherent in the *Godfather* references: although *The Sopranos* characters revere the movie, they are also sensitive to the implicit stereotypes; Tony bemoans the Italian-American "mayonnaisers" and their queries to him about *The Godfather*.

"I don't think people [at the time] realized the extraordinary alchemy: an aging star, a young actor . . . a lot of people in the right moment in their careers. An amazing alchemy was taking place. Making movies is a tough process but this was particularly difficult. It was a great moment in the movie business—a great era—and it all crystallized in this time. Being in the combat zone was daunting, but also absolutely thrilling. We were a little young to appreciate it, as well as being really in the thick of it, day by day. Looking back, it was such an exciting time to be around, in the middle of things. The excitement was such that it defied what you could conventionally call 'enjoying it.' An exciting ride—and at the time you didn't quite realize the import of what you were doing."

—Peter Bart, 2007

APPENDIX I:
THE GODFATHER CREDITS

CAST

Vito Corleone:	Marlon Brando
Michael:	Al Pacino
Sonny:	James Caan
Clemenza:	Richard Castellano
Tom Hagen:	Robert Duvall
Capt. McCluskey:	Sterling Hayden
Jack Woltz:	John Marley
Barzini:	Richard Conte
Sollozzo:	Al Lettieri
Kay Adams:	Diane Keaton
Tessio:	Abe Vigoda
Connie:	Talia Shire
Carlo:	Gianni Russo
Fredo:	John Cazale
Cuneo:	Rudy Bond
Johnny Fontane:	Al Martino
Mama Corleone:	Morgana King
Luca Brasi:	Lenny Montana
Paulie Gatto:	John Martino
Bonasera:	Salvatore Corsitto
Neri:	Richard Bright
Moe Greene:	Alex Rocco
Bruno Tattaglia:	Tony Giorgio
Nazorine:	Vito Scotti
Theresa Hagen:	Tere Livrano
Philip Tattaglia:	Victor Rendina
Lucy Mancini:	Jeannie Linero
Sandra Corleone:	Julie Gregg
Mrs. Clemenza:	Ardell Sheridan

Sicilian Sequence

Apollonia:	Simonetta Stefanelli
Fabrizio:	Angelo Infanti
Don Tommasino:	Corrado Gripa
Calo:	Franco Citti
Vitelli:	Saro Urzí

Director:	Francis Ford Coppola
Screenplay:	Mario Puzo, Francis Ford Coppola
Producer:	Albert S. Ruddy
Director of Photography:	Gordon Willis
Production Designer:	Dean Tavoularis
Costume Designer:	Anna Hill Johnstone
Editors:	William Reynolds, Peter Zinner
Associate Producer:	Gray Frederickson
Music:	Nino Rota, conducted by Carlo Savina

Additional Music

Mall Wedding Sequence:	Carmine Coppola
Songs	
"I Have But One Heart"	Johnny Farrow, Marty Symes
"Luna Mezz' 'O Mare"	Paolo Citarella
"Manhattan Serenade"	Louis Alter
"Have Yourself a Merry	
Little Christmas"	Hugh Martin, Ralph Blane
"Santa Claus is Coming to Town"	Haven Gillespie, J. Fred Coots
"The Bells of St. Mary's"	A.E. Adams, Douglas Furber
"All of My Life"	Irving Berlin
"Mona Lisa"	Jay Livingston, Ray Evans
Baptism Sequence	J.S. Bach
Production Recording:	Christopher Newman
Re-recording	Bud Brenzbach, Richard Portman
Art Director:	Warren Clymer
Set Decorator:	Philip Smith
Casting:	Fred Roos, Andrea Eastman, Louis Digiamo
Post Production Consultant:	Walter Murch
Makeup:	Dick Smith, Philip Rhodes
Hair Stylist:	Phil Leto
Wardrobe Supervisor:	George Newman
Women's Wardrobe:	Marilyn Putnam
Camera Operator:	Michael Chapman
Script Continuity:	Nancy Tonery
Production Recording:	Christopher Newman
Re-recording:	Bud Grenzbach, Richard Portman
Assistant to Producer:	Gary Chazan
Executive Assistant:	Robert S. Mendelsohn
Location Coordinators:	Michael Briggs, Tony Bowers
Foreign Post Production:	Peter Zinner

OAKTREE PRODUCTIONS

Unit Production Manager:	Fred Caruso
Assistant Director:	Fred Gallo
Unit Coordinator:	Robert Barth
Special Effects:	A.D. Flowers, Joe Lombardi, Sass Bedig
Location Service:	Cinemobile Systems, Inc.
Produced by:	Alfran Productions, Inc.

SICILIAN UNIT

Production Manager:	Valerio Deprolis
Assistant Director:	Tony Brandt
Assistant Art Director:	Samuel Yerts

APPENDIX II:
THE GODFATHER TIMELINE

3/5/67	Paramount buys rights to Mario Puzo's book *Mafia* (later renamed *The Godfather*), reported in the *New York Times*.
9/17/69	Paramount exercises their option on the film. "Paramount Pictures probably made the prime deal for a bestseller in modern film history with its $80,000 ceiling for Mario Puzo's *The Godfather*."—*Variety*
11/26/69	*Variety* headline: "Par to Produce *Godfather* Film" "The studio is currently in discussions anent [*sic*] a producer and director for the motion picture, slated for production next year."—*Variety*
3/23/70	Al Ruddy announced as producer in *The Hollywood Reporter* and *Variety*.
4/14/70	Mario Puzo announced as screenplay writer in *The Hollywood Reporter* and *Variety*.
7/70	Italian-American Civil Rights League rally against *The Godfather* in Madison Square Garden.
8/10/70	Puzo completes first full draft of screenplay (and mails copy to Marlon Brando).
9/2/70	*Variety* reports that Paramount won't make the film in New York, the budget is set at $3 million, and that the production is besieged by "members and pseudo-members" of the Italian community. Will start production middle of November, "if all goes well."
9/28/70	Coppola announced as director in *Variety*.
11/70	Filming originally scheduled to begin. Delayed to 1/2/71 with Christmas release.
1/27/71	Marlon Brando (Vito Corleone) signing announced in *Variety*.
2/71	Coppola leaves for London to meet with Marlon Brando, then to Italy to cast Sicily scenes. Production staff moves into offices on the Filmways Studio lot. Production start date moved to 3/29.
2/15/71	Robert Duvall (Tom Hagen) and Diane Keaton (Kay Adams) signed.
2/18/71	Richard Castellano (Pete Clemenza) and John Marley (Jack Woltz) signed. Both had just been nominated for Best Supporting Actor Oscars®.
2/22/71	Coppola casting in Rome. Lunches with Vittorio De Sica. Talia Shire (Connie Corleone) signed.
2/25/71	Coppola returns to the States. Trouble with Manhasset location.
3/1/71	Puzo and Coppola complete second draft of script.
3/4/71	Al Pacino (Michael Corleone) cast. Sterling Hayden (Captain McCluskey) cast.
3/8/71	Preshooting rehearsals scheduled but have to be moved because of Pacino's legal problems with MGM.
3/10/71	Snow machine tested. Brando's first makeup and costume tests scheduled.
3/12/71	Pacino finally cleared to be in picture.
3/16/71	Third draft of script completed (marked 3/29/1971).
3/17/71	Brando's first rehearsal. Informal cast "rehearsal" dinner at Patsy's Restaurant.
3/18/71	Alex Rocco (Moe Greene) signing announced in *The Hollywood Reporter*.
3/19/71	Ruddy's deal with Italian-American Civil Rights League announced.
3/23/71	First unofficial production date (with the second camera unit)—a week earlier than planned to take advantage of predicted snow. Scenes: Michael and Kay outside Best & Co., Hagen abduction outside Polk Toy Store, Michael discovering his father has been shot.
3/29/71	First day of principal photography. Scene: Michael in car with Sollozzo and McCluskey.
3/31/71	Production moved to the Bronx. Scene: Louis' restaurant.
4/2/71	Paramount CEO Stanley Jaffe resignation, effective 8/1, announced in *Variety*.
4/12/71	Brando scheduled to begin shooting at 8 a.m. but misses his plane to New York.
4/13/71	Scene: Exteriors of The Don being taken from the hospital to go home.
4/15/71	43rd Academy Awards ceremony. Coppola wins for his screenplay of *Patton* but doesn't attend.
4/19/71	Scene: The Don assassination attempt.
4/21/71	Scene: Genco Abbandando's death (does not appear in original release).
4/26/71	Scene: Bonasera's Funeral Parlor (Bellevue Morgue).
4/27/71	Thompson and Bleecker streets location, reshooting scenes ruined at the lab: Sonny leaving Lucy Mancini's apartment and "button men hiding out 'at the mattresses'."
4/28/71	Scene: Meeting of the Five Families (location: Grand Central Station).
4/29/71	Rehearsal of Don Vito/Bonasera scene. First "mooning" on set.

4/30/71	Scene: Opening scene of the movie, first scene shot at the Corleone house set ("The Mall").
5/3/71	Scene: Luca Brasi gives The Don the envelope, other wedding scenes.
5/5/71	Scene: Johnny Fontane.
5/7/71	Scene: Brando brought to his bedroom on a stretcher.
5/12/71	Scene: Lucy/Sonny sex scene.
5/13/71	Production returns to Staten Island location for exterior shooting, but rain prevents filming.
5/14/71	Brando told to take a week off; makes plans to go to Tahiti.
5/21/71	Production moved to Long Island. Scene: Woltz.
5/22/71	Scene: horse head.
5/24/71	Production moved back to Staten Island for Connie's Wedding—rain delays.
5/26/71	Scenes: Wedding party.
6/1/71	Scenes: Wedding party.
6/7/71	Scene: Exteriors of baptism.
6/8/71	Scene: Carlo's murder.
6/9/71	Scenes: Completed filming at Corleone Mall (Staten Island location).
6/16/71	Scene: The Don's Funeral (location: Calvary Cemetery in Queens).
6/21/71	Scene: Interiors of baptism.
6/20–22/71	Scene: Assassination of Sonny.
6/23/71	Scene: Sonny beats up Carlo.
6/24/71	Scene: Interior hotel shots. Pacino spends the night at the St. Regis Hotel.
6/28/71	Scene: Kay and Michael in hotel bed together (scene does not appear in original release). Italian-American Civil Rights League leader Joe Colombo shot near Gulf+Western building.
6/29/71	Scene: more hotel scenes, including Clemenza shooting into elevator.
7/1/71	Scene: Murder of Don Barzini, murder of Moe Greene. Wrap party at the Cornish Arms Hotel down the street from YMCA (location of Moe Greene murder).
7/2/71	Scene: Michael's pickup outside Jack Dempsey's Restaurant. Last shot of New York principal photography.
7/15/71	*Variety* announces 50-50 chance that *The Godfather* will be ready for Christmas.
7/17/71	Coppola goes to Italy.
7/20/71	"*The Godfather* will not be available until some time between next March and June."—Frank Yablans, soon to be head of Paramount, in *Variety*. Budget: "a little over $5 million."
7/22/71	Key personnel go to Sicily.
7/24/71	Cast and crew go to Sicily.
8/71	Postproduction begins.
9/71	Coppola screens first assembly, sound effects collection. Paramount booked the film into 800 theaters for mid-December.
11/71	Semifinal version completed.
11/15/71	Paramount CFO, Frank Yablans, sees the film. Coppola notes in his journal, "Evans is so optimistic that I feel hopeful—I'll know in several hours. Several hours later . . . . He liked it."
12/71	Screening for Paramount staff and exhibitors.
2/23/72	Preview screening for the top 500 exhibitors at the Directors Guild of America theater on Sunset Boulevard.
2/25/72	First review (reviewer snuck into preview): rave in *New York Post*.
3/15/72	Premiere at New York's Loews State I Theatre on Broadway in Times Square during snowstorm.
3/23/72	Producers private screening at the Paramount Studio Theatre.
3/29/72	National release—*The Godfather* opens simultaneously in five New York theaters.

APPENDIX III: NOTABLE AWARDS

THEN

1973 Academy Awards®:	Best Actor in a Leading Role:	Marlon Brando (refused)
	Best Writing, Screenplay Based on Material from Another Medium:	Mario Puzo, Francis Ford Coppola
	Best Picture:	Albert S. Ruddy
	Nominated:	
	Best Actor in a Supporting Role:	Robert Duvall
	Best Sound:	Charles Grenzbach, Richard Portman, Christopher Newman
	Best Costume Design:	Anna Hill Johnstone
	Best Actor in a Supporting Role:	Al Pacino
	Best Actor in a Supporting Role:	James Caan
	Best Film Editing:	William Reynolds, Peter Zinner
	Best Director:	Francis Ford Coppola
Directors Guild of America:	Best Director:	Francis Ford Coppola
Golden Globes:	Best Motion Picture—Drama	
	Best Motion Picture Actor—Drama:	Marlon Brando
	Best Screenplay:	Mario Puzo, Francis Ford Coppola
	Best Director—Motion Picture:	Francis Ford Coppola
	Best Original Score:	Nino Rota
	Nominated:	
	Best Motion Picture Actor—Drama:	Al Pacino
	Best Supporting Actor—Motion Picture:	James Caan
Grammy Awards:	Best Original Score Written for a Motion Picture or TV Special:	Nino Rota
National Board of Review:	Best Supporting Actor:	Al Pacino (Tied with Joel Grey in *Cabaret*)
	Best Picture (*nominated*)	
National Society of Film Critics:	Best Actor:	Al Pacino
New York Film Critics Circle:	Best Supporting Actor:	Robert Duvall
Writers Guild of America:	Best Drama Adapted from Another Medium:	Mario Puzo, Francis Ford Coppola

NOW (Lifetime Achievement)

Writers Guild of America:	Second-greatest screenplay ever (after *Casablanca*)
United States National Film Registry:	Selected for preservation, 1990 (the second year of selection process)
American Film Institute:	Second-greatest movie score of all time
Rankings:	Ranked as one of the greatest films of all time:

    American Film Institute (#2, "100 Greatest Movies")
    Entertainment Weekly (#1)
    Internet Movie Database users (#1)
    Sight and Sound international critics poll (#4)

INTERVIEWS

Peter Bart: March 8, 2007

Francis Ford Coppola: February 12, 2007

Sonny Grosso: November 20, 2006

Alex Rocco: January 15, 2007

Fred Roos: March 29, 2007

Al Ruddy: January 8, 2007

Dick Smith: November 15, 2006

Robert Towne: March 11, 2007

BOOKS

Bart, Peter. *Boffo!: How I Learned to Love the Blockbuster and Fear the Bomb.* New York: Miramax Books, 2006.

Biskind, Peter. *Easy Riders, Raging Bulls: How the Sex-Drugs-and-Rock 'n' Roll Generation Saved Hollywood.* New York: Simon and Schuster, 1998

Biskind, Peter. *The Godfather Companion.* New York: Harper Collins Publishers, 1990

Brando, Marlon. *Songs My Mother Taught Me.* New York: Random House, 1994

Cowie, Peter. *The Godfather Book.* London: Faber and Faber Limited, 1997

Evans, Robert. *The Kid Stays in the Picture.* Beverly Hills: New Millennium Press, 2002

Gardner, Gerald and Gardner, Harriet Modell. *The Godfather Movies: A Pictorial History.* New Jersey: Wings Books, 1993

Grobel, Lawrence. *Al Pacino: In Conversation with Lawrence Grobel.* New York: Simon Spotlight Entertainment, 2006

Gross, Terry. *All I Did Was Ask: Conversations with Writers, Actors, Musicians, and Artists.* New York: Hyperion, 2005

Harlan, Lebo. *The Godfather Legacy.* New York: Fireside, 2005

Lavery, David. *This Thing of Ours: Investigating The Sopranos.* Darby, PA: Diane Pub Co., 2004

Malyszko, William. *Ultimate Film Guide: The Godfather.* London: York Press, 2001

Puzo, Mario. *The Godfather Papers: and Other Confessions.* Greenwich, CT: Fawcett Crest Publications, 1972

Puzo, Mario. *The Godfather.* New York: Signet, 1978

Sheridan-Castellano, Ardell. *Divine Intervention and a Dash of Magic: Unraveling the Mystery of "The Method": Behind the Scenes of the Original Godfather Film.* Victoria BC: Trafford Publishing, 2002

Zuckerman, Ira. *The Godfather Journal.* New York: Manor Books Inc., 1972

ARTICLES

Bacon, James. "'The Godfather' Casting Game Continues." *LA Herald Examiner*, October 6, 1970.

Brando, Marlon. "'The Godfather': That Unfinished Oscar Speech." *New York Times*, March 30, 1973

Cameron, Sue. "'Godfather' Biggest Thing Since GWTW, Al Ruddy Says." *Hollywood Reporter*, November 6, 1970.

Cameron, Sue. "Mario Puzo Says 'Godfather' Experience Was Frustrating." *Hollywood Reporter*, February 25, 1972

Canby, Vincent. "Bravo, Brando's 'Godfather.'" *New York Times*, March 12, 1972.

Canby, Vincent. "A Moving and Brutal 'Godfather.'" *New York Times*, March 16, 1972.

Champlin, Charles. "'Godfather': The Gangster Film Moves Uptown." *Los Angeles Times*, March 19, 1972.

Davis, Ivor. "Smuggled into 'Godfather' Screening." *LA Herald Examiner*, March 3, 1972.

Faber, Stephen and Green, Marc. "Dynasty, Italian Style." *California Magazine*, April, 1984s

Gage, Nicholas. "A Few Family Murders, But That's Show Biz." *New York Times*, March 19, 1972.

Heller, Wendy and Willens, Michele. "Life-styles for Waiting in Line to See 'Godfather.'" *Los Angeles Times*, April 16, 1972.

Kael, Pauline. "Alchemy." *The New Yorker*, March 18, 1972.

Kauffmann, Stanley. "On Films: 'The Godfather.'" *The New Republic*, April 1, 1972.

Knapp, Dan. "Coppola 'Godfather' Director." *Los Angeles Times*, October 1, 1970.

Maslin, Janet. "Hollywood Wunderkind's Fall and Rise," *New York Times*, August 25, 1994.

Penn, Stanley. "Colombo's Crusade: Alleged Mafia Chief Runs Aggressive Drive Against Saying 'Mafia.'"

BIBLIOGRAPHY

Wall Street Journal, March 23, 1971.

Pileggi, Nicholas. "How Hollywood Wooed and Won the Mafia." *Los Angeles Times*, August 15, 1971.

Pileggi, Nicholas. "The Making of 'The Godfather'—Sort of a Home Movie." *The New York Times Magazine*, August 15, 1971.

Scott, Tony. "Ruddy Raps Extras Guild, Won't Shoot in Its Jurisdiction." *Variety*, September 2, 1970.

Setlowe, Rick. "Paramount's Gamble Four Years Ago on Mario Puzo Has Really Paid Off." *Variety*, September 30, 1970.

Setlowe, Rick. "Italo American Thesps Picket Par Studio, Protest 'Godfather' Casting." *Variety*, February 11, 1971.

Shanken, Marvin R. "The Godfather Speaks." *Cigar Aficionado*, October, 2003.

Toy, Steve. "Another Sour Note for Acad: Governors Mulling Possible 'Godfather' Music Rub-Out As Not Being Original Score." *Variety*, February 28, 1973

Wayne, Fredd. "'Godfather' Casting: An Italian Uprising." *Los Angeles Times*, February 28, 1971.

Weiler, G.N. "Source Material." *New York Times*, March 5, 1967.

ARTICLES, NO AUTHOR CITED

"Para Buys Puzo's 'Godfather' Tome." *Hollywood Reporter*, January 24, 1969.

"One Man's Family." *Time*, March 14, 1969.

"Par's Bargain Price (80G) For 'Godfather' Rights." *Variety*, September 17, 1969.

"Par to Produce 'Godfather' Film." *Variety*, November 26, 1969.

"Hollywood: Will There Ever Be a 21st Century-Fox?" Time, February 9, 1970.

"How Does Coppola Par Deal Affect His WB Status?" *Variety*, September 28, 1970.

"Paramount Paid Puzo $80 Thou For 'Godfather' Plus Two." *Hollywood Reporter*, September 30, 1970.

"Coppola Says Para Deal 'On Leave' From Warners." *Hollywood Reporter*, October 1, 1970.

"'Godfather' Director Coppola Unhappy Producer Ruddy Has Nixed N.Y. Locale." *Variety*, October 9, 1970

"Fredrickson Aide on Par's 'Godfather.'" *Variety*, October 15, 1970.

"No Stars for 'Godfather' Cast—Just Someone Named Brando." *Variety*, January 28, 1971.

"Brando to Play 'The Godfather,' Evans Announces." *Hollywood Reporter*, January 28, 1971.

"Marley Firmed for 'Godfather.'" *Hollywood Reporter*, February 19, 1971.

"Injunction in Pacino Suit on 'The Godfather.'" *Hollywood Reporter*, March 11, 1971.

"Puzo, Ruddy Deny Friction on 'Godfather.'" *Hollywood Reporter*, March 11, 1971.

"The Making of 'The Godfather.'" *Time*, March 13, 1972.

"Suit Settlement Clears 'Godfather' Role for Pacino." *Variety*, March 17, 1971.

"Rocco for 'Godfather.'" *Hollywood Reporter*, March 18, 1971.

"Par Burns Over 'Godfather' Deal, But Will Rub Out Mafia." *Variety*, March 23, 1971.

"Par Repudiates Italo-Am. Group Vs. 'Godfather.'" *Variety*, March 24, 1971.

"Robert Duvall In 'Godfather.'" *Hollywood Reporter*, March 24, 1971.

"'Godfather' Rolls Today." *Hollywood Reporter*, March 29, 1971.

"Damone Quits Role in Picture 'The Godfather.'" *L.A. Herald Examiner*, April 5, 1971.

"Damone Vacates Role in 'Godfather.'" *Variety*, April 5, 1971.

"A Night for Colombo." *Time*, April 5, 1971.

"Italo Service Club Slaps 'Godfather.'" *Variety*, April 7, 1971.

"Shooting 'The Godfather.'" *Newsweek*, June 28, 1971.

"The Mafia: Back to the Bad Old Days?" *Time*, July 12, 1971.

"Puzo Book Tells About 'Godfather' Experiences Mute Paramount Mafia." *Variety*, December 25, 1971.

"How Gianni Russo Muscled His Way into 'The Godfather.'" *Hollywood Reporter*, February 1, 1972.

"Par's 'Godfather' Date Is Scuttled By London Daily." *Variety*, March 1, 1972.

"Brando's Mute 'Test' Copped Role; 'Godfather' Funnier Than Mafia Picnic." *Variety*, March 8, 1972

"'Godfather' Godsend for Gunmen." *Variety*, March 20, 1972.

"It's Everybody's 'Godfather.'" *Variety*, March 22, 1972.

"'Godfather' Sets Industry Record." *Hollywood Reporter*, March 23, 1972.

"City Troublemaker…" *Seventeen*, April 1972.

"The Godsons." *Time*, April 3, 1972.

"'Godfather' Sparks Queue Gimmicks." *Variety*, April 5, 1972.

"Five More Versions of 'Godfather' Planned." *The Hollywood Reporter*, April 7, 1972.

"The Story Behind The Godfather By The Men Who Lived It." *Ladies Home Journal*, June, 1972.

"Coppola Kicks Back at His Pic-Fest Critics." *Variety*, October 19, 1972.

"Not So Says Al Martino." *LA Herald Examiner*, January 2, 1973.

"Mafia Insisted on Its Own Preview of 'Godfather,' Producer Reveals." *Box Office*, December 17, 1973.

"The Promoter: Frank Yablans." *Time*, March 18, 1974.

"The Producer: Robert Evans." *Time*, March 18, 1974.

AMERICAN ZOETROPE RESEARCH LIBRARY: ARCHIVAL DOCUMENTS

The Godfather Notebook, Francis Ford Coppola

Francis Ford Coppola Journal

The Godfather Screenplay by Mario Puzo, First Draft, August 10, 1970

Francis Coppola Memo, Subject: Special Effects, January 22, 1971

Transcript, preproduction meeting between Francis Ford Coppola, Gordon Willis, Johnny Johnstone, Dean Tavoularis, January 25, 1971

Transcript, preproduction meeting between Francis Ford Coppola, Richard Castellano, Al Lettieri

The Godfather Screenplay by Mario Puzo and Francis Ford Coppola, Second Draft, March 1, 1971

PARAMOUNT PICTURES: ARCHIVAL DOCUMENTS

The Godfather Screenplay by Mario Puzo and Francis Ford Coppola, Third Draft, March 29, 1971

The Godfather Dialogue Continuity Screenplay

VIDEOS AND WEBSITES

Gangland: Bullets Over Hollywood. Image Entertainment, 2006

The Godfather: DVD Collection. Paramount Pictures, 2001

thegodfathertrilogy.com [creator: J. Geoff Malta]

gangsterbb.net

INDEX OF
MEMORABLE LINES

ACKNOWLEDGEMENTS

This book was made possible by the support of so many people: J.P Leventhal, who gave me a shot; Becky Koh, my editor—a calming presence who provided invaluable insight; Madeline, the light of my life; and of course, Josh, who has been patient and supportive throughout.

Risa Kessler at Paramount made this project possible from the outset and was an invaluable ally when it came time to liaise with the studio and other resources. Christina Hahni at Paramount went above and beyond in seeking out the photos for the book. Many thanks. This book could not have happened without you. Thank you, also, to Chris Horton at Paramount.

Anahid Nazarian at the American Zoetrope Research Library was so helpful and hospitable, aiding me in navigating through Francis Ford Coppola's archive of *Godfather* materials and giving me tremendous access to a wealth of information. Gianni Lopez from the Italian Cultural Institute assisted with translations. I wish to thank Kristine Krueger at the Margaret Herrick Library of the Academy of Motion Picture Arts and Sciences for the loan of research materials, as well as the reference librarians there who were always available to answer a query.

Thanks to the astute film critic Kenneth Turan for sharing his thoughts. Some of the people involved in the making of this motion picture were kind enough to provide a comment about the film: Michael Chapman, Robert Duvall, and Stanley Jaffe. Very special thanks to the incredibly generous men who shared their stories and insights on *The Godfather* production in interviews with me: Peter Bart, Sonny Grosso, Alex Rocco, Fred Roos, Al Ruddy, Dick Smith, and Robert Towne.

Finally, mille grazie to Francis Ford Coppola, who magnanimously spent hours relaying his memories of the production. What an honor it was to speak with the maestro of this brilliant film.